GEORGE ELIOT
AND HER TIMES

A VICTORIAN STUDY BY

ELIZABETH S. HALDANE

HASKELL HOUSE PUBLISHERS Lᴛᴅ.

Publishers of Scarce Scholarly Books

NEW YORK. N. Y. 10012

1974

HASKELL HOUSE PUBLISHERS LTD.

Publishers of Scarce Scholarly Books

280 LAFAYETTE STREET

NEW YORK. N. Y. 10012

Library of Congress Cataloging in Publication Data

Haldane, Elizabeth Sanderson, 1862-1937.
   George Eliot and her times.

   1. Eliot, George, psued., i.e. Marian Evans after-
wards Cross, 1819-1880--Biography. I. Title.
PR4681.H3 1974   823'.8 [B]   74-11022
ISBN 0-8383-1848-7

Printed in the United States of America

TRIBUS FRATRIBUS SUIS
D.D.
SOROR

CONTENTS

PREFATORY NOTE

ALTHOUGH, in certain particulars, information regarding the earlier career of George Eliot is here somewhat fuller than in previous lives, it has not been the author's intention to produce a biography which shall in any way compete with that published by J. W. Cross in 1885, supplemented as that was by the collection of her letters. It is of course improbable that this work will ever be superseded. The purpose of the present volume has not been so much to concentrate attention upon the actual events of George Eliot's life, as to consider how the relations of her work to the general aim and effort of her epoch appear after the lapse of nearly half a century. In her life time she was admired, doubtless to excess; since her death she has been depreciated, certainly with injustice. The aim of the following pages is to consider in what that early appreciation was excessive, and in what the subsequent depreciation has been unjust. In order to do this, it has seemed necessary to strip off the accidental advantages which her genius enjoyed, and to see in what form her ideas commended themselves to her contemporaries, and yet were rejected by her successors. But to do this would have little value, if an effort were not made to define what her exact characteristics are seen to be when the fortuitous conditions which first encouraged and then obscured them are removed. The time seems to have arrived when we can contemplate this great writer from a distance, and see her in earlier perspective. For this purpose it is necessary to examine briefly the features of the age which she adorned. We have reached a point at which it is right to consider George Eliot as one of our classics, an artist and thinker to be examined scientifically, without extravagance or prejudice. I have therefore attempted to tell the tale of her life and books, as it presents itself to the mind of the student of to-day.

I have to thank Sir Edmund Gosse for kindly allowing me to reproduce a portrait of George Eliot, hitherto unpublished, by Sir Frederick Burton. Miss Elsie Druce has done the same in regard to a silhouette in her possession. The late Mr. Clement Shorter and others have supplied me with some new information regarding George Eliot's life, and I am much indebted to Professor Basil Williams for criticisms and suggestions. Of those who can recollect George Eliot and who have talked to me about her, I might mention the Earl of Oxford and Asquith and Sir Almeric Fitzroy, who met her as undergraduates, and Mrs. W. K. Clifford, who came into close connexion with her in her young womanhood. Mrs. Orebury and Mrs. C. E. Maurice have also been most helpful in showing me personal belongings and manuscripts.

E. S. H.

CHAPTER I

Introductory

IT is only possible to understand the place George Eliot held in the estimation of her contemporaries if we consider the surroundings in which she lived. The English world some sixty years ago (supposing we take the time at which George Eliot's fame was at its highest) was of course essentially the same world that we see around us to-day ; but if we were transported back to it we should discover surprising superficial differences which we have now forgotten. Perhaps the change has been greatest in dress and demeanour. The ladies would startle us with their volume of crinoline, their skirts descending to the ground, and, indoors at least, trailing far behind along the floor. Their masses of hair, real or artificial, were rolled up in chignons—surely the least beautiful of all modes of dressing the hair—or else they escaped in ringlets on either side. There was no suspicion of bobbing or shingling then ; hats were worn, not pressed over the eyes, but elevated behind to make room for the ball of hair in its silken net. Even the dress of men was more formal and less comfortable than the fashions of to-day. The high silk hat was inevitable even at the seaside, though it had been unwillingly abandoned on the cricket field. The old-fashioned stocks were still common, and elderly gentlemen, at any rate, always wore surtouts and occasionally frilled shirts : younger ones the characteristic side ornaments which became known as the Dundreary Whisker. Tobacco had not advanced much in fashionable esteem ; moralists still spasmodically announced that " nicotine was stealing away the brains of the nation " and hostesses were apt to banish the smoking guests to the kitchen ; while women were being rendered anæmic and subject to fainting fits owing to the practice of tight-lacing which produced the much admired wasp-like waist.

More remarkable than any of these differences would be the aspects of the streets. Saving for the railways, which had struggled into permanent acceptance, the mode of communication had not altered since the time of Alfred the Great. The horse still pervaded the world without a rival, since the recent invention of the " bone-shaker," one immense wheel supplemented by another very small one, tempted none but very bold adventurers. When seen, as it rarely was, in country lanes, this invention awakened mystery and alarm, but no one realised that it was the beginning of all the bicycles, motor cars, chars-à-bancs and motor-lorries that pervade our modern scene. Still less did it occur to anyone that such engines might be bestridden by women.

In the moral, intellectual and political spheres the changes, for being gradual, were not less remarkable. Fifty-five years ago the perennial struggle was going on between Disraeli and Gladstone.

Ireland, that hardy annual, was prominent. Considerable apprehension was felt in regard to the spread of " Puseyism," which, however, was beginning to be accepted as " Ritualism," while in politics " philosophical radicalism " was beginning to be recognised as something less alarming than was anticipated. Towns like Treby Magna were " awakening from the old-fashioned, brewing, woolpacking, cheese-loading " life of the forties and were becoming alive to their political rights. Mr. du Maurier was introducing, in popular form, the draughtsmanship of the dreaded Pre-Raphaelites, and young Mr. Swinburne was shocking the sedate. But the general feeling was that in none of these directions society should go " too far," as Mr. Whistler and Mr. Oscar Wilde were shortly about to do.

There was started in Manchester a Woman Suffrage Society, and Mr. John Stuart Mill had said the emancipation of women was nigh ; but it was not so nigh as was imagined, and women were vainly clamouring for admission to universities to study as doctors. The world, which was feeling towards new departures and yet was all the time restrained and drawn back by convention, found in George Eliot a novelist who exactly diagnosed its complaints and who understood its susceptibilities. At a period when a space had been created by the death of Thackeray and Dickens, this novelist set all England discussing the sympathetic characters of her eminently characteristic " Middlemarch," and when we call to mind the time at

which she flourished we can understand why she
was so universally accepted as the leading novelist
of her day.

If any evidence is required as to how George
Eliot was recognised by her contemporaries who
took the orthodox conservative and conventional
view of her work before it became recognised, we
have only to look at a famous review anonymously
written in a "Quarterly" of 1860. This review
also throws light on the general trend of feeling
on the part of cultivated society at the time. In
it we are told that no good end is to be effected by
fiction of which George Eliot's novels are taken as
the type, which "fill the mind with details of
imaginary vice and distress and crime, or which
teach it—instead of endeavouring after the ful-
filment of simple and ordinary duty—to aim at the
assurance of superiority by creating for itself fanciful
and incomprehensible perplexities."

Truly it was a serious responsibility that rested
on the advanced novelist who gave such anxious
apprehensions as to the effect of her influence.
And we cannot help a feeling almost akin to amusement when we think of the way in which she is
regarded now ; how these "unwholesome books
with their monotonous meanness and indecent
details" are often in the present day spoiled for
their readers by being given as holiday tasks ; is it,
we ask, that our morals have declined or that our
standard of what is fit and proper has altered ?

George Eliot was lacking in what for want of a
better word we call magnetism. She inspired

enormous respect among her appreciative contemporaries as they listened to the words of wisdom
—often real wisdom—that dropped from her lips
at the Priory. Her unconventional life story might
have given a special and human interest to her
personality, but somehow it did not. Her later
years, with the mercurial companion of the greater
part of her life, were so eminently proper and conventional that the criticism poured freely upon it
in early days soon passed away. The shocked and
superior Quarterly reviewer was not long in finding
himself out of date ; people were no longer shocked,
and even the young girl was soon allowed to read
the novels, judiciously selected, that followed one
another in succeeding years ; the older men and
women openly admired her, while the really serious
minded, of whom there were so many, looked to
her for their gospel. She indeed took her place
among the great figures of the Victorian era—
those who like Florence Nightingale, General Gordon,
Tennyson and Her Majesty herself, combined force
of character and genius with the highest possible
ideals. Nowadays we are apt to think that there
was something not quite honest about those times—
that just as so much of the furniture of the day
was veneered instead of being solid, no one was
really quite as high-minded as he appeared to his
contemporaries to be, and that there was an under-
current of pretence in the somewhat self-conscious
attitude of mind. It may have been so in the case
of some of the notables of that period, but it was
by no means the case with the majority. There

was no self-conscious virtue in the work of Miss Nightingale, and there was absolute self-forgetfulness in that of Charles Darwin whose " Origin of Species" appeared about the same time as " Adam Bede."

The truth is that the age was really one in which certain important problems had emerged—problems which never troubled the previous generation, and which it seemed had to be solved. For better or worse we have set aside these same problems as matters of purely speculative interest, which need not concern us now ; indeed the questions are many of them of such a nature that they never do raise themselves before us. The shortness and preciousness of time in which we may do good no longer weighs on our minds, because we are believers in the race rather than the person. The investigating spirit so rules our mode of life that individual sin does not appear the same overwhelmingly dreadful thing, but a matter that may be combated not only through personal influence but by dealing with it in a scientific and curative fashion. Instead of finding moral emotions in every picture she drew, George Eliot would in the present day have found only psychological problems. Her religion was morality as it was to so many of her time. But that morality, however seriously taken and even when touched with emotion, seems in these days a poor substitute for a true spiritual religion which is all pervading and which embraces every aspect of life ; which is above and beyond both science and ethics.

Yet after all George Eliot is what we value most in a novelist—one who lives and understands human beings and their relations and tells us how they live their daily lives and what they think and say. She had, as we shall see, a depressing youth, like so many of her fellow women. For some mysterious reason youth, in the most serious section of Victorianism—more especially the religious section—was regarded almost as a crime. There were human impulses abroad in youth that were deemed naturally evil, and these must be combated and subdued if the child were to grow into a worthy man or woman. Multitudes of young people suffered through the doctrine of original sin and had a morbid bias given to their minds by having their inherent sinfulness pressed upon them. And this it was that made George Eliot—a true lover of children—doubt the wisdom of their having a romance such as " Alice in Wonderland " put into their hands, because it mocked the things children half believed in. This is an attitude which nowadays we cannot possibly comprehend. Childhood has come to its own.

As we should expect, a life of restraint and self-discipline to one naturally full of passion, is not a happy one as the world counts happiness, and in this George Eliot does not differ from many of her contemporaries, especially those of her own sex. From childhood on she struggled after the unattainable and was oppressed by a self-consciousness that made small troubles into great and life a difficult thing. Women had not found themselves. The

French woman knew where she was, and was happy in the knowledge ; the Englishwoman was still seeking and not yet finding ; she was still the parvenu who was looking for slights and full of sensitiveness. George Eliot longed to be a " good and benevolent impulse " to those with whom she could not actually be a beloved friend. Her intimates were first of all the old friends of youth whom she never forgot ; beyond these, many were mere acquaintances who wished to worship at her shrine and obtain admission to her Sunday gatherings. She valued convention—the convention in which she found herself and for which she had an almost superstitious reverence—but at the same time she knew she had in some measure to break free of it and the operation was very painful.

George Eliot was a contemporary of Queen Victoria, and this meant much. The great Queen in her long life and long reign seemed to typify the character of her time. The rough jolly life which we find in Sterne and Smollett had no place in the middle of the nineteenth century. It passed away with the Georges, and with the young Princess came propriety of life and what some term dull respectability. But the remarkable thing is that there also came a galaxy of talent such as the country had not seen since the days of Queen Elizabeth. We can hardly imagine a more brilliant period than when Dickens and Thackeray, Tennyson and Browning and a score of other great writers were at their best.

One wonders whether life was ever such a solemn

or earnest thing as in the fifties, sixties and seventies, and whether conscience was ever so acutely sensitive since the days of the Puritan fathers. Do we now search as George Eliot searched for something worth knowing and remembering in the casual visitor's conversation? Above all do we now record, as she recorded, our results in little notebooks such as not only she but so many men and women (especially women) kept for the purpose, ready to be consulted and thought over at leisure? Such was the atmosphere into which George Eliot was born and in which she lived. Nothing was too slight or unimportant to have a meaning for her; even the casual or careless visitor on the Sunday afternoons at the Priory was often made painfully conscious of his shortcomings as he realised how trivial a simple and unguarded remark sounded in an atmosphere of highest tension. The result was somewhat like that produced by the novice in a silent assemblage speaking to a deaf man through an ear-trumpet.

This great writer obtained almost the greatest success any woman writer has ever had, and yet she was always oppressed by the feeling that she could not do equally good work again. She was too temperamental to be wholly happy or to have a restful life, for it was hard for her to get out of herself and the contemplation of her great problems. A study of her life is all the more interesting for that reason, partly because it typifies the struggles and aspirations of a very distinguished woman, partly because it typifies the struggles and aspirations of a generation at a time of peculiar difficulty.

CHAPTER II

GEORGE ELIOT'S YOUTH
(1819–1839)

THE name of George Eliot has become a household word with us, so much so that, at any rate, future generations will hardly recognise her as Mary Ann Evans, who was born at Arbury Farm on the 22nd November, 1819, six months later than Queen Victoria. She was born " well," that is to say into a healthy stock—just the sort of stock that gives a child the best chance in life. Her father was Robert Evans, the son of George Evans, a builder and carpenter in Staffordshire, though the family came originally from Northorp in Flintshire. We all seem to know Robert Evans intimately, for he was the prototype of two of his daughter's best known characters, Adam Bede and Caleb Garth. He was a type of man such as most of us have come across— a man of great vigour of mind and body to whom work meant all that was worth while in life. Such a one was sure to prosper, but not sure to get rich, and this is what happened to him. He carried on his father's business and did it so well that his excellence was soon noticed by possible employers, as was Caleb Garth's. And Robert Evans was just as devoted to his employer's interest as was Caleb.

His large knowledge of mines, plantations, timber, valuation and measurement made him to be regarded as an ideal land-agent, and this he became to Mr. Francis Newdigate, of Kirk Hallam in Derbyshire, from whom he also held a farm. Later on, his landlord and employer inherited a life interest in the Arbury estate in Warwickshire, and he took Evans with him as his agent. The son of Francis Newdigate was so impressed by his merits that he recommended him to other landlords in the neighbourhood, and consequently Evans became a man of influence and importance as an adviser, probably more useful as well as cheaper than a professional expert.

The time was one when those connected with land were paramount in importance and symbolised all that was substantial and permanent. Probably no one—not even the landlord himself—was as deeply impressed by its enduring qualities and with the crime of tampering with its claims as the conscientious land-agent. Evans was fortunate in his main employer. Sir Roger Newdigate, the owner of Arbury previous to Francis, was a great gentleman as well as a great landowner. He succeeded his brother while a boy at Westminster School, and died at eighty-seven without issue. He represented Oxford for thirty years, of course as a High Tory, owned collieries and promoted the formation of canals. In fact he was the typical good landlord such as George Eliot loved to depict, and such as we have always had set before us as the type which circumstances have unfortunately destroyed. We can see him rebuilding the old home, making it large and lofty " in the Gothic style," just as so many landlords had done to the detriment of their successors at the same happy date, when war made prices high and landlords prosperous ; and we can picture the Gothic house filled with family pictures—Romneys and Reynolds. A man of cultivated taste, he founded the famous " Newdigate "—the prize poem which has encouraged so many would-be poets to write in verse. His later life was cheered by the companionship of his cousin, Francis Newdigate, who succeeded him.

The traditions of the Newdigate family are interesting to any student of George Eliot, because they coloured her conceptions of country life, and gave her that feeling for the past and all that it has given to us, which we find throughout her writings. The first Mrs. Robert Evans, Harriet Poynton, had been " a friend and servant of the family at Arbury," in the conventional expression of the day ; and in this way the family records were preserved, down to the minutest details. Who could be as thoroughly imbued with the feeling of family and all that it entails as the devoted " servant and friend " whose whole life is bound up within the limited circle in which it moves ? The first wife of Mr. Evans died in 1809, at Kirk Hallam, after eight years of married life, and after giving birth to two children, Robert, born in 1802, and Lucy, born in 1805. Four years later, in 1813, Robert Evans married Christina Pearson, by whom he had three children—Christina, born in 1814, Isaac, in 1816, and Mary Ann, in 1819. Thus the future George Eliot was the youngest of a family of five children, and shortly after her birth her half-brother Robert, who must have been only seventeen, became the agent under his father for the Kirk Hallam property and lived there with his own sister, Frances, while the rest of the family moved to Griff on the Arbury Estate. This is the home of her first twenty-one years that George Eliot loved so dearly. The second Mrs. Evans was somewhat superior socially to the first, and as she is usually supposed to bear a resemblance to Mrs. Poyser, we must picture her as a practical " managing " woman with plenty of character. One does not hear of her having any literary proclivities, though she was of yeoman stock and presumably better educated than her husband when he married her ; and as her family, the Pearsons, were admittedly the originals of the Dodsons in " The Mill on the Floss," we can surmise that she had the old-fashioned appreciation of kinship and love of " home truths." Her three married sisters lived in the vicinity. Mr. Cross in his life of George Eliot speaks of her character as forceful, shrewd and practical.

Shortly after Mary Ann's birth her mother became ailing in health and the elder girl was sent to school at Attleboro', a village a mile or two off from Griff, while the other two went to a dame's school close to the estate gates kept by a Mrs. Moore. It is difficult to imagine anything proceeding from such ordered surroundings that was not in itself perfectly

orderly. Rural Warwickshire typifies all that is
established and settled ; its undulating country,
its woods full of blue bells, its fox-hunting, its
manor-houses, its still rivers and canals, all seem
to belie the fact that close by there are manu-
factures, mines, great factory towns and all the
unrest that belongs to them. The great mansions
and parks ringed-in to keep the favoured inmates
from the smallest contact with the common herd,
the picturesque and usually insanitary cottages,
were all typical of this county. The only unorthodox life seemed to emanate from the ugly
little Dissenting chapels with quaint Biblical names ;
but of them the " better classes " took no account.
George Eliot was brought up strictly Church and
Conservative ; she was christened a week after
birth in the church at Chilvers Coton, near Arbury
Farm, which has become famous as Shepperton
Church.

The years of George Eliot's infancy were sad ones
in the history of our nation. The French Revolution had raised hopes in the minds of the workers
in this country which had been dashed to the
ground. They were years of scarcity, of political
discontent and risings in industrial areas, such as
often follow a great war. But, what seems strange
to us in these days of quick and easy transit, though
the Evanses were not really far removed from some of
the busiest parts of industrial England, the country
house and its belongings were as entirely separated
from them as though they had been in a separate
island. The great excitement was the passing of

the coach which ran between Coventry and Nuneaton before the gates of Griff House. There are few now living who remember the excitement of a passing coach and how all who could do so went to change the mail bags and possibly hear the news. The mining village near had little effect on Griff and its inmates : its people were of a different sort and had standards and ways of their own. George Eliot's father, however, had a good knowledge of mines as well as of plantations and crops. How he carried on his manifold duties it is difficult for us to say ; but he was physically very strong, and there are stories of how he himself was able to carry a ladder from one hayrick to another which two men could not manage to carry without help. At the same time he resembled Caleb Garth in being sub-missive to his wife, never forgetting that she was originally of better status than himself.

George Eliot's early books are those which give the best account of the life and doings of country life in the Midlands, and probably nowhere are the outward conditions better described than in " Adam Bede," " Middlemarch," and " Felix Holt." We have the whole of that life set forth in her novels in a way that makes it absolutely real to us. When we read her books we read of real friends, and if we were set down in Griff in the twenties or thirties of last century we should find ourselves quite at home amongst those friends and acquaintances whom we have known for long.

George Eliot herself, when rather a plain-looking,

pale child of four years of age, was already showing
traces of the temperament that was to be her bug-
bear throughout life. Already she suffered from
the self-consciousness that kept her from reaching
out to the happiness that might have been hers.
She related of herself that when only four she set
herself to play on the piano, of which she knew not
one note, in order to impress on the servant a proper
notion of her acquirements and distinguished position ! She was no quick-brained prodigy, but a
poor little girl full of sensibility, who did not yet
know where that sensibility would lead her—or of
the thorns and briars that were to tear the too
susceptible flesh. It was a passionate nature also,
and that was a further trouble, for passion and
sensibility together make a dangerous compound.
All through her life, as her husband points out, she
had to have *one* person who should be all in all to
her and to whom she should be all in all. We know
how true this was in later life. In early days it
took the form of a passionate devotion to her
brother Isaac, three years her senior. The little
sister was not only Isaac's plaything, but, like
Maggie Tulliver, his devoted slave and constant
attendant ; for Mary Ann, like Maggie, was never
quite herself : she was not self-sufficient ; she
always had to stand well with somebody. And yet
she was all the while full of character ; she could not
be altogether subservient ; and this was to make
the tragedy of her life as well as the happiness.
She loved to go fishing in the still, brown streams,
with her big brother, but she never would have

gone fishing by herself as would have done another
boy. Hers was a feminine devotion that demanded
everything and got little but the joy of service ;
and she did not escape the broken heart which
followed an unkind word or the suffering which
came from an unkind act.

One of George Eliot's most touching poems is
" Brother and Sister "—really one of a series of
eleven sonnets which were printed originally for
private circulation in a slim and now rare volume
which appeared in 1869. These sonnets put quite
simply, and without the introspection and self-
reflection that trouble us in many of her poems,
the description of the life of boy and girl devoted
to one another—

> " When our two lives grew like two birds that kiss
> At lightest thrill from the bee's swinging chime
> Because the one so near the other is."

It is all told as vividly as though we saw it before
us. The " little man of forty inches was bound to
show no dread " ; and she, the girl, " now ran, now
lagged behind my brother's larger tread." The
brother was the king, the superior, recognised by
nature, who therefore had the greater share of the
little store of food baked for them by their mother.
He was the elder and a boy ; the time for so-called
gallantry had not come. A story—a true one in
respect of little Mary Ann—is told by her of how,
while the brother sought bait, the girl had been left
" in high charge to mind the rod " on a brown canal
with strict injunctions to snatch out the line did she

see a barge appear.   The child fell asleep and mean-
while the fatal barge came.   Shouts from the
brother made the delinquent draw forth the line,
at the end of which to her and his delight hung a
silver perch.   All recriminations ceased and, instead,
the guilt that won the prey now turned to merit.
" And so I learned luck was with glory wed."

All this is simply and beautifully told ; but, as is
the case nearly always with the grown-up who looks
back and tries to interpret his childhood, it is not
all the truth.   We are never quite straight with
ourselves in these matters.   The account of the
playthings, however, rings true—

> " My doll seemed lifeless and no girlish toy
> Had any reason when my brother came . . .
> I knelt with him at marbles, marked his fling,
> Cut the ringed stem and made the apple drop"—

and the lines conclude

> " But were another childhood world my share,
> I would be born a little sister there."

The break with Isaac was a sad one in his sister's
life.   She felt it acutely and there are those who
tell that she never could read this poem without
tears.   One wonders if Isaac ever realised the
terrible punishment meted out to him in being
associated by the world (though not by his sister)
with the capable, managing but self-loving, self-
sufficient Tom Tulliver, the centre of his own
universe.

Mary Ann joined her sister at Attleboro' school
(Miss Lathom's) and was a boarder for three or four

years. Isaac was sent to school at Coventry at eight years old, for the mother's delicate health resulted in her children being much away from home. Mary Ann was not very strong either and must have required much more careful tending than she got. Very likely such care in childhood would have obviated the delicacy and constant headaches from which she suffered in later years ; but it was not a time when childish ailments were much considered. Of her very early days what chiefly remained in her remembrance was the difficulty of getting near enough to the fire in winter to become thoroughly warm, owing to the circle of girls who sat around a narrow fire-place. She also suffered from " terrors " at night, the terrors which afflicted the proud Gwendolen Harleth in " Daniel Deronda " ; and though the older girls were kind, " all her soul became a quivering fear." The joy was to get home and to see her beloved Isaac again, and hear of his doings since they parted. It was a happy home, for the boy was his mother's pet, she her father's and the elder sister the aunts', and a pleasanter playground than the overgrown farm- house with its old-fashioned garden, its barns and outhouses and long cowshed, could hardly be. It was a busy home too, for Mrs. Evans was not too delicate to be, like Mrs. Poyser, a first-rate cheese and butter-maker.

Was there something in the calm, spacious life of these days that we miss now ? Did children and parents really dwell together as they cannot do now with the constant distractions of outside interests,

telephones and telegrams? A busy man like
Robert Evans, a leader in his community, would
have been at the beck and call of everyone. His
car would have hurried from place to place, from
meeting to meeting of public authorities and private
ventures and charities. A hundred years ago he
drove leisurely along, his little Mary Ann standing
between his knees, taking in far more than he had
any notion of, and picking up the knowledge of human
beings of every sort that was presently to serve her
in such good stead.

Do we ever forget our first " own " book? Often
enough it is a book of quite ephemeral interest and
not worthy to be kept in the inner sanctuary of
memory. But it always is so kept, though sometimes we hardly wish to see it again. In these old
days it was more eventful to receive a book, and
the gift of " The Linnet's Life " published in 1822,
the first present Mary Ann ever received from her
father, was a landmark in her life. " Let anyone
who thinks of me with some tenderness after I am
dead, take care of this book for my sake," she
wrote in it. " It made me very happy when I held
it in my little hands and read it over and over
again." The book still exists : its pictures are
well produced with good woodcuts, the favourite
one of its possessor being that of the Mother Linnet
feeding her young.

It was soon discovered that the little girl was
intelligent and loved books, and a kind friend
brought others. George Eliot, like most of us
older people, compared the books of her day

favourably with those of a later time. There were but few books in her home, but the few were good and valued. Æsop's Fables and all the rest were read and re-read.

So things went on : the seven-year-old girl was taken for a week to Stafford and Derbyshire to her great delight; but the tragedy of life was soon to break upon her. The beloved brother had been presented with a pony which, alas, monopolised his attention to the detriment of the little sister. This was but the beginning of more that was to follow. The girl was sent to a large school at Nuneaton, the town which appeared as Milby in her writings, and there she developed in intelligence on different lines from Isaac, so that Isaac gradually faded into the distance and became a being apart. There were thirty boarders in this school and the principal governess, Miss Lewis, became one of her pupil's dearest friends as well as for many years her constant correspondent. It was she who taught her first to read and care for poetry and George Eliot was always grateful to her.

Children of nine were more developed and self-reliant in those times, or it seems so now when we read of their doings. The time had not yet come when textbooks were supplied by enterprising writers and publishers for every species of instruction, and the youngest scholars had to satisfy their needs with mental food in its natural state and not boiled down to suit their delicate digestion. And the results were not as bad as might be expected. Mary Ann, anyhow, read voraciously without any evident mishap. When only eight a friend lent "Waverley," published thirteen years before, to the elder sister, who returned it before the child had finished reading it. The consequence was, as her friend Miss Simcox tells us, that she set to work to write out the whole story for herself, beginning with Waverley's adventures at Tully Veolan. Her elders were so struck by this unexpected appreciation that the book was got back for her perusal. This is surely a *bona fide* example of youthful precocity.

Little Miss Mary Ann was moved on to yet another school—this one at Coventry and kept by two Miss Franklins, daughters of a Baptist minister. The father resided during his pastorate in a house in Chapel Yard and was the prototype of Rufus Lyon in "Felix Holt." George Eliot was singularly fortunate in her teaching as a girl, and this was one of the best of the schools she attended. From being a slow child she had developed at thirteen into a studious one ; and from acting charades and reading largely she had got a sort of reputation at home. Education, even for girls, cannot then have been at such a low ebb as we are apt to imagine ; for not only was the instruction good at school, but the practical and somewhat sharp-tongued mother, as well as the indulgent father, encouraged rather than thwarted Mary Ann's inclinations.

The staunch churchman and Tory father must have realised the danger of sending his daughter to be under the influence of liberals and dissenters ; and doubtless that influence told, for she conceived the greatest admiration for the aged father of her instructress ; and Miss Rebecca Franklin was a woman of considerable intellectual power. In such a woman we have an example of the old-fashioned preceptress of the best sort—ignorant of science, geometry or psychology—untrained to teach, and yet a real inspirer. And what more can we ask for ? To these good ladies the child was simply the less developed grown-up person who required no special treatment excepting that allowance had to be made for her limitations. And little Mary Ann played her part well and loved her funny grown-up books, and doubtless wrote her essays in the same grown-up language that now seems so odd and stilted.

Anyhow Mary Ann's reading was comprehensive enough. Like Maggie Tulliver she was found per-using Defoe's " History of the Devil "—the Devil always attracts children—and " Rasselas " ; and of course Bunyan's " Pilgrim's Progress," beloved by all generations of young folk in its illustrated form with Apollyon and his great outspreading wings accurately depicted. The wise Miss Franklin saw beyond the shaggy mane and untidy ways and lack of looks—or worse still curls—which were a trial to the tidy practical mother as they were to Maggie Tulliver's mother—herself " the flower of her family for beauty and amiability." She saw that there was something which might a little compensate for these terrible impedimenta in a girl-child—she saw that the child could think and express herself in writing. And so she taught her what she could of composition. Then that most unfortunate of all instructors in these unhappy days when every girl, however disqualified by nature, had to learn the piano—found happiness in teaching a pupil who truly cared for music. The only terrible drawback was when the unlucky victim was called on to show forth her powers in the parlour and do credit to her teacher. Such sad occasions were followed by passionate outbursts of tears while lying prone on the floor of her room.

Thus, like so many others of her kind in days when girls were forced to turn their reflections on themselves and had no outlet in games or exercise, the unlucky Mary Ann with her passionate longings for all that was beautiful and " yearning for something that would link together the wonderful impressions of this mysterious life, and give her soul a sense of home in it," could not but suffer, like Maggie, from " painful collisions," ; and these collisions were to be her lot all through her life.

However, let this be as it might, an outlet for the overpowering emotions had to be found. Girls are usually influenced by their surroundings more than boys, or were in those days, and instead of conceiving a violent revulsion against the religion of her teachers as she might have done, Mary Ann took Paley's " Evidences " to her room and devoured it. Nowadays it seems dry food for a girl, but then it was apparently different. And if something more succulent were needed, there were prayer meetings, in which Mary Ann took a leading part. It was the time when the great Evangelical movement was none too soon shaking up the Church by law established, as well as the dissenting bodies,

Baptist and Methodist, who were beginning to demand religious as well as civil liberty. Coventry was a centre for all this life, and Nuneaton was the scene of a real political riot which brought the well trained girls belonging to a provincial boarding school into personal touch with the politics of the day. There was on the occasion of an election in North Warwickshire a scene such as is described in "Felix Holt." The supporters of the radical candidate occupied the poll and prevented, or made it difficult for the conservative voters to go to the hustings and record their votes. The Scots Greys, who were in the neighbourhood, were called in by the magistrates in these pre-police days ; and the Riot Act was read from the windows of the "Newdigate Arms." In this riot Colonel Newdigate and Mr. Inge were hurt, as well as some of the officers of the Scots Greys : one life was lost, and, as the newspaper account says : " several misguided individuals seriously injured." It is to be noted that the " misguided " non-voters were held of little account ! Few schoolgirls see anything so exciting or exhilarating.

This school life lasted until 1835, when the girl was sixteen. Whether it was a happy life it is difficult to say. The future George Eliot did not seem to be made for happiness of the conventional kind. She was growing up unto " a queer, three-cornered, awkward girl," " sallow and dark " to use her poor mother's expression about this ugly duckling ; she looked so much older than her age that she was taken for one of the Misses Franklin

c

when only thirteen, and one of her schoolfellows
said that it was impossible to imagine her ever
having been a baby : she must have come into the
world fully developed like a second Minerva : her
features were large and fully formed even at an
early age and she had a startlingly serious expression
for a child.   Altogether one cannot wonder that so
unusual a phenomenon did not make friends easily.
Yet she herself yearned for love, as one of the girls
was astonished to discover on reading a poem
written on the blank page of a dictionary.   But if
she did not find love, she learned to write a beautiful
hand—" caligraphy " as it was then called—to
speak correctly if with somewhat formal precision
and not in the provincial dialect used at home.   In
the end her voice had a special sweetness.

One can see it all.   The girl, self-conscious and
introspective, torn in her mind between different
tendencies and inclinations, wanting to be religious
and renounce self, and wanting at the same time
to have approbation and pre-eminence.   Religious
she certainly was in the commonly accepted term
of the word, for she went so far as to wear a peculiar
and unbecoming cap as a token—surely unneeded
in her case, poor child—of her renunciation of the
vanities of this life.   And yet again in her heart she
loved these vanities and had regard even for the
elegancies of ladyhood such as she had seen on her
journeyings with her father.   The end was that she
was admired for her learning and respected for her
qualities ; but it was love she craved for.

Life was going to be a serious thing for Mary Ann

Evans. In January, 1838, both her father and mother fell seriously ill. The father recovered, but later on in the summer the mother died after a painful illness. This was a terrible grief to her daughter. The following year the elder sister, who was in nature something like Celia in " Middlemarch " and very different in character from herself, married a surgeon, and that seemed to break up the home still more. Then Isaac—the once beloved brother—went on his own way and it was a very different way from that of the " little sister." He took up his father's business, hunted and enjoyed himself with his friends, and they were other friends than hers. The elder sister was ultra-evangelical, not just Low Church like her father, and Isaac had become " High " owing to the influence of a tutor at Birmingham. " High " was very far apart from Evangelicalism in those days, and it was new. Therefore the enthusiastic but not wise Mary Ann could not help impressing her views on her brother ; she had not learned that this was not the best way of furthering her aims. The pursuit of pleasure was to her a snare, and the brother was not averse to pleasure. Society was a danger and he was not averse to society. Like Maggie Tulliver, she threw wilfulness and exaggeration even into her self-renunciation : " her own life was still a drama for her, in which she demanded of herself that her part should be played with intensity. And so it came to pass that she often lost the spirit of humility by being excessive in the outward act : she often strove after too high a flight, and came down with her poor little half-fledged wings dabbled in the mud." The path of martyrdom is easier to us than the "steep highway of tolerance, just allowance and self-blame." It is a favourite theme with George Eliot, and it is as true on the large scale of Savonarola as it is on the humble scale of Maggie Tulliver.

When Christina married, the cares of the household devolved on Mary Ann, and she left school and took up her work with the greatest seriousness and zeal. The domestic life had so far had no special claim upon her, and therefore it is all the more creditable to the girl that she made up her mind to show herself a thoroughly efficient housewife, and to carry on the traditions of her mother and her mother's family. The mistress of a busy farmhouse has no light task : her work in the dairy and in the house never seems to be at an end. Her father offered to get a housekeeper to relieve his young daughter from her strenuous duties, but she preferred to do the work herself. And certainly we never could have had the wonderful living accounts of dairy-work and all that it means, from anyone but an experienced dairy-woman. One of George Eliot's beauties was in her large, finely shaped hands—hands such as she often described in accounts of her heroines—and it was said (though this may be apocryphal) that her pride was that one hand was larger than the other, owing to her housekeeping duties in making cheese and butter at Griff.

But the busy woman generally has time for other things, and Miss Evans, as became a pupil of Miss

Rebecca Franklin, took up "good works." She visited the poor, organised clothing clubs and so on, no doubt from the evangelical point of view ; for such things were not as commonly done as now, excepting on a religious basis. And in addition to this, or rather first and foremost, she was pursuing an active intellectual life of her own. She had an Italian master who came regularly from Coventry to Griff—a long journey in those days—and gave her lessons in Italian and German ; besides this she had (also from Coventry) a master for music. And she herself got through an immense amount of miscellaneous reading. This sounds as though it were satisfactory enough ; it would be thought to be so even in these days for a girl whose evident duty it appeared to be to stay at home and look after her father. The long evenings at home when she played to her father who loved music, and also read aloud to him, might be supposed to be happy. But we know from her description of a young woman's life " the slavery of being a girl " when the force was there to do something big in the world ; we know, when " a man's force of genius " was in an individual, how such life galled. She tried to repress her larger self, to put her strength into cultivating her own mind, without having any of the sympathy and help of others which a young man who studies at college has as a matter of course. There was none with whom on such matters she could exchange a sympathetic word.

The commencement of the feminist movement was approaching when women were beginning to speak of their "rights," and, even more, certain men were beginning to assert that they had rights. It was not till long after that John Stuart Mill wrote the "Subjection of Women," but the question was in the air, and almost unconsciously it influenced every thoughtful woman, expecially every young woman. So that when Mary Ann Evans felt her fingers "tremulous from the boiling of currant jelly" or had a drowsy sensation produced by "standing sentinel over damson cheese and a warm stove"; or when she was mending and darning by the fire, her mind was wandering far afield to the regions she longed to explore and could not. . She was becoming conscious that what she called "the slough of domestic troubles" or the *malheurs de cuisine* were becoming a slough of troubles; and that is fatal in the life of a woman situated as she was. If only someone could have told her in what good stead the impressions she was receiving were to prove to her in later life, she might have been in some measure comforted. As it was, all seemed a little dreary and drab; and yet she fully appreciated the home and all it stood for. Mary Ann always required an object on which to pour out her devotion, and at present there was none. Despair seemed to be falling upon her, and yet she was only nineteen and had the best part of life before her. "Her mind," she says, "presents an assemblage of disjointed specimens of history, ancient and modern, scraps of poetry picked up from Shakespeare, Cowper, Wordsworth and Milton; newspaper topics; morsels of Addison and Bacon,

Latin verbs, geometry, entomology and chemistry ; reviews and metaphysics—all arrested and petrified and smothered by the fast thickening anxiety of actual events, relative anxieties and household cares and vexations."

What was wrong was that her life was full to overflowing but with impressions and sensations too keenly felt, and no capacity for setting them in their proper places—powers in plenty but no sense of being able to achieve. There was even a certain sense of dissatisfaction with present social conditions. In those days the differences in manner of life between classes were very marked, and the sense of difference was becoming a conscious and galling fact. Her religion, though it gave her comfort of a sort, cut her off from many pleasures that were open to other girls of her class, and prevented her from associating with them. She paid a memorable visit of a week with her brother in London, but though she worked hard at seeing sights, she would not go to any of the theatres with him and spent her evenings reading and alone. She wrote to her former governess in 1838 : " When I hear of the marrying and giving in marriage that is constantly being transacted, I can only sigh for those who are multiplying earthly ties which, though powerful enough to detach their hearts and thoughts from heaven, are so brittle as to be liable to be snapped asunder at every breeze. The happiest people are those who instead of engaging in projects for earthly bliss, are considering their lives but as a pilgrimage, a scene calling for diligence and

watchfulness, not for repose and amusement."
Such letters seem to us intolerably priggish, and we
have some sympathy with brother Isaac's criticisms.
But we have to remember the time in which she
wrote and the probable views of the recipient of
the letter, which probably modified its tone.

Had Mary Ann Evans had the religion of another
land, she would certainly have been said to have
had the call to a religious life. As it was she
read Pascal and would have made an excellent
Port Royalist. And as a Protestant English girl,
she also applied herself to reading Hannah More.
"The contemplation of so blessed a character,"
she says, "is very salutary." Her ambitions
indeed are high, since, though she fears she cannot
attain to the holiness of St. Paul, "it is very
certain we are generally too low in our aim, more
anxious for safety than sanctity, for place than
purity." And then she bursts forth with "Oh,
that we could live only for eternity!" like a saint
of old or a Bernadette of her own age. Wilberforce's
Life had appeared this very year (1838) in the
portentous form of a five-volume book, and the
girl had begun it expecting a "rich treat," for she
felt that there was a similitude—difficult for us to
follow—between his temptations, or at least *beset-
ments*, and hers, that make his experience very
interesting to her. She prays that she may be as
useful in her obscure station as he was in his exalted
one. "Might she be sanctified wholly!" Her
mind has been clogged by languor of body to which
she was prone to give way, and at this we cannot

wonder when we know of her duties about her nineteenth birthday—" an awakening signal." For the work and anxieties of Michaelmas and " much company " were so great that this gave her little time for other pursuits. Michaelmas, indeed, appears to have been a serious trial, connected as it was with matters " so nauseating " to her, that she required consolation. One pictures the large family gathering consuming the Michaelmas goose with its apple sauce, and other delicacies, and the sensitive girl struggling to do her part and yet keep her soul pure.

Even her music must have been set aside, for she meant to attend an oratorio given at Coventry, but declares that she cannot decide on the " propriety or lawfulness of such exhibitions of talent and so forth, because I have no soul for music." And as a " tasteless person " she goes on to regret that music is not reserved for purposes of strict worship, nor can she think that " a pleasure that involves the devotion of all the time and powers of an immortal being to the acquirement of an expertness in so useless (at least in ninety-nine cases out of a hundred) an accomplishment, can be quite fine or elevating in its tendency."

This is very strange and must really have been artificial, because George Eliot was deeply susceptible to music throughout her later life ; and even two years after this date, when she attended the Birmingham Festival, she was so affected by it that the attention of people sitting near was attracted by her hysterical sobbing. It may be that, like one of her heroines, her enjoyment was not of the kind that indicates a great specific talent—certainly she had no very special technique—but that the "supreme excitement of music was only one form of that passionate sensibility which belonged to her whole nature, and made her faults and virtues all merge in each other."

Miss Lewis was not the only sympathetic friend to whom the girl poured out her religious sentiments and aspirations. Her own family for the most part was orthodox and conforming, but not extreme. There was, however, one exception. Her father's younger brother Samuel had married a Methodist preacher, and this Elizabeth Evans was the prototype of Dinah Morris, one who, consciously or unconsciously, had a great influence on her young mind. She writes to her aunt Elizabeth begging for a "draught from your fresh spring" and, more wonderful still for a girl of her age, asks even for a word of exhortation which she assures her will be taken in good part. Mrs. Fletcher's Life had been sent her by her aunt, who on her part must have been modest in her estimate of her own spiritual condition despite her preaching powers. She laments not only her lukewarmness in comparison with Mrs. Fletcher, but has the highest appreciation of the spiritual state of her niece—an appreciation which was soon to have a sad blow. The niece naturally deprecates her aunt's high eulogies since she felt herself to be far too conscious of her besetting sin which was ambition and desire to stand well with her fellow creatures.

The question of the reading of fiction was one hotly discussed by evangelicals in those days. Mary Ann Evans tried to argue that we must at least read classical fiction in order to understand classical allusions ; and just as we are subject to malign influences all round and yet repel them, we can surely do the same in respect to fiction—that is, receive the good into our minds and repel the rest. But on the whole, as her one-time pupil told Miss Lewis, it is clearly best to drink not of a cup that may perchance prove poisonous even if our object is to deter others from risking life. The future novelist had begun by reading all sorts of books promiscuously, poor child, and now the spirit of repentance had laid hold of her, and she thought with horror of the castles in the air which she had built. She, a Victorian of Victorians, brought up in the paths of strictest piety and evangelicalism, argued the whole question out. " If it be said the mind must have relaxation, ' Truth is strange— stranger than fiction.' When a person has exhausted the wonder of truth, there is no other resort than fiction ; till then, I cannot imagine how the adventures of some phantom, conjured up by fancy, can be more entertaining than the transactions of real specimens of human nature from which we may safely draw inferences. Alas, is it not that there is an appetite that wants seasoning of a certain kind, and that this cannot be indicative of health ? " How conscious was Mary Ann of this sad appetite within her own distorted mind, and the lonely girl is ready to weep at the idea of wasting her time on things that never existed, while she could not know a fraction of those that do exist.

Mary Ann Evans was only a type. In hundreds of homes in England the same heartrending questions were being asked. It may be called a dreary and sterile outlook, but we must remember that it gave a trend to the minds of those who were not overwhelmed by it, that helped them all their lives to care for the real things of life more than the evanescent.

CHAPTER III

Young Womanhood
(1840–1849)

MARY ANN EVANS at the age of twenty-one found
herself, as we have seen, in the centre of a religious
movement which was deeply influencing the society
in which she lived. It was of course possible for
her to have remained secure with the extremer
section of the orthodox school, as represented by
Mrs. Fletcher and Hannah. More, whose writings she admired ; but, unfortunately, she was
brought into contact with a whole multitude
of doctrines which were not only to disturb
her faith, but to threaten the happiness of her
family life.

Darwin had not of course as yet published his
devastating " Origin of Species," but people were
reading Carlyle and were soon to read their Darwin.
Carlyle affirmed his belief in forceful language, but
he was a moralist and pantheist rather than a devout
Christian. Ruskin admired the form and the spirit
that caused Christianity to exist, but we could not
call him an orthodox believer. Then there was the
" Broad " school arising, with its Cloughs, Kingsleys,
Matthew Arnolds, Seeleys and so many others.
Even Tennyson joined in the general admiration of
an " honest doubt " which may have more faith

than half the creeds ; and Browning had much the same outlook.

All this was very well, but it opened the way for the strictly religious and orthodox of two distinct sorts who took up a stand of frank opposition to these laxer views. The Oxford Movement had begun fourteen years before, and was culminating about this time (1841) with the publication of " Tract XC " : this school was to have momentous effects on religious life in England. There was also the evangelically orthodox school to which belonged the majority of ordinary English people, especially of the middle classes ; and which, through its powerful Press and organised opinion, did yeoman service against the Tractarians on the one hand and the Broad church or "unbelievers " on the other.

It was impossible for a sensitive young woman like Mary Ann Evans to live in a time like this without being profoundly influenced by it. She began to read that dangerously doubting believer Pascal, and gradually made her way on to other theological writers and critics. Her own first effort in authorship took the strange form of a religious poem on death, published in the *Christian Observer*, the editor of which was astute enough to detect a slight unorthodoxy in the writer's conception of the sacred text. There was a wonderful standard in those days ! If fiction were more or less banned, Miss Evans's general reading was voluminous. Most of the great poets were consumed, and Wordsworth was now as ever her favourite amongst them all. But it was religious matters that interested her most,

and she had a great scheme for making an Eccle-
siastical Chart of a comprehensive kind which would
give every sort of information about the chronology
of the Apostolical and Patristical writings, schems
and heresies—a scheme which possibly betokened
youth rather than experience, but which proved a
valuable exercise for a serious student of history.
The Newdigate family opened up their valuable
library for her use ; otherwise she would have been
hard put to it to procure books. She "hedged
herself in " over this work, and just ventured forth
with joy occasionally to read the Oxford Tracts, the
" Lyra Apostolica " and the " Christian Year."

Perhaps fortunately, a chart was suddenly published by another, and that left the girl historian
out of work. She then ventured to emerge from
her theology to read the " Faerie Queene," " Don
Quixote," and Mrs. Somerville on Physical Science.
But after that she attacked Isaac Taylor, then
reputed to be one of the most " eloquent and pious
of writers." The Taylor family were certainly
counted to be of the elect : there were Ann (Mrs.
Gilbert) and Jane, both of whom wrote irreproachable moral and religious poetry for children. But
Isaac, the line-engraver, ventured into deeper regions,
for he carried his studies into philosophy, and even
became a candidate (though an unsuccessful one)
for a chair of Logic and Metaphysics in Edinburgh.
His best known work is his " History of Enthusiasm,"
but it was that on " Ancient Christianity and the
Oxford Tracts " that Mary Ann " gulped down in
reptile-like fashion." What it was in this book that

had so dire an effect on her beliefs it is difficult for us to understand, but the early Fathers were dealt with in what then seemed a critical fashion, and tended to suggest difficulties to a mind prepared to receive them. Anyhow, the book was discussed with the Rev. Mr. Sibree, a Nonconformist minister in Coventry, and the difficulties grew rather than solved themselves. Quite gradually there came to be a different tone in the letters to Miss Lewis, Miss Evans's constant correspondent and religious confidante. The religious side becomes less prominent, and poetry and other forms of literature are now freely discussed. The writer gradually became aware of what in literature was worthless, and even if recommended to her by her friend, she ruthlessly discarded it, saying : " Why should she feed on the broth of literature when she can get strong soup—such, for instance, as Shelley's ' Cloud,' the five or six stanzas of which contain more poetic metal than is beat out in all Mr. B.'s pages." This must have been truly disconcerting to her correspondent.

Till now, Mary Ann Evans's life on the whole had been quiet and uneventful, but after 1840, when she had reached her twenty-first year, there was to be a considerable change. So far she had been living in the country, and country life meant isolation in a degree it is difficult for us to realise. Trains, bicycles and motor-cars have changed rural conditions much ; but the first change, the advent of the locomotive, was the most surprising change of all : " Would not a parcel reach you by railway ? "

a query tentatively addressed to Miss Lewis at Nuneaton, was the first significant token of what was about to transform the whole mode of life. Mr. Evans was greatly affected by the alteration in respect of his business as valuator, as crowds of navvies with their pickaxes were soon cutting their way along the new roads. But this change came along with another, for Mr. Evans had decided to hand over his home and the management of Sir Roger Newdigate's estate to his son Isaac, who had of late been helping him, and who was now married. Therefore in the early spring of 1841 Mr. Evans removed from Griff, which had been his daughter's home practically all her life, to Foleshill Road, near Coventry, where the two settled in a semi-detached suburban villa with a garden, which was made as like the beloved old garden at Griff as possible, but which meant town life instead of country.

To her beloved friend, Miss Lewis, Mary Ann Evans writes :

" My only reason for writing is to obtain a timely promise that you will spend your holidays chiefly with me, that we may once more meet among scenes which, now I am called on to leave them, I find to have *grown in* to my affections. Carlyle says that to the artisans of Glasgow the world is not one of blue skies and a green carpet, but a world of copperas fumes, low cellars, hard wages, ' striking ' and whisky ; and if the recollection of this picture did not remind me that gratitude should be my reservoir of feeling, that into which all that comes from above or around should be received as a source of fertilisation

D

for my soul, I should give a lachrymose parody of the said description, and tell you all-seriously what I now tell you playfully, that mine is too often a world such as Wilkie can so well paint—a walled-in world furnished with all the details which he remembered so accurately, and the least interesting part thereof is often what I suppose must be designated the intelligent ; but I deny that it has even a comparative claim to the appellation ; for give me a three-legged stool, and it will call up associations— moral, poetical, mathematical—if I do but ask it, while some human beings have the odious power of contaminating the very images that are enshrined as our soul's arcana."

This change of abode meant living in a centre of some activity, commercial and intellectual, a town of factories and mills, and a society of busy, active people. The change was great to one with George Eliot's sensibility to surroundings, and we are conscious of the fact that her attitude of mind changed with her change of life. Her ways of life also necessarily altered, and she became much more fastidious as regards her home surroundings than before. The town was small in those days, having, perhaps, not more than 30,000 inhabitants, but it was full of ancient traditions as well as modern industries.

What affected Mary Ann Evans most of all throughout her life was not so much her surroundings as the nature of the friendships made by her, and now at last she found congenial spirits with whom to converse. The days of the influence of Miss Lewis were waning, and the letters to her after this date are explanatory of the new influences in her own life, rather than confidential as before. She had the sense of loneliness that comes most acutely to the mind of the young, and at the same time, hard as she worked at things domestic as well as those of the intellect, she felt the precious moments going by without any adequate return. She was still of the old days as regards the social and domestic demands made upon her, while longing to spread her wings and fly ; but attempted flights did not carry her far.

Now, too, she became more conscious of the misery around her, and longed to give a hand at something beyond the clothing club and the other ordinary charities of the day. The misery to be seen in the streets made her wonder whether she had the right to engage in " mental luxury "—the luxury for which she pined. In a slightly later generation, Octavia Hill, another woman of the same type and passionately devoted to poetry, under the same impulse turned to the active social work in which her name became famous. George Eliot, whatever may have been her inclinations, remained in the main a student ; she collected a good library of her own, besides having access to other books, and had masters to help her. The Rev. T. Sheepshanks, head master of the Coventry Grammar School, taught her Greek and Latin, both of which she thirsted to know. She continued her studies of modern languages—French, German and Italian— under Signor Brezzi ; and Mr. Simms, the organist of St. Michael's, Coventry, and a fine musician, instructed her in music, just as Rosamond Vincy, in " Middlemarch," was instructed by one who " might have been a noted Kapell-meister." One of her biographers, Mathilde Blind, says that archæology, for which she had so many opportunities of study in Warwickshire, had little attraction for her compared with music, about which she constantly speaks in her novels. The same writer, who wrote soon after George Eliot's death, and who had opportunities of gleaning much personal information, tells of an abortive love story, the first of many passions to which that difficult nature was subject. This engagement, or semi-engagement, was one which her father refused to countenance, and it is supposed that he was justified in his attitude as events turned out. Mary Ann sadly assented, as daughters usually did in those days, but we know nothing further of the matter.

Miss Evans soon made friends with some of the more intelligent of the residents in Coventry. First of all there was a Mr. Bray, a wealthy ribbon manufacturer with a taste for literature and much bitten by the new " science " of phrenology. He was an author and had written volumes entitled the " Education of the Feelings " and " The Philosophy of Necessity." Then Mrs. Bray, though herself religiously disposed, was also interested in speculative matters, and occasionally wrote for publication, though usually on such practical questions as kindness to animals, a matter in which George Eliot helped her long years afterwards by supplying her with the funds necessary for publication.

But in addition to the Brays themselves, there was a brother and sister of Mrs. Bray, who were also writers and religious inquirers. The brother, who was named Charles Hennell, had published in 1838, " An Inquiry Concerning the Origin of Christianity," a book which explained the origin of Christianity by natural causes and was thought worthy of being translated into German with a preface by Strauss. Then the sister, Sara Hennell, became Mary Ann Evans's very dear friend. She was highly strung and nervous, and brought all the ardour of feeling into her metaphysical speculations.

It was Charles Hennell's writings that had the greatest effect on George Eliot's mind, following as they did on doubts of origins set on foot by her previous reading. In him she met with the utmost freedom of investigation as regards Biblical criticism and the philosophy of Christianity, though the writer disclaimed there being no permanent value to be derived from the Biblical record, and held that the teaching of Jesus represents no sudden break from the previous teaching of philosophy. All this impressed the girl greatly, and it is difficult for us nowadays to realise what it meant to her in her struggles after enlightenment to find that others were travelling the same road. Then the home at Rosehill, the residence of the Brays, was a charming one and there were occasionally visitors of distinction and breadth of view, such as George Combe (whose outstanding fame has somewhat vanished), and yet greater ones like Emerson and Froude. The quiet, gentle-mannered girl with her pale face but expressive eyes, loved her talks in the old-fashioned garden, and was for the first time appreciated as she deserved.

Delightful as this new life was, it soon brought difficulties with it. Miss Evans had been, as we have seen, in the habit of pouring out her soul to Miss Lewis. But in a letter written in November of 1841, she says : " My whole soul has been engrossed in the most interesting inquiries for the last few days, and to what result my thoughts may lead, I know not—possibly to one that will startle you ; but my only desire is to know the truth, my only fear to cling to error. I venture to say our love will not decompose under the influence of separation, unless you excommunicate me for differing from you in opinion. Think—is there any *conceivable* alteration in me that would prevent your coming to me at Christmas ? I long to have a friend such as you are, I think I may say, alone to me, to unburthen every thought and difficulty—for I am still a solitary, though near a city."

This shows how her new views were likely to be regarded even by her closest friend. The course which was most likely to be pursued by a young woman in a case like hers, was outwardly to have conformed, whatever might have been her beliefs. But George Eliot had something of the martyr, as well as of the logician, in her nature. It was impossible for her to hold an equivocal position and to her mind the simple and obvious thing to do was to cease going to church. This was an unforgivable offence in the eyes of her father as an orthodox churchman of the old school, and it brought about a family crisis. Things came to such a pass that Mr. Evans wished to dispose of the house and go to live with his still orthodox married daughter; while Mary Ann was to go to Leamington and try to support herself by teaching.

To us this seems a desperate remedy for a venial offence; but such an offence seemed heinous in middle-class Victorian circles, and when it became known it would have been the subject of endless criticism and gossip. The daughter felt it all keenly, ready as she was, in words at least, to face her own difficulties of " doleful lodgings " and of being made a " gazing-stock." Mrs. Pears, another sister of Mrs. Bray, who had indeed first introduced her to the fatal Bray family with the innocent view of influencing them for good, was to have been her companion.

The " cool glances " and exhortations to the " suppression of self-conceit " were hard to bear, but they only made George Eliot " wrap more closely round her the warmth of determinate purpose." And, indeed, perhaps she was trying enough to the parent who never conceived that he should beget a child—and above all a woman-child—who would strike out in such unusual and uncomfortable lines, and be so uncompromising in her expression of her views. He had done all in his power to give her a happy and comfortable home, and why should she, his " little wench " of days gone by, that he loved so much, shake the conventions of what to him was civilised life, by breaking with the

essential conditions on which it was held ?   There was
also the more trying sorrow of those like the good
Mrs. Elizabeth Evans, the preacher, who had been
so uplifted because of her niece's spiritual condition
not long before, and now found her in what she
termed "a crude state of free-thinking." The
Rev. Mr. Sibree pleaded with her in vain.   The
situation was indeed tragic enough, and as usual
Mary Ann, like Maggie Tulliver, felt it all most
keenly once the deed was done beyond repair.
The father at length, however, relented sufficiently
to withdraw the house from the agent's hands, and
his daughter went to pay a visit to her brother and
his wife, the Isaac Evans, at Griff. She must have
felt this sufficiently trying, but she received from
her relatives " unlooked for blessings—delicacy and
consideration," and she began to recant her sad conclusion about the indifference to her of the world,
for even her acquaintances at her beloved Griff
were kind and smiled on her despite her terrible
heresy. So, though still convinced that she must
learn to be "independent of what is baptized by
the world external good," she began to consider
whether her own conduct had been free of reproach.
Had she shown the respect and regard due to her
father's opinion—the father she loved so well ?
She regretted her impetuosity, just as Maggie
Tulliver used to regret it, and was only too glad
when what she felt her banishment was over ; and
as she and her father were both equally miserable,
she returned home on the understanding that she
would go to church as before.   Later on she,

like all of us, was wise, and regretted her action, or at least her way of carrying it out. Looked at from a distance this episode throws a curious light on the manners and customs of the day.

After this date things went well, and between voluminous reading and housekeeping, time passed happily. Correspondence was always a pleasure, though we cannot but wish the well-turned sentences a little less consciously well turned. There was at least one little expedition in 1843 with the Hennells and another friend, Miss Brabant, daughter of a Dr. Brabant of Devizes. The last acquaintance had important consequences, because Miss Brabant had at the instigation of Joseph Parkes of Birmingham, a prominent liberal and advanced thinker, and other friends, undertaken the translation of Strauss's *Leben Jesu*; but on becoming engaged to Charles Hennell, she persuaded George Eliot to take over the task.* This was a further step in the direction in which Mary Ann Evans was tending to go. But as usual her views were thoroughly thought out, and her position almost painfully *rangé*. She realised that the first impulse of the young is to withhold the slightest effort at compromise with what they conceive to be error : that the relief of throwing off the burden of rejected beliefs or dogmas thrust upon us is so great, that we feel a longing to make everyone share in our discoveries. And then she realised further that we gradually make the discovery that we are only

* George Eliot paid a visit to Dr. Brabant after his daughter's marriage in order to supply her place. The visit was not, however, wholly successful.

passing through a process which does not entitle
us to take any such extreme steps. We see, as she
says, that speculative truth begins to appear but
the shadow of individual minds—that even we
ourselves can hardly, e.g. afford to part with crutches
that have helped us, and that to do away with
what we have regarded as incrustations of error is
often to destroy the vitality of the whole body.
" It is the quackery of infidelity to suppose that
it has a nostrum for all mankind, and to say to all
and singular ' Swallow my opinions and you shall
be whole.' " We have the same penetrating questions meeting us everywhere in the various circles
of seriously minded people at this period, whether
amongst the Tractarians, the Broad Church, or
the Evangelicals and Dissenters. Men and women
fought through it with their heart-blood.

It is a phase which, in looking back at those
days, we are apt to forget, because there were so
many circles—and circles which produced enduring
work that stamps the period, in which it meant
nothing. What was it to Dickens or to Thackeray
or Disraeli ? It did not exist. But to Carlyle, to
Newman, to Manning, to Browning, even to Tennyson, and to so many minor figures, it meant everything. And now that these struggles are so far
away; now that the growth of science and the
acceptance of the principle of evolution have changed
our point of view, even though the new attitude of
mind may not be properly defined and may still
leave the relation of the spiritual to the material
vague and unsatisfactory, there is no longer that

tense interest in the struggle that seemed to those
of the previous generation one of life and death.
Anyhow Mary Ann Evans shared to the utmost in
the pains that the time-spirit put upon her. She
argued and argued. She saw so clearly that if one
does not conform to prescribed ordinances, hitherto
respected and sacred, others do not comprehend ;
they relax not in the same way from conviction
but from letting the essentials go ; and not one
person but many suffer. How are we to act ? The
same old answer comes to the struggling girl. We
cannot fight against freedom of inquiry. We must
sow good seed when we can, and not root up tares
which will inevitably bring the wheat along with
them—we must remember St. Paul's teaching about
the conduct of the strong to the weak. And so
she went to church, worked away at her Strauss
translation—six pages a day—not feeling quite
sure, or sure at all, that she was doing the right
thing.

There were other friends at Coventry who were
shocked at Mary Ann Evans's new departure as
well as her near relatives. She had been giving
German lessons to Miss Sibree, a young lady a little
older than herself, and there was much controversy
with the father, and consequent fears that the
lessons might be discontinued. Of course German
Biblical criticism was so formidable a menace to
orthodoxy at this time that this is not wonderful.
But Miss Blind tells us that before tackling the
" Inquiry Concerning the Origin of Christianity "
Mary Ann read through the whole of the Bible from

beginning to end. And another friend, Miss Edith Simcox, says that one day when walking near Foleshill she paused to clasp her hands with a wild aspiration that she might live " to reconcile the philosophy of Locke and Kant," and that years afterwards she remembered the very turn of the road when these words were spoken. This shows the mental atmosphere in which she was living.

Disputations may have formed a great part of the intercourse with the Brays and their friends, but there was mercifully a certain amount of diversion too, and already the future George Eliot had begun to relate the conversations of labourers, farmers and butchers that she observed and remembered so well. In 1843 she went with some of the party to Tenby and at this watering place she actually attended a public ball, the first and last that we hear of, perhaps because partners were scarce and the results consequently disappointing.

In a ball-room Miss Evans might not have been specially attractive. Even in youth we are told that her beauty was but in expression, and in a quantity of soft, pale-brown hair which one hears was on one occasion cut in order that Combe might the better observe her bumps ! Her head was massive, her features powerful and rugged, her mouth large but shapely, the jaw singularly square for a woman. Her complexion was sallow—pale but not fair—and her blue-grey eyes, constantly changing in tint and expression, were small and not beautiful. But everyone agrees that what was striking was the play of light and shadows on the face, and the mobility of the mouth. Thus the whole face lightened up in conversation so that its inherent plainness was not noticed. A low, deep voice "vibrating with sympathy" was also a great attraction. Altogether she was of the type of plain woman who often improves with age as the character stamps itself on the outward figure. We are constantly told of the charm she exercised over those with whom she conversed in later years. She had dignity combined with a somewhat sad expression—"bishop-like" as Lord Morley described her to the present writer. She was about middle height, but looked taller than she was, since she had a well-poised, slight figure. Her health was never robust, and she was, as we have seen, highly nervous and excitable. Thus, despite her great mental vigour, she had all the susceptibility and passion of what is held to be the feminine nature, and it was this that made life so specially difficult to her: in these early days she often "wept bucketfuls of tears." Later on, as we shall see, she reached the power of governing herself and in a measure her passions. But her sympathy was so keen, and her power of entering into the lives of others so unusual, that all through she bore the sorrows of others as well as her own, a faculty that gave her a quite unwonted power of friendship. George Eliot always had friends—intimate friends—both men and women. This was no doubt a great source of happiness to her, but it was also a trial. In some cases passion was apt to find its way in ; in others the very keenness of her feelings made the relationship almost unendurable. The worst of a sympathetic nature is that it draws to itself all that there is to tell, and sometimes more than that.

* * * * *

The work Miss Evans had undertaken was no sinecure, and she sickens at the idea of having Strauss on her hands for a lustrum instead of saying good-bye to him in a year. She is inclined to vow that she will never translate again if she lives to correct the sheets for Strauss. Her work required much patience, will and energy, as well as study, for she had to teach herself a good deal of Hebrew (later on useful enough to her) and she was often tempted to relinquish her task. It was only the constant encouragement of friends that enabled her to continue the " soul-stupefying labour." Strauss did not really appeal to her emotional and spiritual nature. Her " leathery brain " had to work at " leathery Strauss "; and she goes on " I am never pained when I think Strauss right— but in many cases I think him wrong, as every man must be in working into detail an idea which has general truth, but is only one element in a perfect theory—not a perfect theory itself." Then again the emotional Miss Sara Hennell writes of her friend that " she is Strauss-sick—it makes her ill dissecting the beautiful story of the Crucifixion, and only the sight of the Christ-image and picture makes her endure it." The image mentioned refers to a copy of Thorwaldsen's crucified Christ which she greatly valued, and which stood over her desk in her study at Foleshill where she worked at that time, and from the window of which she had an expansive view of the country.

Between nervousness about her work, headaches, and the anxiety which was growing about her father's health, she was in the year 1846 beginning to suffer greatly. Sometimes, however, she had little expeditions which set her up for the time, such as one with the Brays to Atherstone Hall where she had the pleasure of meeting Harriet Martineau for the first time. She greatly admired some of Miss Martineau's work, such as " The Crofton Boys " and " had some delightful crying over it " which brings before us the time at which such " pleasures " existed in abundance !

So things went on unhappily enough, with constant hopes and fears about her work—work that worried her, though well and carefully done, because it was not in her view important enough to demand the sacrifice of her whole soul. That is what she craved for, to have demanded of her something more—something through which she could give expression to that soul, cabined and confined, which was yet struggling to be free. Strauss with his abstract views, translation with its limitations, were a poor substitute for the self-expression which she demanded.

The book was brought out by Mr. Chapman in 1846, but this publication itself was a matter of anxiety. The guarantors of funds had somewhat forgotten their promises, but the generous Mr. Joseph Parkes had not done so : he and Mr. Hennell paid £300 towards the publication. Directly the book was out its excellence was recognised, and the translation obtained a certain amount of fame ; while the translator received the moderate sum of £20. In the end the whole edition was sold and others were issued later so that the guarantors may have been recouped.

At last the troubles were over : " the dull ass does not mend his pace for beating ; but he *does* mend it when he finds that he is near his journey's end. I am determined from henceforth to live in and love the present of which I have done too little," she exclaims ; " My poor adust soul wants refreshment," she says to Miss Hennell ; " I do not know *one* person who is likely to read the book through—do you ? Next week we will be merry and sad, wise and nonsensical, devout and wicked together." Strauss himself sent a good letter and preface, and the translator was happy, and meant to set to at once in characteristic fashion to refresh her soul by reading her Shakespeare through from end to end.

The galled neck is thus out of the yoke, and in May, 1846, there was a visit to the Hennells at Hackney, and an evident desire for fun though " we are as ignorant as Primitive Methodists about any of the amusements that are going." " Please," she writes to Mrs. Bray " to come in a very mischievous, unconscientious, theatre-loving humour " —a different spirit from that of a few years earlier when Mary Ann sat poring over her books when her brother Isaac went to the play, and when she disregarded her appearance so much as, in her own words, " to go about like an owl." Soon after this her father's health began to fail and he and she paid a visit to Dover together. All that autumn was a happy time for Mary Ann Evans, as she had an encouraging letter from Strauss and good reviews. The translation was anonymous, and it must have been a pleasure as well as amusement to the translator to hear herself spoken of as " a man who has familiar knowledge of the whole subject " ; and of the work as having been taken part in by " a discerning and well-informed theologian."

That there was a light-hearted side to the serious young translator is evidenced not only from the above but also from an amusing *jeu d'ésprit*. She describes the supposed visit of a dry-as-dust German professor and his search for one who would be both his wife and translator. All efforts proved vain, for he looked for a young lady who was sufficiently ugly, and who yet possessed sufficient capital to provide him with tobacco and *schwarzbier* and to print his books. This paragon he of course found at Coventry, and her friends are invited to the wedding ! Then there was in 1847, the happiness of another stay in London when she heard the " Elijah " and " I Puritani " to her great delight. They were given in Exeter Hall : " I look upon it as a kind of sacramental purification of Exeter Hall, and a proclamation of indulgence for all that is to be perpetrated there during the month of May," she says. These were the days when " May-Meetings " were famous in evangelical circles.

E

Miss Evans corresponded with another philosophical friend, Mr. John Sibree, the son of the Rev. Mr. Sibree before spoken of, who had been sent to a German University, and who translated Hegel's " Philosophy of History." The Sibrees were all warm friends, more particularly Mary, her German pupil, who applied to her for counsel as to religious matters. Instead of leading her into the devious paths dreaded by her friends, she gave her the sound advice first to give more attention to arithmetic which she professed to teach, and only after this was done to settle her religious views ! She also rather characteristically beseeches her young friend, who presumably was in the habit of subjecting her own views to those of an older generation, to love and venerate the old but on no account to trust their application of their gathered wisdom ; since a worn-out, dried-up organisation can never be as rich in inspiration as one fraught with life and energy. This is the outlook of the modern image-breaker, and its truth is illustrated in the case of the unfortunate Maggie Tulliver who has to live, after her father's failure, with parents who have lost all their vitality and power of grappling with new circumstances, and accordingly has herself to suffer most deeply. We have the same motive with Gwendolen Harleth and her mother, and Romola in respect of her father. The age of rebellion was beginning, the age when youth demanded its rights as well as its duties ; and George Eliot, with all her passion for tradition, was one of the greatest rebels. The worst of it was that the old reverence and devotion were all the time present with her, and consequently we have that terrible clashing of different tendencies which made her life a constant warfare. For her friends she might be sure, for herself she never was quite sure, and usually regretted her action when it was too late.

It is difficult to believe that George Eliot had any cause to reproach herself in reference to her father during these last years of his life, for she appears to have been a devoted daughter, reading aloud to and caring for him in every way. Sometimes they travelled together, and sometimes she left her unorthodox and rationalistic theology, and deigned to read Richardson whom she adored, or Disraeli whom she detested. " Young Englandism," she says, " is almost as remote from my sympathies as Jacobitism, as far as its force is concerned, though I love and respect it as an effort on behalf of the people." Of " Sybil "—a book which one might imagine might appeal to her altruistic instincts— she says that " the man hath good veins, as Bacon would say, but there is not enough blood in them " —a curious criticism and hardly a just one. She was never likely to appreciate Disraeli except as an upholder of Israelism, and at this time she was quite devoid of any theory of race, such as later on took so great a hold on her. She appreciated his " tirades against Liberal principles as opposed to popular principles," but she considered that his views were buoyed up by windy eloquence, and that races were bound in time to degenerate just as privileged classes degenerate from continual inter-marriage. When we think of it, it seems strange that Disraeli and she wrote at the same time and of the same people, so absolutely divergent are they in outlook and spirit. But in spite of the tremendous hold he got on the English people, Disraeli was never English, and George Eliot was English to her backbone. George Sand, on the other hand, appealed to her greatly. She would never go to her writings as a moral code, she says, but she " cannot read six pages without feeling that it is given to her to delineate human passion and its results, and some of the moral instincts and their tendencies, with such truthfulness, such nicety of discrimination, such tragic power and withal, such loving gentle humour, that one might live a century with nothing but one's own dull faculties, and not know so much as those six pages will suggest."

The question of love and its meaning was coming very vividly before her, though she cannot make up her mind to agree with George Sand on the subject. Rousseau might, she writes, have been guilty of all sorts of *bassesses*, but " it would not be the less true that Rousseau's genius has sent that electric thrill through my intellectual and moral frame which has awakened me to new perceptions—which has made men and nature a fresh world of thought and feeling to me ; and this not by teaching me any new belief." Rousseau was always a favourite with George Eliot, and when we remember that both had the same passionate nature and warring instincts we need not wonder. George Eliot, unlike him, was usually able to hold hers in check, but it was a constant struggle. She often fell back on the *De Imitatione Christi* which with its cool air as of cloisters, "makes one long to be a saint for a few months"—the few months is typical —" Verily its piety has its foundation in the depth of the divine-human soul."

All her numerous early letters are a curious study. Even the earliest are carefully written—one would say too carefully for the modern view of letter-writing as being a delightful way of wasting time— but though they occasionally have humour, and always thought, they are usually lacking in charm. Charm is an elusive quality, and it is hardly possible to say how and why it comes. Perhaps it has to do with the power of self-forgetfulness and concern with him one speaks to rather than oneself, and yet many delightful letters are egotistic. But possibly the egotism is not self-conscious. George Eliot's letters are well worth perusing—she had a passion for utterance—but one has too much the sense of listening to an oracle even if that oracle is a girl in her twenties. She pictures to a correspondent two sorts of letters—one of simple affection giving a picture of all the details a loving heart pines for, the other the purely intellectual, carried on for ghostly edification in which each party puts salt on the tails of all sorts of subjects. Hers are almost always of the latter type.

At the date we have reached (1848) the world was politically alive and palpitating with interest, and the young woman sympathised with the "revolutionary ardour," and had no use for the "sages

whose reason keeps so tight a rein on their emotions
that they are too constantly occupied in calculating
consequences to rejoice in any great manifestation
of the forces that underlie our everyday existence."
It seemed to her a wonderful thing that she should
live to see a really great movement after conceiving
that the era was what St. Simon calls a critical
epoch, and not an organic one. " I would consent,
however, to have a year clipt off my life for the sake
of witnessing such a scene as that of the men of the
barricades bowing to the image of Christ ' who first
taught fraternity to men.' " " Lamartine," she
continues to Mr. Sibree, " can act a poem, if he
cannot write one of the very first order." Too
hastily she assumed that our working classes are
inferior to the mass of the French people, whose
mind is so full of ideas on social subjects, and who
really desire *reform*. She saw selfish radicalism and
brute sensuality rather than a true sense of justice,
and therefore assumed that a revolutionary movement in England would be destructive rather than
constructive. All we can hope for, she considers,
is slow political reform : " We English are slow
crawlers." Her judgment was often warped by
personal idiosyncrasies.

It is doubtful if George Eliot ever really understood the working people as a whole, and the reason
probably was that she had only come into touch
with the characteristic country people, and not with
those with whom she had much intellectual sympathy. Also she belonged essentially to the comfortable bourgeois classes. And the enlightened

people amongst whom she dwelt were all rather apt
to take the superior air of those who knew what was
for the people's good. Probably the later develop
ment of the " 48 " revolution was also disillusioning.
For Louis Blanc she had an immense admiration—
she worshipped the man who could say—" L'inégalité des talents doit aboutir non à l'inégalité des
retributions mais à l'inégalité des devoirs " so that
in a way she entered into the revolutionary spirit.
Emerson was one of her great heroes and she had
the happiness of seeing him with the Brays and
accompanying the party to Stratford : " The first
man I have ever seen ! " she exclaims, and Carlyle's
eulogium on him delighted her. And again, after
she wrote a notice on the " Nemesis of Faith " for
a local paper, she was delighted to receive a " charming note from Froude, naively and prettily request-
ing her to reveal herself."

But however much she thought and wrote in
private letters, Mary Ann Evans's constant desire to
utter seemed to be always thwarted, and she longed
for her chance to come. " I possess my soul in
patience for a time, believing that this dark, damp
vault in which I am groping will soon come to an
end, and the fresh green earth and the bright sky
be all the more precious to me." Her father was
ill and unable to amuse himself, and she hardly felt
free to follow her own bent for an hour. She
struggled against the tendency to " look black,"
she " needed the Jesuits' discipline of silence."
Her friend Miss Hennell sent her a letter from
Newman who was one of whom she had, in spite of

the total difference in outlook, the deepest appreciation. "His soul is a blessed yea. The highest inspiration of the purest, noblest human soul, is the nearest expression of the truth. These actual volcanoes of one's spiritual life—those eruptions of the intellect and the passions which have scattered the lava of doubt and negation over our early faith —are only a glorious Himalayan chain, beneath which new valleys of undreamed richness and beauty will spread themselves." It was these valleys she longed for.

The father's illness continued and was a terrible strain on the daughter's health and spirits. She did all the nursing herself after the manner of the day, and did it well. She had begun to translate Spinoza's 'Tractatus Theologico-Politicus' and that was a relief to her when she could get at it. It showed the present tendency of her mind to apply herself to one who was in every way so different from Strauss. The translation was never published.

Her father grew weaker and the end came on May 31st, 1849. "What shall I be without my father?" she exclaims in grief. "It will seem as if part of my moral nature were gone."

CHAPTER IV

DIFFICULT YEARS
(1849–1854)

Now that Mary Ann Evans was left alone, the question arose what was to be her future. She had a small—very small—annuity, and plenty of real friends, and these friends came to the rescue. The Brays were going to travel, and they took her to Geneva where she was settled in a *pension* a little way out of the town.

It was a great change for the provincial girl who was young still, though she felt so old, and the Swiss landlady tried to make her feel more like her age by compelling her to dress her hair in the newer fashion ; to abandon the ringlets which are shewn in the early silhouette and adopt the fashionable side pads as introduced by the Empress Eugénie. But Mary Ann was difficult to attire, and she counted herself " uglier than ever." However the change did her good, removing the depression of spirits and " terrors " from which she had been suffering, and turning her mind on new things. Her letters from this *pension*, and the next in Geneva, kept by M. and Mme. d'Albert, are natural and human. This one is to the Brays :—" About my comfort here, I find no disagreeables, and have every physical comfort that I care about. The family seems well-ordered

65

and happy. I have made another friend too—an elderly English lady, a Mrs. Locke, who used to live at Ryde—a pretty old lady, with plenty of shrewdness and knowledge of the world. She began to say very kind things to me in rather a waspish tone yesterday morning at breakfast. I liked her better at dinner and tea, and to-day we are quite confidential. I only hope she will stay—she is just the sort of person I shall like to have to speak to—not at all ' congenial,' but with a character of her own . . . I have quiet and comfort—what more can I want to make me a healthy, reasonable being once more ? I will never go near a friend again until I can bring joy and peace in my heart and in my face—but remember that friendship will be easy then."

M. d'Albert, her landlord at Geneva, was an artist by profession, and we owe a well-known portrait to his skill. He also translated most of her books into French and kept up his friendship to the end. The surroundings were homely and pleasant, because Mme. d'Albert had two boys in whose future George Eliot took an interest, and there was music which she loved. Even the little housemaid, Jeanne, appealed to her. Of course Voltaire and Rousseau were read in these their own surroundings, but from Spinoza she " had been divorced for several months," and her interest in him for the time being waned. Typically, however, she attended science lectures and took " a dose of mathematics every day " to prevent her brain from " becoming quite soft." The only dread apparently was the prospect of a return to the gloom, the *ennui*, the platitudes of England. It had to be, of course : for one thing funds were not too abundant, and Mary Ann Evans even thought of selling some of her books, though this expedient was not resorted to. But she would not have minded the return if she could just have seen some manifest woman's duty before her—as she put it : " Some possibility of devoting myself where I may see a daily result of pure calm blessedness in the life of another." Her filial duties had gone ; life seemed barren and pointless ; and yet she felt she could perform if the chance were only given her.

So at length the tedious journey back was taken with the help of good M. d'Albert, and the Jura mountains were crossed in sledges as in the olden days. Miss Evans went straight to her kind friends the Brays, at Rosehill, but her premonitions had been but too correct, for the sensitive nature soon felt the misery of east wind and dust and missed the glories of the Alps. Coal fires and carpets and comfort did not make up for these : and a visit to Isaac and his wife did not induce her to remain with them. " Oh, the dismal weather and the dismal country, and the dismal people ! " she exclaims. " It was some envious demon that drove me across the Jura." These are things that many feel but few put into words : some such words were being said by husband and wife in a house in Cheyne Row just about the same time.

There really was no cause for this terrible depression, for the Brays, whom George Eliot always liked, offered to make her their guest for sixteen months from April, 1850, to Novenber, 1851 and with this offer she more or less complied even though it was her strong desire to be a free lance and write on philosophic subjects. She got into touch with Mr. Chapman, of the *Westminster Review*, who had published her Strauss, and with Mr. Mackay his assistant editor, and inquired about the boarding house kept by Mr. and Mrs. Chapman in the Strand. As a result, Mr. Chapman and his assistant paid a visit to Rosehill in October, 1850, and in the following January a review by Miss Evans on " The Progress of the Intellect," a book written by Mr. Mackay, appeared in the *Westminster Review*. Thus the young writer seemed fairly started on her way as a philosophical essayist, the rôle she had always pictured for herself.

This is so momentous a period in George Eliot's life that we must try to arrive at the new influences that were being brought to bear upon her, and the effect that these had on her susceptible character. She had learned a good deal at Geneva, had got a somewhat larger view of life than the conventional one presented by her quite intelligent, but also quite limited circle at Coventry. She came back to it seeing what its limitations were, and desirous of breaking forth into the larger world, now she had no domestic duties to restrain her. Hence, though she had her nominal home with her friends the Brays at Coventry, it was understood that this was quite a temporary arrangement to be carried on till she moved permanently to London. With the editor of the *Westminster Review*, Mr. Chapman, she had been brought into close touch over her work, and had evidently come to know him well ; and when she paid a long visit to London in January, 1851, she stayed at his house. Chapman states in his diary that on arrival early in January " her manner was friendly but formal and studied." However, her music was a great attraction, and she read Latin and German with her host.

John Chapman's history was curious. He was born near Nottingham, ran away from home, landed in Australia, returned to England and married in 1843, when he began his studies in medicine. However, he soon deserted medicine for publishing, and after a time removed from Clapton to the Strand, where he settled about 1850. His house had business premises below, and a dwelling house above, and he took in a certain number of boarders to help to meet the necessary expenses. The back of his house abutted on Somerset House. It was this house that became famous as the centre of a literary côterie. Here there came from time to time, often on Monday evenings, Thackeray, Dickens, Carlyle, Lewes, Thornton Hunt, Spencer, Francis Newman, Froude, Emerson, Harriet Martineau, Mrs. Gaskell, Sir David Brewster, W. R. Greg, Forster, and Louis Blanc—a galaxy of Mid-Victorian talent. As these writers centred to a great extent round the *Westminster Review* it is worth while narrating its rather interesting history.

The *Westminster Review* was started by Jeremy Bentham in 1824 as the organ of the Radical party,

the literary editor being Mr. Southern and the
political, Dr. Bowring. But the personality of
James Mill, the father of John Stuart Mill, dominated
the periodical. It had on the whole rather a struggling existence, but after it was incorporated with
the *London Review**, it succeeded in securing as its
most famous editor John Stuart Mill†, who was
assisted by an Aberdonian named John Robertson.
There were now many distinguished contributors
such as Roebuck, Grote, Edwin Chadwick, Mrs.
Austin, Bulwer Lytton, Leigh Hunt, Harriet Martineau and Carlyle. Despite the excellence of its
matter, the *London Review* failed for funds, and it
once more became the *Westminster* in 1836, and was
edited by a Mr. Hickson. He got as contributors
G. H. Lewes, Hill-Burton and W. R. Greg. The
whole scheme was probably an anxious venture,
for Hickson was glad to sell it to Mr. John Chapman
for £350. Chapman gathered around him as contributors such men as Froude and Mark Pattison,
and later Frederic Harrison and Pater as well as
others mentioned before, and made it a real success
on the literary side. He must have had true
editorial gifts, for not only did he carry on the
magazine for many years, but he even managed to
edit it from Paris long after this date, and after
he migrated there and practised as a doctor amongst
the English colony. Certainly he had an extraordinary attraction for both men and women, as far
as social relations go. His manner was exceedingly

* The *London Review* started in April, 1835.
† J. S. Mill did not think it compatible with his office at the India
House to be publicly acknowledged as editor.

agreeable ; he was tall and handsome, with one of the long beards admired more then than now, and a fine head.

The consequence of their close association was that Chapman saw a great deal of his boarder ; they walked constantly together before breakfast in the Park, and as Mr. Chapman was on dubious relations with his wife, jealousies arose. It was a strange and Bohemian household into which Mary Ann Evans had plunged ; its freedom from convention appealed to a young woman struggling after liberty ; while the opportunities it gave for meeting those who had been but names to her before, were like the opening up of a new world to her. She remained till near the end of March, and it is clear that the situation was a strained and difficult one. She herself was extraordinarily susceptible, and Chapman's views of what was seemly were odd. But if he was not a good husband his wife was difficult in nature, a bad housekeeper, and constantly nagging, so that every little event was magnified and distorted.

The visit was over towards the end of March and Miss Evans returned to Coventry, but apparently with a mind disturbed and upset. Was this the great world into which she was possibly to enter, and was she to mingle with the literary world with which she had come into touch, not as a mere onlooker as before, but as one who might be asked to play her part in it and one who had within her the capacity to do so ? Were the old conventionalities of rural and provincial town life but conventionalities which might be discarded, just as she had discarded the religious views which now seemed to her effete, and to belong to a past generation ? Her passionate nature had been restrained by the deep philosophic studies in which she had hitherto been engaged, and she thought she could get satisfaction through them alone. Suddenly there surged up in her those human and wayward impulses, so long repressed by her early training. She noticed with wonder that in the new life the relations between men and women were the pivot on which other relations moved.

George Eliot, we must remember, had from her childhood up been influenced by the ascetic and Christian attitude, which, indeed, was fundamentally hers to the end. Renunciation was what she sought for, the death that was to bring life. But the struggle with wayward impulses was also never ceasing, and sometimes they mastered her for the moment ; when this occurred she had to exert all the power which was within her to regain her self-command. This was perhaps the bitterest part of a bitter young life, and yet it had its recompenses, for at length she came into touch with the outside world of which she dreamed, and for which she had so often longed in the quiet hours spent beside her father. Now at last she found the sympathy which had been lacking heretofore.

The work that Mr. Chapman had in view, and in which he wished to get Miss Evans's assistance, was the publication of a *catalogue raisonné* of philosophic literature—his own philosophic publications particularly—and also the reviving and resuscitating of the *Westminster Review* as a periodical of Liberal views in philosophy and literature. The *Review* he intended ultimately to purchase, and the purchase was completed in October, 1851. The first essential in his plan was to issue a good prospectus, and in this he also wished Miss Evans's help. Naturally all this work and the high esteem for her capabilities from a man whom she regarded as a competent authority, and who held a prominent place in literary London, was a matter of great moment to the young provincial woman.

After Miss Evans's return she carried on her work on the catalogue through correspondence, but in the end of May Mr. Chapman paid a visit of about a fortnight to Coventry, staying with the Brays at Rosehill, where Miss Evans was. The idea of her going to help with the *Westminster* was in both their minds. But any suggestion of this sort roused keen objection on the part of a jealous wife. When at Coventry, Chapman discussed the matter up and down in his usual early morning walks with Miss Evans. She was anxious to go, and willing either to board at the Strand or live elsewhere in London ; she was deeply concerned about the pain she had caused, but still she was anxious to take up the work, and this man who had the power of fascinating those with whom he came into touch also attracted her, though she must have known in her heart that he was as regards passion untrustworthy and un-stable. Though Miss Evans had none of the ordinary outward attractions of womankind, she had the sympathetic soul that drew both men and women to her. And she had also the passionate nature that was all the time crying out for recognition and reciprocity. She had all her life longed to know that others cared for the things she cared for—and that they cared as she wished them to care—and now at last her chance had apparently come. She was skating on thin ice, but she was endeavouring to be mistress of herself and, on the whole, succeeding.

The prospectus in which she helped was a good deal criticised by J. S. Mill, who wrote sarcastically about it ; Martineau was cold, but others like Froude and Greg were more appreciative. Martineau seemed to think that Chapman was descending from the high literary plane to a more commercial level, a stricture that did not seem deserved. It is incidentally rather curious to hear that when John Stuart Mill recommended Chapman to ask Miss Brontë to write an article on modern novelists, Miss Evans, who at this time did not appreciate Charlotte Brontë's work (as she did later on), disapproved of the suggestion ; it was finally handed over to Lewes, though Chapman thought him lacking in that " thoroughness of thought and earnest purpose " for which he sought. In the middle of August Miss Evans and Mrs. Bray came to London from Devonshire, where they had been staying, to see the Exhibition, and at that time things were more or less amicably arranged for Miss Evans's return to the Strand in the end of September, when she was to become the assistant editor of the *Review*. Chapman paid two other visits to Coventry before everything was finally settled ; and it now seemed as if things were simply on a business footing, and there was prospect of happier relations at home. Miss Evans's view of the running of the *Review* was that Chapman should not take much part in writing for it, as he would thereby lose power and influence with the contributors. As matters turned out, however, he wrote a considerable number of articles, and George Eliot was also a contributor besides doing the editorial work. In addition to his work as editor, the publishing part of Chapman's business was considerable. He brought out a number of books that attained fame, such as Emerson's Essays, with a preface by Carlyle, and Froude's " Nemesis of Faith."

Bohemian as might the company and talk occasionally be, there was certainly plenty of interest in the life at 142, Strand. There were also constant visits to opera, concerts and picture galleries. Lectures from Froude were attended, books such as Spencer's " Rights of Women " were read aloud : the last-mentioned being " all admirable and true, but dry and dull," according to Chapman. Then there was a great meeting on the question of sales of books and the rates of profits, at which Dickens took the chair : the question was a critical one to authors at this time, and the meeting was so much of a success, being attended by the great ones of the earth, that at the close Mary Ann sat down to the piano and greeted Mr. Chapman with the strains of " See the Conquering Hero Comes " ! The meeting apparently had an excellent effect, for the questions between authors and booksellers as to rates of retail profits were for the time being settled to their mutual satisfaction.

Herbert Spencer was one of the frequent visitors to the Chapmans. He had just produced his "Social Statics," which, Miss Evans says, Lewes pronounced the best book on the subject. Then her old friend Dr. Brabant (the father of Mrs. Charles Hennell, with whom she had lived for a short time after his daughter's marriage in 1842) reappeared, and took her to the Crystal Palace and theatres. Lewes, a constant visitor, was already well known by his "History of Philosophy," and in a less degree by his novels, and he wrote many articles for the magazine. Chapman had attended a private performance of "The Critic" at Miss Kelly's Theatre, at which there had acted Mr. and Mrs. Lewes and Thornton Hunt: a trio who were seriously to affect Miss Evans's life.

All letters just now are full of business, of getting, or attempting to get, good articles for the *Review*, going sometimes to the theatre—for Spencer was editing the *Economist* on the other side of the Strand and sent the tickets—of meeting Carlyle, who was difficult to catch for the *Review*, but who recommended Browning, the poet, as a contributor, and so on. One of Miss Evans's own articles was a review of Carlyle's "Life of Sterling." Harriet Martineau was kind and cordial but evidently not sympathetic: "I have no doubt she is fascinating when there is time for talk," as the young editor puts it. Miss Parkes, one of George Eliot's closest friends to the last as Mme. Belloc, "is a dear,

ardent, honest creature." Cobden lectured on the
" Abolition of the Taxes on Knowledge," but Miss
Evans was disappointed. Mazzini's speeches are
" better read than heard." " Grote is very friendly
and has propitiated J. S. Mill, who will write for us
when we want him." " We had quite a brilliant
soirée yesterday evening. W. R. Greg, Forster (of
Rawdon), Francis Newman, the Ellises and Louis
Blanc were the stars of greatest magnitude. I had
a pleasant talk with Greg and Forster." Greg was
" much pleased to make my acquaintance." In
the letters we are struck by the number of people
of interest that Chapman collected at his house and
the richness of the times that produced so many men
of first and second degrees of eminence. Evidently
it was all delightful to the intelligent young woman
and she made the most of it.

One sometimes wonders what was the great
attraction to so varied a collection of literary people.
Chapman was carrying on his publishing business
and magazine without any capital to speak of, and
for long after this few contributors were paid. One
of those who took part in the book-selling section
of the establishment was William Hale White, a shy
young man who was to play a prominent part in
the work of interpreting to the world the inwardness
of the intellectual and religious life of his time.
Perhaps no one has given such a veracious and
moving account of what serious and earnest young
manhood passed through during that momentous
period of heart-searching in the latter part of last
century as the writer who became known to us as

Mark Rutherford. One can conceive how the shy, awkward youth when he first came to Mr. Chapman's house was drawn towards Miss Evans whom he found *vis-à-vis* to him at luncheon. Her qualities appear to have struck him at once, and especially the manner in which she greeted a trifling remark made by him, so as to give it some importance.

However it was with Hale White, a real and close—one might say affectionate—friendship was formed with Herbert Spencer. " I went to the Opera on Saturday—' I Martiri ' at Covent Garden—with ' my excellent friend, Herbert Spencer,' as Lewes calls him. We have agreed that there is no reason why we should not have as much of each other's society as we like. He is a good, delightful creature, and I always feel better for being with him." And later : " My brightest spot, next to my loved *old* friends, is the deliciously calm *new* friendship that Herbert Spencer gives me. We see each other every day, and have a delightful *camaraderie* in everything. But for him my life would be desolate enough. What a wretched lot of old shrivelled creatures we shall be by and by. Never mind—the uglier we get in the eyes of others the lovelier we shall be to each other."

Herbert Spencer was just a year younger than his friend, who was then (1852) almost thirty-two. Spencer was clearly interested in Miss Evans, and gives an amusing account of how, following on her inquiries as to the authorship of " Social Statics," she and Chapman had set about finding him a wife. The desired introduction, according to Spencer, took place ; but the young lady (who actually was Miss Evans) proved too highly intellectual—indeed he described her as " morbidly intellectual. A small brain in a state of intense activity "—and nearly as combative as himself. " So," he concludes, " I do not think the spirit will move me." Spencer, the cold-hearted, who had never been in love, had, all the same, been impressed by the lady; impressed first, it is true, by her powers of drafting a resolution at the famous booksellers' meeting ; and he went so far as to describe her as the most admirable woman, mentally, he had ever met. " We have been for some time on very intimate terms," he says. " I am very frequently at Chapman's, and the greatness of her intellect conjoined with her womanly qualities and manner generally keep me by her side most of the evening."*

The association with this remarkable man was one of the most important elements in George Eliot's life, and it is interesting to have his conclusions about her character and appearance, because he had every opportunity of studying both at close quarters, though he studied all as an outsider and unmoved. Unfortunately for her, it was not the same with the more emotional woman. For her it was almost impossible to be in such close relation with a man whom she admired without another element coming in, and we now know from personal testimony that it did come in, however ardently she tried to suppress it.

This is how Spencer describes Miss Evans in

* Autobiography, Vol. I. p. 395.

writing of her later on : " In physique there was, perhaps, a trace of that masculinity characterising her intellect ; for though of but the ordinary feminine height, she was strongly built. The head, too, was larger than is usual in women. It had, moreover, a peculiarity distinguishing it from most heads, whether feminine or masculine ; namely, that its contour was very regular. . . . Her face was remarkably transfigured by a smile. The smiles of many are signs of nothing more than amusement ; but with her smile there was habitually mingled an expression of sympathy, either for the person smiled at or the person smiled with."

This is the almost unanimous testimony of all observers, as is the description of her voice—a contralto of low pitch and naturally strong. Spencer likewise at once observed what was very marked at all times in George Eliot's life—her intense domestic affections. " The activity of these last," he continues rather cynically, " largely conduced to the leading incidents of her subsequent life." He saw clearly in the acute examination he made of this woman, whom he clearly regarded as an interesting phenomenon but no more—that she had an intense desire to be in harmony with the society around her, and that the throwing off of early beliefs and the antagonism that was thereby aroused, was but a phase, and a temporary one. Her natural desire was for agreement, and she deprecated harsh judgments, and was ever ready to forgive. Her bane, indeed, as he considered, was not to judge too hardly of others, but to criticise herself too harshly :

this constant self-criticism led to undue depreciation and distrust of herself—and we might add self-consciousness.

All this criticism is just, as is the praise accorded by the same observant psychologist. For he gives his subject great credit for her humility in not displaying her knowledge, considerable as it was, for having an extremely good memory combined with a quickness of apprehension that made acquisition easy, and some (though less) ability in organising that which she acquired. Thus her constructive imagination, though it could create characters and represent mental states, was, he considered, less satisfactory with plots ; and her speculative faculty " was critical and analytic rather than sympathetic." " She had remarkable capacity for abstract thinking, which so seldom goes along with capacity for concrete representation, even in men " ; and, he adds, " among women, such a union of the two as existed in her, has, I should think, never been paralleled."

This curious friendship was a very different one from that which existed between Miss Evans and Chapman, where there was plenty of reciprocity ; but it was remarkable enough in its way. Spencer and the lady sang together—she joining in with that gentle voice to which she never gave full scope, and they walked up and down the terrace, for which Chapman had a key and which was shut off by a gate from one of the courts in Somerset House in the pre-Embankment days. And there they discussed the Comtian classification of the Sciences, though they also considered the problem of why there were no lines or wrinkles on Spencer's face, which apparently involved a lengthy account of his whole philosophy. In his mind the two were simply good comrades, whose minds were set on things higher than love in its concrete form, and when reports naturally arose about their relationship, since both were still moderately young, he dryly remarked that " these reports were untrue." So they were on one side.*

But George Eliot was not a woman to resent what was, after all, a matter in which there was no blame attached. Spencer did not, with all his perspicacity, realise that he was playing with fire, that is, with a passionate woman ready to burst out on the smallest provocation. One only hopes she saw something of the humour of the situation, for with this self-sufficient philosopher it had its humorous side. The real esteem in which George Eliot held him is revealed by the fact that for a time he alone held the secret of the authorship of " Scenes of Clerical Life," on which he had difficulty in meeting Chapman's questions. He was certainly to be trusted, and the two were close friends at the last. And Spencer always prided himself on the fact that he suggested to George Eliot to write novels, for he thought she had the necessary qualifications for doing so. Then she did not believe him.

The work undertaken by Miss Evans in respect

* After George Eliot's death newspaper paragraphs appeared implying that Spencer had been one of her suitors. Spencer went so far as to consult his friend Mr. Potter as to whether he should publish the whole truth and nothing but the truth, and was concisely told by him : " My dear Spencer, you will be eternally damned if you do."—" My Apprenticeship," by Beatrice Webb, p. 31.

of the *Review* often seemed to her drab and tedious, though she had a certain satisfaction in the progress of the periodical and its improved sale. There were certain women contributors with whom she came into touch, like Harriet Martineau, whose article on " Niebuhr " George Eliot thought admirable. " After all she is a trump—the only Englishwoman that possesses thoroughly the art of writing." Miss Parkes introduced her to Barbara Smith, afterwards Mme. Bodichon, with whom she had many common interests. And in the year 1852 she came across for the first time a greater Englishwoman still in Florence Nightingale, whose fine qualities she at once recognised. " There is," she says, " a loftiness of mind about her which is well expressed by her form and manner." Florence Nightingale was not yet in the limelight. Two years had yet to elapse before the war in the Crimea was to give her her chance. Just now she had paid her short visit to Kaiserswerth and was struggling—how hard, few prople knew—to get her liberty and continue her training. The " mountains of difficulty " that she sometimes spoke of were gradually being overcome, not for herself alone, but for whole generations of young womanhood which were to succeed her. She was just six months younger than George Eliot, and was now thirty-two, but the difficulties she had to contend with were on the social side even greater than her contemporary's, for she was born into a yet more " sheltered " surrounding, and even at this time had only reached the compromise accorded her by her mother when she was allowed one part of the year to pursue her " fancies." It is not recorded that the two ever became friends, though George Eliot was keenly interested in her work. But she was in close touch with the other women mentioned (Barbara Smith and Bessie Parkes), who worked so keenly for the education of women, and later on she also came into relation with Emily Davies.

George Eliot always had the sense of the physical and physiological differences between men and women that the younger generation was beginning to think exaggerated. She considered that it required much and careful thought to understand their influences, and dreaded rash experiments in the direction of equality in education. Like her contemporaries, she stressed the value of the moral influence that might be exerted by the woman and the benefits that differences of function founded on primary differences might provide. And the new doctrines of higher education for women seemed to overlook these facts. There was always to her a certain fear of " unsexing " the woman—that unnecessary fear so long as men and women are what they are, the newer school declared. Still, later on she gave £100 to what is now Girton College, as " from the author of ' Adam Bede,' " for she believed that only by opening to women the same store of acquired truth as to men can we reach the same grounds of judgment for both sexes.

It was not all work in these days, for there were occasional expeditions away, and one wonderful one to Edinburgh in October to stay with the Combes. George Combe was a faithful friend to George Eliot, and his comfortable house in Edinburgh was a delight to her. " I am tipsy with pleasure," she says, " an elegant home, glorious fires, and a comfortable carriage—in short, quite the circumstances to nourish sleek optimism." Mrs. Combe was a daughter of Mrs. Siddons, and her husband devoted his talents and means to popularising his views on phrenology and education. He may well be called the first Eugenist as a distinguished mental specialist has told us,* for he insisted on great caution in contracting marriage in consideration of the prevalence of hereditary diseases, and pointed out that the union of suitable parents was conducive to favourable offspring. Combe himself, when engaged to Priscilla Siddons, had her head phrenologically examined, risking thereby the loss of her considerable fortune as well as herself! He had his own head examined also to ascertain that conditions were suitable, and, wonderful to relate, the marriage turned out a thoroughly satisfactory one! His books passed through a dozen editions, and his views were adopted so far as to cause school children to be tested for their future vocations by the nature of the conformation of their heads—a kind of test now undertaken by psychologists in a different fashion.

George Eliot thoroughly enjoyed the beautiful views and the calm of Edinburgh society, where Combe did the talking and the company assented,

* Sir J. Crichton-Browne.

like the people talked to by Socrates in Plato's dialogues. He was indeed in his way an apostle —" an apostle, it is true, with a back and front drawing-room, but still in earnest." Then Miss Martineau was visited, and Miss Evans trudged round to see her cottages and the mountains of Cumberland. Then back to Rosehill for ten days before returning to London and fog and headaches, while working away at articles on Taxation, reading German for Chapman, and having talks with Lewes. Nowadays she gets out of spirits with the *Review* and would be glad to run away from it altogether. But, though there was plenty of intercourse with interesting men and women, and discussions of authors such as the Brontës, with their " preternatural power " (" Villette, Villette, have you read it ? " she exclaims, " and Lewes says it emanates from a ' plain, provincial, sickly-looking old maid ! ' "), as well as visits from scientists like Huxley, there is an atmosphere of unrest.

If Herbert Spencer and she were not to be more than friends, he influenced her life more than he knew by bringing George Henry Lewes to call upon her at the end of 1851. Before that she had casually seen him (" a sort of miniature Mirabeau in appearance " she says) in a shop. This was to prove a momentous friendship, but not for some time later. As a companion Lewes was extremely attractive, interested in, and well informed upon, a variety of subjects, and an admirable mimic ; it was impossible to be dull in his company. We cannot therefore wonder that his advent on the scene was a great addition to the attraction of life at Chapman's house in the Strand where the wheels did not by any means always run smoothly : this new friendship, indeed, was to prove the turning point in her life and to change all her plans.   Lewes had already arrived at a considerable degree of fame in the literary world in which George Eliot was moving. He had published his " Biographical History of Philosophy " which, being written in simple and comprehensible style, had a popular success.   Then some years before he wrote two novels, " Ranthorpe " and " Rose, Blanche and Violet," which are now forgotten.   But he was likewise a voluminous contributor to the periodical literature of the day, and wrote well.   As he was the literary editor of the *Leader* newspaper (a weekly paper, somewhat resembling the *Spectator* in form and of advanced views like the *Westminster*, which had a short but distinguished life) his criticisms carried weight. Indeed his favourable review of Spencer's " Social Statics " encouraged the friendship with the author, and Lewes was Spencer's constant companion in his Sunday rambles.

Lewes, who was now living apart from his wife, had had a varied career, for he was the grandson of a comedian and had strong inclination for the stage in which he might have excelled, but that his figure was unfortunately slight and unimpressive and his voice ineffective.   He was educated in England but spent some years in Germany and France when about twenty-one.   He began to study medicine, but could not stand the operating-room, and in the end merged into journalism. He married a Miss Jervis, a young lady of good family. He was not a profound thinker, but had remarkable versatility, was interested equally in all sorts of subjects—the drama—literature and biography, and finally chemistry and biology. Indeed, though he had a clear intellect and sharp wit and a good style, he was more of a populariser of science and philosophy than an original writer : it is probably true that he had not the qualifications necessary for the latter, and hence he has been set down as a brilliant amateur. Spencer clearly influenced him in respect of his excursus from the pure Comtism with which he started, into the psychology which was his chief interest latterly. His best known work, written soon after this,* "The Life and Works of Goethe," has made Goethe known to innumerable Englishmen ; and as the book, without being profound, is eminently interesting and readable, it has passed through very many editions. This is the man who, absolutely without physical attraction, had a special quality of his own that drew people to him.

Thus was Mary Ann Evans drawn to this man, genial and amusing as he was, and she came to like him and more than like him, though she does not confess it. And then as time went on the subject of divorce is mentioned. She says that Mr. Bray of course highly approves of the recommendations of the Commissioners on Divorce. But divorce was still a difficult thing for Mr. Lewes and others, and

* In 1855.

no more is said about it. In a letter she writes : "People are very good to me. Mr. Lewes especially is kind and attentive, and has quite won my regard after having had a good deal of vituperation. Like a few other people in the world, he is much better than he seems. A man of heart and conscience wearing a mask of flippancy." George Eliot was restless, and even meditated taking a journey to Australia with her half-sister and her family, after her brother-in-law's death. But a visit to the coast with Miss Barbara Smith did her good, and her spirits once more rose. She had fully decided to remove from the Strand, and finally did so, taking up her abode in lodgings at 21, Cambridge Street, Hyde Park Square.

We have not much to tell us regarding the actual reasons for the change of house in October, 1853, after a holiday away, but it is clear that Miss Evans was not happy or satisfied in her life and work, and she wished something different. It was in November that she told Mr. Chapman definitely that she desired to give up any connexion with the editorship of the *Westminster*, though he begged her to carry on till April. She was busy with the translation of Feuerbach's "Essence of Christianity" and intended to publish a book on "The Idea of Future Life" which was even advertised but never produced. She was in close touch with Mr. Lewes, and in April Lewes fell ill and was ordered complete rest, so that George Eliot undertook some of his work as well as her own, while he went to recuperate with his friend Arthur Helps in Hampshire. She

G

prepares her friend Mrs. Bray for the possibility of her wishing to go to the Continent without saying why. She tells Mrs. Bray that she expects Lewes back again, though " his poor head—his only fortune—is not well yet," also that there is no chance of her being able to pay her a visit before her midsummer visitors arrive. But she did pay the visit, and enjoyed it. In July the translation of Feuerbach appeared with her real name on the title page, the only time her own name appeared in print excepting in a privately published edition of her poem—" Brother and Sister," in 1869. On July 20th, 1854, the Brays received this letter : " Dear Friends—all three—I have only time to say goodbye and God bless you. *Poste Restante*, Weimar, for the next six weeks, and afterwards Berlin. Ever your loving and grateful Marian."*

The die was cast.

It was probable that it had been cast before this, as Mr. Oscar Browning states, though unknown to her friends. Relations with Lewes were certainly close in the course of the latter part of her stay at the Strand, though it is a time in regard to which we have little record. George Eliot's nature, as we have seen, required an object for her devotion. Chapman was unstable in character ; his admirations moved themselves from one to another, and at this time there was another on whom his devotions had specially fixed themselves. How those things influenced George Eliot we cannot tell, but we can understand how difficult and unsatisfactory her

* George Eliot spelt her name " Marian " in later years.

position must have been. She was left with the burden of work for the *Review* on her hands, and with the financial side more than dubious. She managed, indeed, not alone to do for herself, but even to help needy relatives, but the exertion must have been great, and she had always that craving for love and sympathy that made her life specially lonely. Had Mr. Lewes been free, all would have been well, but he was not free in the eyes of the law.

The story is not an uncommon one, or was not in those days when marriage was much more permanent and absolute than now. During the ten years before George Eliot met him, Lewes had been living with his wife in a curious unconventional set. Several young couples, including Lewes* and his wife, and Leigh Hunt's son, Thornton Hunt and his wife, were dwelling together in a large house in Bayswater and naturally seeing a good deal of each other. They were " advanced " in their views and far from restrained in their conduct. Lewes's wife deserted him and her three children for Hunt, who forsook his own wife. Lewes was forgiving and took back his wife, but she left him again, giving him to understand that her decision this time was final. Lewes was thus left with his three children to care for alone.† Of course in the present day the

* Both Lewes and Hunt wrote for the *Leader*, and another of the company, Edward Pigott, chiefly financed the paper.

† Mrs. Lynn Linton in her Reminiscences (" My Literary Life " —1899) gives an account of the curious company in the house in Queen's Road. Lewes, she says, was a singularly plain man, deeply pitted with the smallpox, with narrow jaws and somewhat drawn-in cheeks. He had bright, vivacious and well-shaped eyes, a quantity of bright brown hair and a flexible mouth. She states that he was startlingly free in speech and had little reticence of any sort—that

situation would have been simple, for Lewes would have divorced his wife. But it was only in 1857–8 that in England marriage could be dissolved without a special Act of Parliament. A husband petitioning for such an Act was required first to sue for a separation, and to bring an action for damages against the seducer of his wife. Divorce, therefore, was only possible for the rich. When the law was altered, Lewes had put himself out of court by his union with another, and at this time it was impossible for him to face the necessary steps. One wonders whether some of Miss Evans's friends, who were comparatively well off, might not have helped in the matter, but both the parties concerned were full of independence and believed that they were entitled to deal with the situation in the simple way in which it presented itself to them, especially as there was no objection on Mrs. Lewes's part. To many people the extraordinary success of the union justified the means of bringing it about. To others it seemed wholly wrong to defy the law of the land as well as of the Church, especially as the question of

legal obligation in marriage meant nothing to him or to Hunt. But she disliked Lewes, and in contrast professed to admire Hunt's nature, though she could not but allow that he loved where he should not : he was " irregular " but not licentious, she says. To Lewes, life, she considered, meant love and pleasure. " In work and in idleness, in the *sans façon* of Bohemianism and in the more orderly amusements of conventional society—in scientific discussions and empty persiflage, he was equally at home ; and wherever he went there was a patch of intellectual sunshine in the room." The lightness and versatility of Lewes, and the wonderful expressiveness of his eyes, made one forget the rest. Agnes Lewes, she calls " that pretty rosebud-like woman, whose ' *dona fatale di bellezza* ' worked its usual tale of woe to all concerned. Mrs. Hunt, she terms, " One of the sweetest and best women that ever lived," which certainly does not make Hunt's desertion of her the less culpable.

a change in the law was being discussed, and as it turned out, it would only have meant a delay of two or three years to wait till the law was altered. It is one of the matters on which people will always disagree according to their respective outlooks. It was undoubtedly a break with society as it existed at that time, even more than it would have been now, and the tragic side of it was that though it probably was not at all so with George Lewes, it was to the last a real trial to George Eliot. Long afterwards, when a second marriage gave her a legal name, it was carried out in the most orthodox and conventional manner possible.

*   *   *   *   *

The life in the Strand had been highly emotional and almost hysterical at times : it was certainly not healthy in any sense, but it was a revelation of what life and love meant to one who came to it from outside. Now it seemed as if a haven of rest had been found. George Eliot was never meant to live alone : she always required someone on whom she could lean, and whom she could wholly love : she poured out her experiences to her women friends in early days, but this did not suffice her. She required something more in order that her whole nature might develop as it did develop. And with Lewes the development was little less striking. His mercurial disposition seemed to gain in stability by association with her steady outlook, and he was enabled to do better work thereby. His belief in her gave her the confidence she needed, and he tenderly watched over her physical health. And to his children, on the other hand, she was a devoted mother : more devoted she could not be. To Miss Hennell she says : " The intense happiness of our union is derived in a great degree from the perfect freedom with which we each follow and declare our own impressions," and to Charles Lewes (Mr. Lewes's son) she writes : " Let us hope that we shall all— father and mother and sons—help one another with love." And long after, in 1865, she writes : " Dear George is all activity, yet is in very frail health. How I worship his good humour, his good sense, his affectionate care for everyone who has claims on him ! That worship is my best life." As Mr. Cross says in his " Life " : " No words that anyone else can write, no arguments anyone else can use, will, I think, be so impressive as the life itself." Her friends the Brays were much distressed by the news they received through the short communication quoted above, and it took long to reconcile her old friends to the step. Fourteen months later she wrote to Mrs. Bray : " If there is one action or relation of my life which is and always has been profoundly serious, it is my relation to Mr. Lewes . . . We cannot set each other right in this matter (the subject of the marriage laws) in letters, but one thing I can tell you in a few words. Light and easily broken ties are what I neither desire theoretically nor could live for practically. Women who are satisfied with such ties *do not* act as I have done. That any unworldly, unsuperstitious person who is sufficiently acquainted with the realities of life can pronounce my relation to Mr. Lewes immoral, I can only understand by remembering how subtle and complex are the influences that mould opinion. But I *do* remember this ; and I indulge in no arrogant or uncharitable thoughts about those who condemn us, even though we might have expected a somewhat different verdict. From the majority of persons, of course, we never looked for anything but condemnation. We are leading no life of self-indulgence, except indeed that, being happy in each other, we find everything easy. We are working hard to provide for others better than we provide for ourselves, and to fulfil every responsibility that rests upon us." And so to another friend, Mrs. Peter Taylor, she tells of a great boy of eighteen who calls her " Mother," as well as two other boys almost as tall who write to her under that name, and begs that anyone who has regard for her will cease to speak of her by her maiden name.

Certainly in her writings no one asserted more strongly the inviolability of the marriage vow, and on dedicating it to him she wrote on the manuscript of " Adam Bede " : " To my dear husband, George Henry Lewes, I give the MS. of a work which would never have been written but for the happiness which his love has conferred on my life."

CHAPTER V

The New Life
(1854–1857)

It was indeed a new life on which George Eliot was embarking. There were no illusions. The woman who had gone with a man who could not be her husband, knew the risks she was taking, the certain condemnation of the world and the possibilities of disaster. On July 20th, 1854, when the two embarked for Antwerp in lovely summer weather, all this was present to her.

In what she says of her journey there is nothing but delight. All seemed fresh and wonderful to the little-travelled woman who thirsted to see the world and all that it contained—the great pictures that she had read of, the various spots sacred to the memory of those men who were so constantly in her thoughts, Goethe, Schiller and Wieland. Weimar meant much to her in days when the memory of such men was fresh, and when others such as Strauss, who had greatly influenced her in former days, were still living there.

Then her companion was full of vivacity and keenness looking out for what would help him in his "Life of Goethe," but also prepared to start off on any conceivable topic, philosophic or scientific, and give apparently the most lucid exposition of each.

In these respects he reminds us of one of the eighteenth century encyclopædists.

They must have been an odd-looking couple. He shaggy, small and lightly built, padding along like a Skye terrier ; she, massive in appearance and impressive in manner ; he mothering as well as adoring his companion and shielding her from the cold winds of the world so far as was in his power ; she grateful for and responsive to every attention given her. Arthur Helps, the " sleek man, with close-snipped hair and a quiet humorous way of talking like his books " unexpectedly arrived at Weimar in the end of August, and, good friend as he was, accompanied them in their expeditions. It is believed that it was Helps, the man of the world, who had served in high Government circles at home as well as writing agreeable and wise books, who advised the two to call themselves man and wife.

The Court of Weimar, that august body, very naturally did not appreciate their position at first ; but at the close of their visit Lewes, at least, was invited to the Palace, where he charmed the Grand ducal party by his conversation. Ilmenau—that historic and charming spot, the Kickel-hahn, and Goethe's tiny wooden house, were duly visited : Wagner's most celebrated operas, then compara- tively recent, were heard : Liszt conducted "Ernani " and his talk delighted the two visitors who both loved music. The whole account of this journey is full of happiness and interest, and no one could have profited more than George Eliot from meeting famous people and seeing historic sights. Berlin was the next stage in their journey, and here they came to know the famous scientific men of the day like Liebig, du Bois Reymond and Johannes Müller, as well as artists like Rauch the sculptor, Dessoir the actor, and many others. All doors were open to the many-sided Lewes with his varied interests. When we read of the life in Berlin, the concerts, the operas and the rest, we realise how much literary and artistic life in Germany meant. And during the cold winter there were long evenings when the two read together : Shakespeare, Goethe, Heine and Macaulay, " with German Pfefferküchen and Semmels at the end."

Altogether the months spent in Germany—the two remained there till March of 1855—were not only beneficial but helpful in a literary way, for both George Eliot and Lewes were working and writing hard. Lewes, of course, was occupied with his " Life of Goethe," which he had begun before, but was rewriting with a view to completion ; and she was composing an article for the *Westminster* on Victor Cousin's " Madame de Sable," besides finishing the translation of Spinoza's " Ethics." George Eliot's Journal gives us a list of books read at this time, English and German, which makes us feel what serious study meant in those days. And this was regarded as a time of relaxation, combined as it was with visiting, theatre and concert-going. Altogether there were eight happy months of exile before the world of convention in England had to be faced again. One feels convinced that there was relief in being away from the voice of criticism that was sure to descend on the heads of the errant couple from the respectable middle-class England of that day, where the outside of the platter was kept meticulously clean.

Germany, however, did something else for George Eliot. It was at Berlin that a momentous event took place in her life. One evening whilst she was rummaging amongst a number of papers brought out from England, she came across something that she had attempted to do a long time before. Mary Ann Evans had thought of writing about the people and country she knew so well in her youth, and with this in view, she wrote what was to be an introductory chapter to a future work of fiction. She showed it to Lewes, probably half in fun, and he, with his keen sense of literary value, was struck with its power ; and though it seemed to him that there was no indication of dramatic power, there was at least something that indicated that the writer might have it in her to write a novel. Had he lived a little later and seen the rise of the " kail-yard " and other descriptive studies of rural life, he might not have concerned himself so much about the absence of dramatic capacities, but rejoiced in the keen powers of observation applied to ordinary country life. However, nothing was attempted in the meantime, for this was considered a by-play and not the serious part of the day's work.

The serious part was serious enough when the two got back to Dover, where haltingly they paused before entering London and all the complications London life would bring. There George Eliot waited

whilst her husband did his business. She wanted
to be alone for a while and think out her future, as
she told herself whilst she again took up her translation of Spinoza.* She told herself likewise that
she was stronger in body and calmer in mind since
she started on her new life, and was ready to face
what might come. She was only too glad when she
was offered some reviewing for the *Westminster
Review*, which gave her further occupation. Presently the move to London was made, but as that
was not wholly satisfactory, the two once more
moved to East Sheen, and finally to 8, Park Street,
Richmond, where they were to settle for a period
of three years.

Had it only been themselves who had to be
supported their future life would have been easy.
But there were the three sons of Mr. Lewes who
had to be educated and their mother to be assisted.†
The pair thus settled down to work and to use
the material accumulated in Germany which was so
specially helpful for the book on Goethe. George
Eliot's writing was mainly for the *Westminster*, but
she also contributed to the *Leader*. It was a
strenuous life, for there was but one sitting-room for
the two, and the woman, who was all nerves, was
almost driven wild by the scratching of the other
pen. The great relief came with the success of
the Goethe ; but still the mistress of the little house
kept the purse-strings carefully closed and " doled
out her sovereigns with the pangs of a miser."

* Her translation of the " Ethics," though announced, was never
published.
† She survived her husband.

Her friend, Barbara Smith, tried hard to bring her into the political arena and persuade her to join the army of women struggling for the right of women to their own earnings. So obvious a right had George Eliot's sympathy, but she was never attracted by the public work that was occupying the minds of most of her friends. That was not her way of dealing with the problems of womanhood. She had the sense that there were other powers moving within her, powers of creation that might take definite form before very long.

Another great Victorian novelist was starting on his career at this same time. George Meredith, though younger than George Eliot by almost a decade, was setting to work on fiction at nearly the same date. The " Shaving of Shagpat " had just appeared, and George Eliot was an appreciative critic of the new author. So far as we know, they were never friends. The contrast between the two novelists is astounding, and yet both were psychologists analysing the inmost being of their contemporaries and predecessors : the one dealing with the super-civilised society of the day, showing forth its virtues and foibles and its essential meaning and humour below a surface which was but a veneer of polite convention, the other taking the simple essentials of common life as it is lived day by day by those who hardly knew what society meant excepting as a vague and distant background, and performing for it the same office.

The need of money has been at all times a useful and impelling force as regards authorship, and it certainly was so with George Eliot. In May, 1856, she and Lewes set off for visits to Ilfracombe and Tenby. The reason the seaside was chosen was that the versatile Lewes was now deep in biological work, and writing his " Seaside Studies." George Eliot, without being herself scientifically disposed, was greatly interested in all this, and thoroughly enjoyed the expeditions it entailed, just as she loved the beautiful country round, where masses of wild flowers delighted her. She was being pressed to write further critical articles for the *Westminster*, but now for the first time she cried a halt, and said she did not wish to occupy her time with other work since she was anxious to begin her fiction and this gave her a favourable opportunity of doing so.

So far, one would have imagined that fiction writing was far removed from her powers. There was little trace of imagination in the serious and well-thought-out articles written for the most part between 1855 and 1857 in the *Westminster* and other reviews, and re-published in the " Essays," though no doubt there is evidence of a well-stored mind and a great gift of expression and literary acumen. The articles seem to us to be lacking in the sacred fire of genius, or at least of imaginative genius ; and to-day the " Essays " are not much read. But how few such essays are read after seventy years have passed and with them much of the interest of the subjects treated of ? They are read only if their subjects are dealt with as something not of ephemeral interest, or else if they are written in a specially attractive form. George Eliot never lacked ideas : they teemed from her wonderful brain, but she had not the gift of expressing them easily or lightly. She wrote once, many years later, to Frederic Harrison of " the severe effort of trying to make certain ideas thoroughly incarnate,"* and in her essays one has this sense of overwhelming effort.

The lightest of her essays were published in a little book for private circulation in 1919 under the title " Early Essays." These represented George Eliot's first attempts in literature—attempts which date from the early days in Coventry before the writer went to London. Even her friend Mrs. Bray saw that something was being evolved and believed that it was a novel that was in prospect. Possibly the notes found in Berlin had even then been begun, but if the Essays were the only literary effort they still show considerable imagination. They purport to come from the " Notebook of an Eccentric," and to be published by a friend after his death, and are written in a style that would seem to be taken from a generation before the author's own. There is likewise rather a beautiful little fairy tale, such as we do not associate with an author who had a certain dread of imaginary writing for children in her later years.

In the later Essays there is a good deal of scathing sarcasm of a kind that reappeared no more in George Eliot's later writings. The unfortunate poet Young, of the " Night Thoughts," suffered severely ; but perhaps he was fair game. Anyhow, his religious

* " Frederic Harrison," by Austin Harrison.

and moral spirit is declared to be low and false, and
his thoughts the reflex of a mind in which the
higher human sympathies were inactive. He is
compared unfavourably with Cowper, in which
judgment all must agree. Mr. Buckle is treated in
a similar way and termed " a conceited, ignorant
man." Lord Morley truly said of George Eliot :
" Universal benevolence never lulled an active
critical faculty, nor did she conceive true humility
as at all consisting in hiding from an impostor that
you have found him out." She had indeed : " a
remarkably strong, hard, masculine, positive judging
head."

Another subject of George Eliot's criticism was
a figure who held a prominent place in London
society, but whose star has so completely fallen
from its orbit that the object of the satire seems
hardly worthy of the sharp darts she aimed at it.
Dr. Cumming was then preaching in London on
Armageddon and the literal interpretation of
Biblical prophecy, as well as on the strict verbal
inspiration of the sacred volume, and attracting to
himself crowds of hearers. George Eliot, rather
unfairly, takes his preaching as typical of evangelical
teaching, which she represents as that in which a
smattering of science and learning passes for profound instruction, platitudes are accepted as wisdom,
and unctuous egoism as God-given piety. In a
sense this was true : there was this element in the
religion of the day : but if it applied to Dr. Cumming's teaching it did not represent evnagelical
religion at its best. The writer knew the best side

of evangelicalism as she remembered it in her youth ; she depicted it with consummate skill and sympathy in the religion of Dinah Morris and Seth Bede. Oddly enough, however, this was the article above all others that attracted the general attention and interest of the world, and impressed George Lewes with the fact that the writer had true genius and not mere talent in her productions. Therefore it served a useful purpose, and we may be grateful for the criticism of a man who would now be termed a fundamentalist and who appears to have really influenced the opinions of the day.

The essay on Heine, on the contrary, gives George Eliot a subject worthy of her steel. Satire, wit and humour were her favourite subjects at this time ; and the contrast between the two last, their respective qualities and natures, is a topic on which she loved to dwell, and to which she applied all her powers. She discusses these qualities as they reveal themselves in different nationalities. As criticism the article is admirable, and it has just that sympathetic touch as regards the man and his terribly suffering life, and even his occasional lapses into coarseness, that makes it specially valuable.

George Eliot had to keep up her reputation for masculinity, and she succeeds sometimes too well, as women are apt to do when they ignore their womanhood. She wrote anonymously and besought any friends who recognised her pen to keep their knowledge to themselves. There were indeed few who did recognise it. In those days, for her particular work, it was essential that her sex should

H

be concealed—or else it was supposed to be, which amounts to the same thing. George Eliot was not a breaker-down of barriers : she was far too much a child of her time. When she did leap over fences she suffered too deeply for the act to wish to repeat it.

There are biographical articles, such as that on Carlyle's " Life of Sterling," which have still considerable interest. But one of the most interesting things in regard to these articles is the just view the writer takes of the value of biography and of the form it should take. Here she gets away from the conventions of her time which prescribed, as she says, a dreary three- or five-volumed compilation of letters and diary in detail, and advocates a real " life," setting forth briefly and vividly the man's outward and inward struggles, aims and achievements, so as to make clear the meaning which his experience has for his fellows. A few such lives the world possesses, and they have, she believes, been more influential in the formation of character than any other kind of reading. Harriet Martineau's autobiography had been the origin of much of George Eliot's dislike of the ordinary biography of self-glorification, but in her own case this had the somewhat unfortunate result that many letters and papers that might have thrown light upon her real life have been destroyed. In 1861 she writes to Sara Hennell : '" I have destroyed almost all my friends' letters to me, because they were only intended for my eyes and could only fall into the hands of persons who knew little of the writers, if I allowed them to remain till after my death. In proportion as I love every form of piety—which is venerating love—I hate hard curiosity ; and unhappily, my experience has impressed me with the sense that hard curiosity is the more common temper of mind."

So far, George Eliot seemed in her writings to regard her public from an absolutely impersonal point of view. She was not writing for that public as a woman who had lived and loved, and suffered all the pangs of a life of sensibility ; but as one who was all the time hiding that personality under a mask of masculinity and even hardness which was not her own. For a more feminine woman it would be almost impossible to find. A further article written in 1856 on " Silly Novels by Lady Novelists," just before her own first work of fiction was sent to the press, was even more artificial in tone. In it the writer speaks of the frothy, prosy and pious or pedantic woman's novel of what she calls the " mind and millinery " species. This style of novel she terms only excusable because she imagined that destitute women turned novelists as they turned governesses, because they had no other ladylike means of getting their daily bread.

The writer knew better : she has the grace to recognise Jane Austen as an exception, and a brilliant one ; but she might have remembered others like the Brontës, who certainly gave us no sort of " medical sweetmeat for Low Church young ladies." Even in those days women had distinguished themselves in what has been almost the only form of any real artistic work in which they have equalled, and decisively excelled, the work of men, and this deserved to be recognised.

The article runs on : " The real drama of Evangelicalism, and it has abundance of fine drama for anyone who has genius to discern and reproduce it, lies among the middle and lower classes. Why can we not have pictures of religious life among the industrial classes in England as interesting as Mrs. Stowe's pictures of religious life among the negroes ? " This is the question that the writer herself was about to answer in the best possible way, by showing that it could be done. And even now the method was in her mind, for she goes on to censure the way in which rural life is usually approached and the wrong impression most people have of it. " The notion that peasants are joyous, that the typical moment to represent a man in a smock-frock is when he is cracking a joke and showing a row of sound teeth, that cottage matrons are usually buxom, and village children necessarily rosy and merry, are prejudices difficult to dislodge from the artistic mind which looks for its objects into literature instead of life."

One would have thought that at that time so soon after the " hungry forties," and while agricultural wages were miserably low, people might have realised what the actualities were. But George Eliot's summing-up, if severe, is true. " The selfish instincts are not subdued by the sight of buttercups, nor is integrity in the least established by that classic rural occupation, sheep-washing. To make men moral something more is requisite than to turn them out to grass." She felt the *seriousness* of

misrepresenting the life of the common people, and
here her moral feelings came in as well as her artistic.
For, as she writes, " Art is the nearest thing to life ;
it is a mode of amplifying experience and extending
our control with our fellow-men beyond the bounds
of our personal lot. All the more sacred is the task
of the artist when he undertakes to paint the life
of the people."

This indeed, was the goal of George Eliot's art.
She had beneath, and running through her artistic
productions a deep sense of the responsibility which
lay upon her to teach as well as to entertain, to
interpret the true meaning of human life in all its
aspects as well as to depict its external developments.
She prepared herself for this, just as she prepared
herself for the literary side of her work. In one of
the articles reprinted in the " Essays," the " Address
to Working Men by Felix Holt " written for *Blackwood's Magazine* in 1868, the moral, or rather
didactic vein is painfully prominent. The newly
enfranchised working man of '68, with all his
grievances and aspirations, was not likely to appreciate being lectured by those who had none of his
troubles to bear. Not that there is any definite
intention to lecture in this article. It is an attempt
to put the situation fairly and squarely before those
who are going for the first time to exercise their
vote—to urge on them the care and precaution with
which they should go about the task of making
things better, so that public order may not be destroyed and " so that no fatal shock may be given
to this society of ours, this living body in which

our lives are bound up." And she tells of the
Election Riot she saw as a girl, and warns them
against producing any such disorder by giving
ignorant and brutal men the belief that with power
in their hands they can do pretty much what they
like. " I am a radical," she says ; " and what is
more, I am not a radical with a title and a French
cook, or even an entrance into fine society. I expect great changes, and I desire them. But I don't
expect them to come in a hurry, by mere inconsid-
erate sweeping. A Hercules with a big besom is a
fine thing for a filthy stable, but not for weeding a
seed-bed, where his besom would soon make a
barren floor." And then she makes a strong appeal
to the men by means of their Unions to fulfil their
duties as parents, and demand that the children be
sent to school and not to let their little ones " be
turned into breadwinners, often at cruel tasks,
exposed to the horrible infection of childish vice."

Indeed a just appeal ; but was the writer thinking
of the other responsibility, that of the employers
and ratepayers, and was not the way of Lord
Shaftesbury, who was battling with all these difficulties, the true one—to prevent the employment
of these children ? Again we must remember the
struggles of those who in two or three years were to
bring about compulsory free education, and thus
make it possible for every child to have the advantage
of being taught to read and write : in the old days
what chance had the poor parent to keep his child
at school until it was equal to the strain of bread-
winning ?

This gives some idea of the nature of the " Essays " which have proved of no ephemeral interest like so many magazine articles of the day. Many of them would seem to deal with matters now past and gone, and others, like the " Three Months in Weimar," are slight and transient in their character. Their interest is of course in relation to their author and her future work, and they are still read from this point of view.

For now at last at the mature age of thirty-seven, the long apprenticeship was over, and the possibilities that had seemed but possibilities, were developing into something greater. George Eliot herself gives an admirable account of how the new step was taken, in a memorandum which she wrote. " It had always been a vague dream of mine," she writes, " that some time or other I might write a novel ; and my shadowy conception of what the novel was to be, varied, of course, from one epoch of my life to another. But I never went further towards the actual writing of the novel than an introductory chapter describing a Staffordshire village and the life of the neighbouring farm-houses ; and as the years passed on, I lost any hope that I should ever be able to write a novel, just as I desponded about everything else in my future life. I always thought I was deficient in dramatic power, both of construction and dialogues, but I felt I should be at my ease in the descriptive parts of a novel." Then she goes on to tell of that evening in Berlin when something led her to give the descriptive chapter she had written to Lewes, who was at once taken with it, and advised her to try her hand at fiction ; and then after they returned to England, when Lewes was struck with her success in other sorts of writings, (i.e. in her articles), he had the impression that it was worth while going on with efforts in this direction. " He began to say very positively, ' You must try and write a story,' and when we were at Tenby he urged me to begin at once. I deferred it, however, after my usual fashion, with work that does not present itself as an absolute duty. But one morning as I was thinking what should be the subject of my first story, my thoughts merged themselves into a dreamy doze, and I imagined myself writing a story, of which the title was ' The Sad Fortune of the Reverend Amos Barton.' I was soon wide awake again and told G. He said, ' Oh, what a capital title ! ' and from that time I had settled in my mind that this should be my first story."

This gives a clear account of how the " story " was only brought to birth through the encouragement and sympathy of her ever-helpful companion, without whose assistance and even pressure, the world might have been bereft of some of its best imaginative literature. He told her that her effort might be a failure, for he was convinced that though it could not be *poor* it might lack the highest quality of fiction—dramatic representation. And all who read her previous essays in literature would probably agree with Mr. Lewes—neither her critical articles nor her letters would give one the idea that there was, concealed behind these admirably measured sentences the wealth of sympathy, imagination and dramatic power that eventually was found there. Had George Eliot, when she was the simple Mary Ann Evans, living a peaceful life in the provinces, met her fate earlier, it may be that she would have produced her masterpieces earlier. But we cannot believe that they would have been the same masterpieces, that she did not gain in depth of feeling and understanding by those long years of study and of struggle.

Anyhow the story itself is a touching and delightful one—how the " Silly Novel " article being duly sent off, George Eliot began her tale on September 22nd ; how in the course of a walk in Richmond Park she told Lewes that she had thought of writing a series of stories containing sketches drawn from her own observation of the clergy and calling them " Scenes of Clerical Life," the first of which was to be " Amos Barton." He thought the idea an excellent one—fresh and striking. About a week afterwards when she read him the first part of "Amos" he no longer had any doubt of her ability to carry out the plan. The scene at Cross Farm satisfied him that she had the element he had been doubtful of—the power to write good dialogue. There was still the question of whether she could deal equally with pathos ; and that was to be decided by the mode in which she treated Milly's death. " One night G. went to town on purpose to leave me a quiet evening for writing it. I wrote the chapter from the news brought by the shepherd to Mr. Hackit, to the moment when Amos is dragged from the bedside, and I read it to G. when he came home.

We both cried over it, and then he came up to me and kissed me, saying, ' I think your pathos is better than your fun.' "

The story was finished on the 5th November and they had, before it was written, decided to send it to Blackwood ; even though it might, to begin with, be rejected and have to be rewritten. Lewes wrote the very next day, November 6th, to John Blackwood, as for a friend who desired his good offices with him. He also stated his own opinion that " such human pathos, vivid presentation and nice observation, have not been exhibited (in this style) since the ' Vicar of Wakefield.' " He explained that this would be the first of a " series of tales and sketches illustrative of the actual life of our country clergy about a quarter of a century ago—but solely in its *human* and not at all in its *theological* aspects " holding that " since the ' Vicar ' and Miss Austen we have had no stories representing the clergy like every other class, with the humour, sorrows and troubles of other men. He (i.e. the author for whom he wrote) begged me particularly to add that—as the specimen sent will sufficiently prove—the tone throughout will be sympathetic, and not at all antagonistic."

Mr. John Blackwood's reply was as follows : " I am happy to say that I think your friend's reminiscences of clerical life will do. If there is any more of the series written I should like to see it, as until I saw more, I could not make any decided proposition for the publication of the Tales, in whole or in part, in the *Magazine*. This first specimen, ' Amos Barton,' is unquestionably very pleasant reading. Perhaps the author falls into the error of trying too much to explain the characters of his actors by description instead of allowing them to evolve in the action of the story : but the descriptions are very humorous and good. The death of Milly is powerfully done, and affected me much. I am not sure whether he does not spoil it a little by specifying so minutely the different children and their names. . . . At first I was afraid that in the amusing reminiscences of childhood in church there was a want of some softening touch, such as the remembrance of a father or mother lends, in after years, to what was at the time considerable penance. I hate anything of a sneer at real religious feeling, as cordially as I despise anything like cant, and I should think this author is of the same way of thinking, although his clergymen, with one exception, are not very attractive specimens of the body. . . . If the author is a new writer, I beg to congratulate him on being worthy of the honour of print and pay."

The correspondence goes on in the same strain. Mr. Lewes rather adroitly suggests that his " clerical friend " (he afterwards explains to Mr. Blackwood who was " pleased to hear that as he supposed he was a clergyman " that this was not so) was somewhat discouraged, but that he would send a further story when written, and that he himself rated the first story more highly. Blackwood replies that he has been misunderstood, and that he does appreciate the work and will go on at once with the series. Lewes is satisfied and only begs that his negotiations should be kept secret and the anonymity preserved. On Christmas Day, 1856, "Mr. Gilfil's Love-Story" was begun and in the January *Blackwood* " Amos Barton " appeared, being honoured by receiving the first place in the then famous " Maga." Now Mr. Blackwood lets himself go in regard to praise. He even gives way, at the instance of his brother, over the naming of Milly's children and, best of all, encloses a cheque for fifty guineas and puts forward suggestions for future publication. The " author " replies : " Your letter has proved to me that the generous Editor and publisher—generous both in word and in deed— who makes the author's path smooth and easy, is something more than a pleasant tradition. I am very sensitive to the merits of cheques for fifty guineas, but I am still more sensitive to that cordial appreciation which is a guarantee to me that my work was worth doing for its own sake."

The anonymous author seems to have completely mystified the world. " It will be curious," Blackwood says, " if you should be a member [of a club] and be hearing your own praises," so that he had no suspicion of her being a woman, though one wonders that the careful enumeration of Milly's children to which he objected did not itself suggest the fact. When Lewes read the first part of " Amos " to a party at Helps', they were all sure she was a clergyman and a Cambridge man. Blackwood even hunted up a clue through Eliot Warburton's brother. As to criticisms such as that scientific illustrations were brought in (it is early days for this objection to appear) George Eliot writes to her publisher : " If

it be a sin to be at once a man of science and a writer
of fiction, I can declare my perfect innocence on
that head, my scientific knowledge being as superficial as that of the ' practised writers.' " And then
comes the choice of the name—the " George " was
taken from Mr. Lewes and the " Eliot " as a " good
mouth-filling, easily pronounced word."—" Whatever be the success of my stories," she writes to
Mr. Blackwood, " I shall be resolute in preserving
my *incognito*—having observed that a *nom de plume*
secures all the advantages without the disagreeables
of reputation. Perhaps, therefore, it will be well to
give you my prospective name, as a tub to throw
to the whale in case of curious inquiries : and accordingly I subscribe myself, best and most sympathising
of Editors, Yours very truly, George Eliot."

The correspondence between the author and her
publisher is in all respects agreeable and friendly,
but about one thing the former is adamant, and
that is the alteration of anything in relation to the
delineation or development of her characters ; for,
as she says, her stories " always grow out of psychological conceptions of the dramatis personæ. For
example, the behaviour of Caterina in the gallery
is essential to my conception of her nature, and to
the development of that nature in the plot. My
artistic bent is directed, not at all to the presentation of eminently irreproachable characters, but to
the presentation of mixed human beings in such a
way as to call forth tolerant judgment, pity, and
sympathy. And I cannot stir a step aside from what
I *feel* to be *true* in character."

A new page seems to have been turned—the old worries over finance and the criticism of friends appear to have passed and the delights of prosperity, in however mild a form, have come in their place. One likes to think of the happy couple going off to Cornwall and the Scilly Islands armed with their great book box full of everything from Mrs. Gaskell's Life of Charlotte Brontë to Sophocles and other classics.　One of the greatest satisfactions of a stroke of luck to George Eliot was also the power of helping her friends and relations, and she is able already to ask her brother—though so estranged— to pay £15 of her tiny income to help a half-sister, who had lost a child with fever, to have a change of air.　It was from Jersey that she wrote the charming epilogue to " Mr. Gilfil's Love Story," where she tells of the old vicar's later life, and of how " with all his social pipes and slipshod talk, he never sank below the highest level of his parishioner's respect " —the sort of human character that the author had come to love.　And for description we have little better than her own account of the charms of the country in Jersey in May.　She writes in her Recollections : " There is a charming piece of common, or down, where you can have the quietest, easiest walking, with a carpet of minute wild flowers that are not hindered from flaunting by the sandy rain of the coast. . . . The first lovely walk we found inland was the Queen's Fern Valley, where a broad strip of meadow and pasture lies between two high slopes covered with wood and ferny wilderness. When we first saw this valley it was the loveliest springtime : the woods were a delicious mixture of red and tender green and purple. . . . When the blossoms fell away from the orchards my next delight was to look at the grasses mingled with the red sorrel ; then came the white umbelliferous plants, making a border or inner frame for them along the hedgerows and streams. . . . Everywhere there are tethered cows, looking at you with meek faces—mild-eyes, sleek, fawn-coloured creatures, with delicate downy udders."

CHAPTER VI

George Eliot as a Novel Writer: Her First Novels
"Scenes of Clerical Life" and "Adam Bede" (1857–1858)

In the midst of a life of marvellous calm, success was about to dawn on a woman who had never dreamt of anything of the sort. So far she had nearly reached her fortieth year—the best of her life was past—and though she had written and thought far more than most women of her time, she had only somewhat faintly interested the readers of serious magazines, and had left the large world outside untouched. To be admired of that limited section of the community was the height of her ambition, and now she was beginning to receive the praise of men such as William Makepeace Thackeray, and it almost took away her breath.

What was it, then, that laid hold of the imagination of the English world in this truly amazing fashion? Was it that all through a life of strenuous work and devotion to duty in the conventional sense of the word, there was a real life of passion surging through the veins of the young woman and demanding the expression which now for the first time it received? There had indeed been critical phases in her life. There were the uncontrollable griefs of childhood, the differences with her father in girlhood, and above all, those passions of young womanhood that ended in the union with Lewes.

Anyhow it is clear that we have in George Eliot's career an unusual combination of a life of thought and passionate impulses only partially held in bounds. But more than that we have in her a woman who from the circumstances of her early years had been able to lay hold of the lives of her fellow countrymen and fellow countrywomen at a critical time in their history ; and who from her intimate study of these lives and the whole circumstances which surrounded them, was able to write of them as they appeared to an understanding observer. There had been others, no doubt, who had taken the same subjects, but always with a difference. Jane Austen, a little earlier, with her marvellous power of depicting the virtues and foibles of the well-to-do, no doubt knew the ordinary people of the land in her quiet country life. But they made no appeal to her excepting as a part of the setting that enabled others—those of real importance—to move about with ease and grace. The Brontës, again, knew them, as with their insight of genius they could not fail to know them, and they sometimes came forth uncompromisingly true to nature, raw and even brutal. But they are the products of another sort of surroundings, different from any with which Mary Ann Evans was in touch. The Brontës had little in common with the calm, still life of the rich pasture lands, where tragedy and comedy ran one into the other in almost imperceptible amalgamation. Farmers,

I

rich and to all appearances prosperous, struggling
craftsmen and tradesmen, and above all, clergy,
lawyers and doctors such as are met with in every
little provincial town, were the material out of
which George Eliot dug her ore. Her methods were
old-fashioned : her style was direct as the Bible :
there were none of the modern allusionary modes of
hinting at things not told. But what people
recognised in her tales was truth : and at first, at
least, she was content with that and did not trouble
to point the moral or paint the lily with the mature
reflection of the philosopher.

One wonders if these early tales could have been
written during the period of " Sturm und Drang "
in London. The descriptive parts had indeed been
begun in the early days in Warwickshire, but the
" Scenes from Clerical Life " inherently belong to
the peaceful life by the seaside, the cheap but snug
lodgings, and the pleasure of knowing that the man
with whom the writer's life was bound had discovered a parasitic worm in a cuttle-fish. " No
cause for headaches now ! " as she exclaims in
writing to her friend, Mrs. Bray :

" You may wonder how my face has changed in
the last three years. Doubtless it is older and
uglier, but it ought not to have a bad expression,
for I never have anything to call out my ill-humour
or discontent—which you know were always ready
to come on slight call—I have everything to call
out love and gratitude." And again : " I am very
happy in the highest blessing life can give us.
The perfect love and sympathy of a nature that

stimulates my own into healthful activity. I feel, too, that all the terrible pains I have gone through in past years, partly from the defects in my own nature, partly from outward things, has probably been a preparation for some special work that I may do before I die. That is a blessed hope to be rejoiced in with trembling, . . . I am contented to have lived and suffered for the sake of what has already been."

Amos Barton of the "Sad Fortunes"—could there be a more truthful account of that commonplace and irritatingly stupid man that we know so well? He is the curate of Shepperton Church, and Shepperton is the Chilvers Coton where George Eliot was baptized. Milby, the market town near, where the clerical meetings took place and the Book Society was established, is quite recognizable as Nuneaton, then a big, straggling village rather than a town. The Reverend Amos himself was supposed to have as his prototype the curate who was at Chilvers Coton during George Eliot's girlhood. She revels in the description of the church at Shepperton as it was in the old days, " with its outer coat of rough stucco, its red-tiled roof, its heterogeneous windows patched with desultory bits of painted glass." " No benches in those days; but huge, roomy pews round which devout churchgoers sat during ' lessons,' trying to look anywhere else than into each other's eyes."

Those who have lived long enough to cast their memory back to similar scenes, love to have them brought to mind. But in George Eliot's writings it is the human beings whose doings or sayings interest us most, and at the period at which the story opens, the situation is revealed in an admirable conversation in the Cross Farm between its owner, old Mrs. Patten, who had got rich chiefly by the negative process of spending nothing, and her epigrammatic neighbour, Mrs. Hackit, who " declines cream ; she has so long abstained from it with an eye to the weekly butter-money, that abstinence, wedded to habit, has begotten aversion," and who has brought her knitting. " No frivolous fancy knitting " is it, " but a substantial woollen stocking ; the click-click of her knitting-needles is the running accompaniment to all her conversation, and in her utmost enjoyment of spoiling a friend's self-satisfaction, she never has been known to spoil a stocking." The gentlemen of the party were Mr. Pilgrim, the doctor from the nearest market town, and Mr. Hackit, who thought " preaching without the books no good, only when a man has the gift, and has the Bible at his fingers end." " It does as much harm as good to give a too familiar aspect to religious teaching." Mrs. Patten " hates the sight o' women going about trapesing from house to house in all weathers, wet or dry, and coming in with their petticoats dagged and their shoes all over mud." No one was to join in " tracking " in *her* house, so that Evangelicalism as exemplified by the Rev. Mr. Barton was clearly not held in high esteem.

The unfortunate Mr. Barton in his dressing-gown of maize—" Maize is a colour that decidedly did *not* suit his complexion "—had a lovely wife who had much to suffer—a large, fair, gentle Madonna— " the flowing lines of her tall figure made the limpest dress look graceful." She had six children, with another coming, and not the wherewithal to clothe them ; and to make matters worse, her husband became mildly enamoured of a Countess with a foreign name, who settled herself upon them and made their difficulties greater, even causing a scandal amongst the parishioners. A wonderful account is given of Mrs. Barton's care for her children. " Everything else one can turn and turn about, and make old like new ; but there's no coaxing boots and shoes to look better than they are." How could this have been written by a man ? Poor Mr. Barton ! He " had not the gift of perfect accuracy in English orthography and syntax ; which was unfortunate as he was known not to be a Hebrew scholar, and not in the least suspected of being an accomplished Grecian," and " though he thought himself strong, he did not *feel* himself strong." The Tractarian movement had begun to be felt even in these backward parts and as an evangelical he would " like to have taken in the *Christian Observer* and the *Record* if he could have afforded it." " His very faults were middling—he was not very imaginative even—all was of a drab dullness." Then comes the development of the story, the routing of the Countess by the servant maid Nanny, and then the tragedy of Milly's death surrounded as she by her children, Patty, Chubby, and Dicky and the rest—a tragedy which

few can read without tears ; and yet it is a pathos
which has no exaggeration, for it seems to come
naturally, just as Milly's life came naturally, without any consciousness that she was a pathetic
object at all. Hers is perhaps one of the most
beautiful and simple death-scenes in the English
language. The epilogue, which was an after-
thought, seems to spoil it : we should like the story
to end as such stories do in real life, without a
conclusion.

There is one scene, that of the clerical dinner party
at the vicarage where the various types of clergy
meet—from the Reverend Archibald Duke, who
takes the gloomiest view of mankind and thinks
the immense sale of the " Pickwick Papers," then
just published, one of the strongest proofs of original
sin, to the excellent Mr. Cleves, " the pastor beloved,
consulted, relied on by his flock," who has hereditary
sympathies with the chequered life of the working
people—that brings to mind those other " Scenes
of Clerical Life " that were being written at exactly
the same time by another great writer, Anthony
Trollope. Trollope does not worry about " movements," or the deeper side of religious life, but he
does give us a most accurate description of the life
of the clergy in England at the selfsame time.
Had Trollope been a man learned in literature and
philosophy, he might have gained in depth. But
we should have missed something in his straight-
forward writing—writing that tells us just what we
want to know about the people we see and meet in
everyday life. The two writers are a contrast,

inasmuch as George Eliot digs down to the foundations and has them in view while she describes the outward play of action ; while the other is content to relate the comedies and tragedies of life simply and naturally without troubling to ask the deeper question of how they have come to be there.

" Mr. Gilfil's Love-Story," the next of the series, deals with an earlier date and brings us into touch with more aristocratic circles—never quite so real to their author as the rather humbler folk—since it mainly concerns the ward of Sir Christopher Cheverel, Maynard Gilfil, who has just entered the Church, and who falls in love with Lady Cheverel's beautiful Italian protégée, Caterina Sarti. Sir Christopher's nephew and heir, Captain Wybrow, however, amuses himself by flirting with Caterina, (who prefers him to Mr. Gilfil), while he engages himself to another. The tragedy ends by the sudden death of Wybrow, and Caterina's wandering off in despair. In the end Gilfil secures his bride (though she is marked for death) and has a short married life. He is ever afterwards known as the beloved old vicar of Shepperton. Cheverel is clearly Sir Roger Newdigate of the family in whose employment George Eliot's father, Mr. Evans, was for so many years, and Cheverel Manor is Arbury, which Sir Christopher rebuilt in the Gothic style, just as was done by Sir Roger. We know of the immense impression Arbury Park made on Mary Ann Evans as a girl ; she often visited it with her father, sometimes waiting for him in the housekeeper's room and hearing the legends of the house from those who

frequented it, and then admiring its grey loveliness
as it stood four-square veiled in beautiful trees and
surrounded by pleasant lawns. And in later girlhood
she was allowed to browse in its fine library ; for
the Newdigates we saw to be a family of culture. In
the " Love-Story " it is thus described : " A charming picture Cheverel Manor would have made that
evening, if some English Watteau had been there to
paint it : the castellated house of grey-tinted stone,
with the flickering sunbeams sending dashes of
golden light across the many-shaped panes in the
mullioned windows, and a great beech leaning
athwart one of the flanking towers, and breaking with
its dark flattened boughs the too formal symmetry
of the front ; the broad gravel-walk winding on
the right, by a row of tall pines, alongside the
pool—on the left, branching out amongst swelling,
grassy mounds, surmounted by clumps of trees,
where the red trunk of the Scotch fir glows in the
descending sunlight against the bright green of
limes and acacias ; the great pool where a pair of
swans are swimming lazily with one leg tucked
under a wing, and where the open water-lilies lie
calm accepting the kisses of the fluttering light
sparkles ; the lawn, with its smooth emerald greenness, sloping down to the rougher and browner
herbage of the park, from which it is invisibly
fenced by a little stream that winds away from the
pool and disappears under a wooden bridge in the
distant pleasure-ground." This description, evidently lovingly made, gives the tone to the story.
There is no poverty or sordid care here. Sir

Christopher is the splendid old gentleman the writer remembers, who deals fairly with his people while assuming a peremptory and somewhat overbearing manner. He typified the " old school " at its best, and George Eliot loved the old school.

For herself, the author preferred " Amos " to " Mr. Gilfil," and after the lapse of seventy years most people will agree with her. " Mr. Gilfil " has a genuine plot, but the plot is rather a strain on our imagination, and the tale does not develop so naturally as the other. Captain Wybrow is rather too much of a stage villain, and his death is too opportune to be convincing. But Maynard is a wholly delightful character.*

The next tale, and the last, is one which had the least favourable reception when it first appeared in *Blackwood's Magazine*: " I sent off the first part of ' Janet's Repentance,' " its author writes, " but to my disappointment Blackwood did not like it so well—seemed to misunderstand the characters,

---

* Lady Newdigate-Newdigate in " The Cheverels of Cheverel Manor," tells us a good deal of the family history, which George Eliot probably picked up on her visits to Arbury and worked into " Mr. Gilfil's Love Story." The Lady Cheverel of the story is Sir Roger Newdigate's second wife, a fascinating woman and good letter writer. The original of Caterina was the daughter of a collier on the property with a beautiful voice whom Lady Newdigate trained with a view to her becoming a professional singer. Lady Newdigate became much attached to the girl, who was prosaically named Sally. But Sally's triumph was short, for she fell ill (whether love-smitten or not, we do not know) and had to go abroad. An Italian named Motta, formerly Lady Newdigate's singing-master, spent much time at Arbury teaching her. Sally finally recovered and returned to Arbury, and married Mr. Bernard Gilpin Ebdell (Mr. Gilfil, the vicar of Chilvers Coton). She did not die early like Caterina, but had twenty-two years of married life. There was also an heir to Sir Roger, a Mr. Parker, who would have succeeded had he lived, but who, though resembling him in appearance, has no other connection with Captain Wybrow.

and to be doubtful about the treatment of clerical matters. I wrote at once to beg him to give up printing the story if he felt uncomfortable about it, and he immediately sent a very anxious, cordial letter." But George Eliot was very sure of her ground. She was willing only to make superficial alterations in the proofs and not to change them materially. " The collision in the drama is not at all between ' bigoted churchmanship ' and evangelicalism, but between irreligion and religion. Religion in this case happens to be represented by evangelicalism ; and the story, so far as regards the *persecution*, is a real bit in the religious history of England, that happened about twenty-eight years ago." And then she explains that her sketches both of Churchmen and Dissenters, with whom she was equally acquainted, are drawn from close observation in real life, and not at all from hearsay. " If I were to undertake to alter language or character, I should be attempting to represent some vague conception of what may possibly exist in other people's minds, but has no existence in my own. As an artist I should be utterly powerless if I departed from my own conceptions of life and character." She offers to close the series in the magazine if Mr. Blackwood thinks well, and in this case she would " accept the plan with no other feeling than that you have been to me the most liberal and agreeable of editors."

In " Janet's Repentance " we come back to the later date—the thirties—and meet some of the same people as in " Amos Barton." The scene is the town of Milby (Nuneaton) and the story centres round the division of opinion over the work of the new Evangelical curate, Mr. Tryan, who is a devoted and earnest clergyman, but who is opposed and persecuted by the supporters of the snuffy old curate, Mr. Crewe. Mr. Tryan's character is finely drawn. George Eliot disclaimed his being taken from any clergyman, living or dead, though a Mr. Jones wrote to Mr. Blackwood assuring him that he was certainly sketched from his brother. It is anyhow clear that the whole story had some basis in tales that George Eliot had heard in her youth, both from what she herself says and from its convincing nature. "I think I told you that a persecution of the kind I have described did actually take place, and belongs as much to the common store of our religious history as the Gorham controversy, or as Bishop Blomfield's decision about wax candles. But I only know the *outline* of the real persecution. The details have been filled in from my imagination." The marvel is why anyone should object to any relative being identified with so selfless and beautiful a character as Mr. Tryan's.

One of the most ardent of Mr. Tryan's opponents is Robert Dempster, a lawyer of a low and offensive kind who helped to prepare a scurrilous poster and to organise a hostile crowd. He is given to drink and ill-treats brutally his noble wife Janet. "Her grandly-cut features, pale with the natural paleness of a brunette, have premature lines about them telling that the years have been lengthened by sorrow, and the delicately-curved nostril, which seems to quiver with the proud consciousness of power and beauty, must have quivered to the heart-piercing griefs which have given that worn look to the corners of her mouth." She, too, in desperation had taken to drinking, and the bitterness of her mother's grief over her daughter's sad fate is one of the most poignant parts of the tale. In a final fit of anger Dempster turns his wife out of doors in her nightdress and she seeks refuge with one of Mr. Tryan's adherents. He comes to know of her and helps her to quit herself of the demon that possessed her, and so she becomes one of Mr. Tryan's loyal supporters. Her husband is mercifully thrown from his dog-cart when drunk and nearly killed, and Janet watches over him in his last hours, while both remember that they once loved one another. Mr. Tryan succumbs to his heavy labours at last, for his frame was none too strong. There is a beautiful account of his funeral, and the simple gravestone— " a meagre memorial, that tells you simply that the man who lies there took upon him, faithfully or unfaithfully, the office of guide and instructor to his fellow-men. But there is another memorial of Edgar Tryan, which bears a fuller record ; it is Janet Dempster, rescued from self-despair, streng-thened with divine hopes, and now looking back on years of purity and helpful labour. The man who has left such a memorial behind him must have been one whose heart beat with true compassion and whose lips were moved by fervent faith."

But it must not be thought that " Janet's Re-pentance " was all tragedy, or Mr. Blackwood's stricture might have been justified. There is the delightful Miss Pratt : " an old maid with a cap, a braided ' front,' a backbone and appendages," the one blue-stocking of Milby, who possessed no less than five hundred volumes and dabbled a little in authorship, " though it was understood that she had never put forth her full powers in print." But above all there is the handsome but scolding Mrs. Jerome, the wife of well-meaning Mr. Jerome, the kindly Dissenter who was a firm supporter of the Evangelical Mr. Tryan, and who told him : " You shall not be wantin' in any support as I can give. Before you come to it, sir, Milby was a dead an' dark place ; you are the first man i' the Church to my knowledge that has brought the Word o' God home to the people ; an' I'll stan' by you, sir," which he did with great effect, for Mr. Tryan was one of those men whose weakness it is to be too keenly alive to every hard wind of opinion ; to wince under the frowns of the foolish.

Then there was the little Lizzie Jerome, one of George Eliot's delicious creations such as make one long for her to have had little ones herself to play around her. " If Janet had had babes to rock to sleep—little ones to kneel in their nightdresses and say their prayers at her knees—sweet boys and girls to put their young arms round her neck and kiss away her tears, her poor hungry heart would have been fed with strong love, and might never have needed that fiery poison to still its cravings. Mighty is the force of motherhood. It transforms all things by its vital heat ; it turns timidity into fierce courage and dreadless defiance into tremulous submission ; it turns thoughtlessness into foresight, and yet stills all anxiety into calm content ; it makes selfishness become self-denial, and gives even to hard vanity the glance of admiring love. Yes ; if Janet had been a mother, she might have been saved from much sin, and therefore from much of her sorrow."

This is one of the tales of George Eliot that has much practical wisdom as well as human pathos. " I'd rather give ten shillin' an' help a man to stand on his own legs, nor pay half-a-crown to buy him a parish crutch ; it's ruination to him if he once goes on the parish " ; and again, Mr. Tryan " can't abide to preach to the fastin' on a full stomach." The sane and sensible form of preaching is to maintain that the least attractive but best form of self-mortification is that which " wears no hair-cloth and has no meagre days, but accepts the vulgar, the commonplace, and the ugly whenever the highest duty seems to be among them."

It is generally allowed that these Tales are to be reckoned as amongst George Eliot's best writing, and as freer from didactic reflections than many of her later works. No one can say that they are free from philosophic thought : that is the case with none of her writings, and no one who cares for her work would have it otherwise. We have plenty of good art without this thought ; we could even in her time delight in plenty of unphilosophic fiction. Though Thackeray is full of his own reflections on the situations that he presents, that reflection is comparatively simple, and concerns the obvious faults and virtues of society as he knew it. Meredith was about to give us something different—hard nuts to crack—but his writings are subtle and understanding, rather than philosophical. We do not feel with him that there is tremendous moral and religious truth being developed through the simplest action. One has to go to the Victorian poets to find just this sentiment, or else to the writers who are not novelists. " Writing is part of my religion," says George Eliot at this time, " and I can write no word that is not prompted from within." One can imagine Trollope smiling over this as he set himself to accomplish his daily tale of pages.

This was the end of the " Tales of Clerical Life," for the last one, " The Clerical Tutor," did not develop, owing to Mr. Blackwood's discouragement about the beginning of " Janet " (he came round in the end)—the only thing for which posterity will censure her publisher. George Eliot, however, writes to him : " I have a subject in my mind which will not come under the limitations of the title ' Clerical Life,' and I am inclined to take a larger canvas and write a novel." And then : " My new story haunts me a good deal, and I shall set about it without delay. It will be a country story—full of the breath of cows and the scent of hay." This foretells the dawning of " Adam Bede."

Success seemed to have come both to Lewes and herself. Blackwood increased his offer for the " Scenes " from £120 to £210, and Lewes's " History of Philosophy " reached a new edition. " Goethe " was in its third edition, and on the last day of 1857

George Eliot writes : " My life has deepened un-
speakably during the last year : I feel a greater
capacity for moral and intellectual enjoyment ; a
more acute sense of my depression in the past ;
a more solemn desire to be faithful to coming duties
than I remember at any former period of my life.
And my happiness has deepened too : the blessedness of a perfect love and union grows daily. . . .
Few women, I fear, have such reason as I have to
think the long sad years of youth were worth living
for the sake of middle age."

Thus the year 1858 opened auspiciously, and a
very favourable review of the " Scenes " in *The
Times* came as a pleasant New Year's gift. " But
at present fear and trembling predominate over
hope." Dickens's letter, in which he speaks of " the
exquisite truth and delicacy, both of the humour and
the pathos of these stories " was especially cheer-
ing. But he was too clever a novelist not to see
the " womanly touches in this moving fiction . . .
If they originated with no woman, I believe that
no man ever before had the art of making himself
mentally so like a woman since the world began,"
Thackeray, however, was not as discerning as
to sex. Froude wrote appreciatively, though he
again did not guess the sex of the writer ; Mrs.
Carlyle's letter was characteristic, for the book
had helped her through one of the most wretched
nights of her life, which for her was saying a good
deal. She adroitly conceives Mr. Eliot as " a man
of middle age, with a wife from whom he has got
those beautiful *feminine* touches in the book—a

good many children and a dog! Not a clergyman, but brother or first cousin to a clergyman." The testimonies were so agreeable that the incognito became almost oppressive, even though well preserved in discreet letters to the writer's friends : the authorship was at last revealed under oath of secrecy to John Blackwood.

Blackwood was even shown the MS. of the next novel, which he naturally was keen to get for his magazine ; but, true Scot as he was, he first of all wished to get an account of the story ; for the wise publisher evidently had a certain anxiety about the perfect propriety of the plot. And his prognostications were justified, for, strange as it seems, " Adam Bede " was, in those Victorian days, as completely banned from the shelves of the young person's library as was Zola some time later. And meantime Nuneaton was becoming all agog over the authorship of the " Scenes " ; and was beginning excitedly to discuss who was who. Lists of who was who were indeed drawn up, reaching the alarming number of half a hundred ; and amongst these we may well believe that there were mixed feelings about the likenesses. George Eliot was not as safe as she had hoped to be under her incognito. She did indeed assure her publishers that even she could not supply a key to her tales, for she alone knew from what a combination of subtle shadowy suggestions they were formed. But this did not suffice for excited Warwickshire. Most writers of this genre do start by writing almost unconsciously from nature and memory ; and

K

probably most have the same rather trying experiences when their characters are identified.

The usual remedy for all such troubles was to go
abroad and forget them ; and this was done with
great success. Nüremberg and Munich, professors
galore, and all sorts of interesting people came
their way. The charming Liebig delighted them
with his manners ; Strauss, the old acquaintance,
was re-visited, all arranged by the wonderful Lewes,
who acted as a skilful courier, smoothed over
every difficulty, and also delighted his friends by his
attractive talk. Then the pleasure of the travels was
enhanced first by the fact that the new novel was
going on steadily ; and chapter after chapter was
being read to the helpful companion ; and by the
fact that in an attack of illness at Munich she " was
nursed so tenderly " by the same devoted hand.

The journey was carried on to Vienna and Prague
and finally stopped at Dresden, where six delightful
weeks were spent undisturbed by visitors. Here
both were " as happy as princes—are not "—
George writing in the far corner of a big salon where
presumably the scratching of his pen disturbed no
one ; she at her *Schrank* in her own private room,
shut tightly in behind closed doors. Both wrote
and wrote, and she, rising at six, managed to
finish the latter part of the second volume of
" Adam." They took time, of course, to visit
beautiful pictures, and George Eliot gives a vivid
account of how she was overcome by the sight of
the famous Madonna Cabinet, and had to hurry out
of the room. But all delightful things must come

to an end ; and from Dresden the travellers returned home, reaching Richmond on September 2nd, 1857. The manuscript of " Adam Bede " went off in the early part of the following year, and a period of suspense followed till Blackwood, the ideal publisher, wrote to offer £800 for the copyright for four years, giving warm praise to the book. " *Jubilate !* " exclaims the author.

If we had nothing but the " Scenes " and " Adam Bede " we should still have had a very famous writer, and probably " Adam Bede " is still the most read of all George Eliot's works. It is both an interesting story and a human document that all can understand. It is a real novel too, and not just a " short story." English people like a novel and are not very fond of short stories, perhaps because they have not often the art of writing them, as have, for instance, the French.

The germ of " Adam Bede " was a story told long ago of her own experiences by the author's Methodist Aunt Evans (the wife of her father's younger brother). We remember that this was the aunt who was her correspondent and confidante in the old days when she begged her for a word of exhortation, and when Elizabeth Evans had great hopes of the promising niece whose religious experiences were so remarkable—hope destined in her view to be sadly disappointed. " We were sitting together," George Eliot says in telling of its genesis, " one afternoon at Griff, probably 1839 or 1840, when it occurred to her to tell how she had visited a condemned criminal—a very ignorant girl

who had murdered her child and refused to confess ;
how she had stayed with her, praying through the
night, and how the poor creature at last broke out
into tears, and confessed her crime. My aunt
afterwards went with her in the cart to the place
of execution ; and she described to me the great
respect with which this ministry of hers was regarded by the official people about the jail. The
story, told by my aunt with great feeling, affected me
deeply, and I never lost the impression of that
afternoon and our talk together ; but I believe I
never mentioned it, through all the intervening
years, till something prompted me to tell it to George
in December, 1856, when I had begun to write the
'Scenes of Clerical Life.' "

In talking of the book, when once it was decided
not to make it one of the " Scenes " but a book in
itself, the Leweses always called it "My Aunt's
Story." Dinah, who was the prominent character
in its first conception, was not like the aunt in appearance. The latter was a very small, black-eyed
woman who, when her niece knew her, was elderly,
had given up public work and become more subdued and gentle than in the days of her active
ministry and bodily strength, when she could not
rest without exhorting and remonstrating with
recalcitrant sinners in season and out of season.
" I was very fond of her," George Eliot writes, " and
enjoyed the few weeks of her stay with me greatly.
She was loving and kind to me, and I could talk to
her about my inward life, which was closely shut
up from those usually round me. I saw her only

twice again, for much shorter periods—once at her own home at Wirksworth in Derbyshire, and once at my father's last residence, Foleshill." Dinah is one of the most tender and beautiful of George Eliot's characters and the beauty is not spoiled by exaggeration as it easily might have been. She is one of those holy women—" succourers of many " —who go through life doing the simple tasks that come to their hands, and just because of that, the tasks come first to them, because wherever there is trouble people at once turn to where they will certainly get help. Probably many of them had, like Aunt Evans, a more fiery early existence. But these things pass with really good women like Dinah Morris.

" Adam Bede " has, like the " Scenes," a special value of its own as a picture of English rural life, accurate to the last degree. Perhaps the author does not touch the lowest stratum of rural life, like Hardy, but if so, that is the only exception to her large embrace. The relations between land-lord and tenant, farmer and cottager, have been peculiar to this country, and the changes in recent years in these relationships have been great, and will become greater as years go on. No one could understand them better than a land steward's daughter who, through her father, had been brought into touch with every class. And, besides, the father had begun his career as of the humbler craft of carpenter. Adam Bede, the hero—if so he may be called, for there are many prominent figures in the story—is a young carpenter of diligence and capacity, who from force of character makes his way to being foreman in a timber yard near. Instead of caring for his master's daughter, he is carried away by the attractions of Hetty Sorel, the egotistical and pretty young niece of a neighbouring farmer, Mr. Martin Poyser, with whom she lived. Dinah Morris is Mrs. Poyser's niece, but neither her exertions nor Adam's can turn Hetty's thoughts to higher things.

The old Squire is a typical selfish landlord of the old days, but the heir, Arthur Donnithorne, a generous, impulsive young man, is beloved by all. Unfortunately Arthur almost unwittingly becomes enamoured of Hetty ; and Hetty, who has a passion for luxury and believes she will eventually be his wife, yields to him. Adam finds the two together in the wood, and after a tumultuous scene and a fight, Arthur promises to write to Hetty, and goes off to his regiment without Adam's knowing how far things had gone. Hetty is miserable, engages herself to Adam, but, as time goes on, she realises that she cannot conceal her condition, leaves home on a pretext of visiting Dinah, goes to Windsor just to find Arthur left with his regiment for Ireland and has to wander back. In the course of her wanderings her child is born, and she allows it to die. She is arrested for child-murder, condemned to death, and Dinah is with her till near the time of execution when Arthur, overwhelmed with shame and grief, succeeds in getting a reprieve. Adam finally marries Dinah.

There is the makings of a whole tragedy here,

and George Eliot uses it to the utmost. Adam—the fine craftsman and high-minded man—is clearly taken from her father, Robert Evans. But her own account is this : " The character of Adam Bede and one or two incidents connected with him were suggested by my father's early life : but Adam is not my father any more than Dinah is my aunt. Indeed, there is not a single portrait in ' Adam Bede ' ; only the suggestion of experience wrought up into new combinations. When I began to write it, the only elements I had determined on, besides the character of Dinah, were the character of Adam and his relations to Arthur Donnithorne, and their mutual relations to Hetty—i.e. to the girl who commits child-murder—the scene in prison being, of course, the climax towards which I worked. Everything else grew out of the characters and their mutual relation."

Adam was much more like her father than George Eliot allows—so her contemporaries said, who recognised many of his traits in this fine representation of the best type of British working man who has true pride in his work. " A large-boned, muscular man nearly six feet high, with a back so flat, and a head so well poised that when he drew himself up to take a more distant survey of his work, he had the air of a soldier standing at ease. The sleeves rolled up above the elbow showed an arm that was likely to win the prize for feats of strength ; yet the long, supple hand, with its broad finger-tips, looked ready for works of skill." Does a woman ever draw a perfectly conceived picture of a man ?

This is always disputed ; but certainly George Eliot had studied her father to good effect. So far, at least, as Adam's relationship to his worthless father and rather irritating and querulous mother went, it seems as if the conception had been perfect. Lisbeth, his mother, had never learned the lesson not to talk to an angry or drunken man, and her voice became choked with sobs when she mourned over her drunken husband and her son's insistence on doing his father's work, though he had to work all night for it ; and finally it reached a sort of wail, " the most irritating of all sounds where real sorrows are to be borne, and real work to be done."

But as to Adam's relation to the pretty, vain little Hetty, the circumstances may be different. Leslie Stephen says that one characteristic of female writing is the kind of resentment with which the true woman contemplates a man unduly attracted by female beauty, and that Adam Bede's passion for Hetty produces an exposition of the theory. " Ah, what a prize the man gets who wins a sweet bride like Hetty ! How the men envy him who come to the wedding breakfast and see her hanging on his arm in her white lace and orange blossom. The dear, young, round, soft, flexible thing ! Her heart must be just as soft, her temper just as free from anger, her character just as pliant. If anything ever goes wrong it must be the husband's fault there : he can make her what he likes—that's plain. . . . Every man under such circumstances is conscious of being a great physiognomist. Nature, he knows, has a language of her own which she uses

with strict veracity, and he considers himself an
adept in the language. Nature has written out his
bride's character for him in those exquisite lines
of cheek and lip and chin, in those eyelids, delicate
as petals, in their long lashes curled like the stamen
of a flower, in the dark, liquid depths of those
wonderful eyes." Then come George Eliot's reflections which, though they are not as constant in
" Adam Bede " as in her later novels, are always
there weighing and balancing in the light of the
eternal, and they are those of a woman critic, not
of a lover. " Nature has her language and she is
not unveracious ; but we don't know all the
intricacies of her syntax just yet, and in a hasty
reading we may happen to extract just the very
opposite of her real meaning. . . . One begins to
suspect at length that there is no direct correla-
tion between eyelashes and morals ; or else that
the eyelashes express the disposition of the fair
one's grandmother, which is, on the whole less
important to us." Mrs. Poyser, of the keen eye
for facts and readiness to state them, puts it in a
few terse and plainly spoken words : " She's no
better than a peacock, as 'ud strut about on the
wall and spread its tail when the sun shone if all
the folks i' the parish was dying : there's nothing
seems to give her a turn i' th' inside, not even when
we thought Totty had tumbled into the pit."

It is in dialogue that George Eliot excels when
she wishes to bring out the spirit of the country-
side. In her best dialogue she seems to forget herself, ceases to be a spectator, and identifies herself

with the company, taking pure joy out of doing so. The dialogue of Mrs. Patten and her neighbour in " Amos Barton " and of Mrs. and Mr. Jerome in " Janet's Repentance " are admirable, but they are surpassed by that of Mrs. Poyser and Martin Poyser, her husband, and their cronies. Mrs. Poyser, the sharp-tongued, capable wife, has a gift of epigram quite her own, and she uses it well. This is her description of a slatternly neighbour : " A poor soft thing wi' no more head-piece nor a sparrow. She'd take a big cullender to strain her lard wi' and then wonder at the scratchins run through. . . . Her house all hugger-nugger and you'd never know, when you went in, whether it was Monday or Friday, the wash draggin' on to the end o' the week ; and as for her cheese, I know well enough it rose like a loaf in a tin last year. And then she talks o' the weather bein' i' fault, as there's folks 'ud stand on their heads and then say the fault was i' their boots." This shows how country life had bitten into the writer's inmost self : every bit of her description comes home to the housewife's soul. And Martin Poyser is nearly as good : " It a'most makes your fingers itch to be at the hay now the sun shines so," he observed one Sunday as they passed through the Big Meadow. " But it's poor foolishness to think o' saving by going against your conscience. There's that Jim Wakefield, as they used to call ' Gentleman Wakefield,' used to do the same of a Sunday as o' weekdays, and took no heed to right or wrong, as if there was nayther God nor devil. An' what's he come to ? Why, I saw

him myself last market-day a-carrying a basket wi'
oranges in't." " Ah, to be sure," said Mrs. Poyser,
emphatically, " you make but a poor trap to catch
luck if you go and bait it wi' wickedness."

But quotations from the Poysers might go on
indefinitely. Mrs. Poyser's drastic dealing with the
old Squire who came to suggest putting a new tenant
into the farm, is a wonderful account of how a man
with all the awful dignity of a squire in those days,
could be routed by a woman's tongue. " It's a
pity but what Mr. Thurle should take it, and see if
he likes to live in a house wi' all the plagues o'
Egypt in't—wi' the cellar full o' water, and frogs
and toads hoppin' up the steps by dozens—and the
floor rotten, and the rats and mice gnawing every
bit o' cheese, and runnin' over our heads as we lie i'
bed till we expect 'em to eat us up alive—as it's
a mercy they hanna eaten the children long ago."
Then there are her aphorisms that have become
classic : " It wants to be hatched over again and
hatched different," quoted soon afterwards by
Charles Buxton in the House of Commons to George
Eliot's satisfaction. " You're mighty fond o' Craig,
but, for my part, I think he's welly like a cock as
thinks the sun's rose o' purpose to hear him crow."
Then again there are the little Poysers—the delightful fat Totty and her brothers Marty and Tommy
(George Eliot knew just the right names for her
children) whose doings and sayings are just the
doings and sayings of real fat, healthy children who
find speckled turkeys' nests and upset bowls of
starch over the ironing sheets.

Bartle Massey, the caustic woman-hating school-master, is a character clearly drawn from life. His name is one of the few real names used by George Eliot, for Massey was her father's school-master, and had, it is said, some of his characteristics. " I'll have nobody in my night-school that doesn't strive to learn what he comes to learn, as hard as if he was striving to get out of a dark hole into broad daylight. . . . I'll not throw any good knowledge on people who think they can buy it by the sixpence 'orth and carry it away with 'em as they would an ounce of snuff." Vixen, his dog, was the only female he allowed to be in his house, and she was there under protest, especially as she had the indiscretion to produce a litter of puppies : " I tell you there isn't a thing under the sun that needs to be done at all but what a man can do better than a woman, unless its bearing children, and they can do that in a poor make-shift way ; it had better ha' been left to the men."

Not one character in the book is a failure. Take for instance the Rev. Adolphus Irwine, the pluralist Rector. " He really had no very lofty aims, no theological enthusiasms ; if I were very closely questioned I should be obliged to confess that he felt no serious alarm about the souls of his parishioners. . . . On the other hand, I must plead, for I have an affectionate partiality towards the Rector's memory, that he was not vindictive—and some philanthropists have been so : that he was not intolerant—and there is a rumour that some zealous theologians have not been altogether free from that blemish; that although he would probably have declined to give his body to be burned in any public cause, and was far from bestowing all his goods to feed the poor, he had that charity which has sometimes been lacking to very illustrious virtue—he was tender to other men's feelings, and unwilling to impute evil."

But it is Dinah who is the central character, as George Lewes saw at once. To her there was no half-way house: men were lost or saved, and she set herself to save the sinner. The beauty of her sermon in the beginning of the book preached on the village green can never be forgotten: it was written with the author's heart blood, " with hot tears as they surged up in her own mind," as she puts it. " She stood and turned on the people. There was no keenness in the eyes; they seemed rather to be shedding love than making observations; they had the liquid look which tells that the mind is full of what it has to give out, rather than impressed by external object. She stood with her left hand towards the descending sun, and leafy boughs screened her from its rays: but in this sober light the delicate colouring of her face seemed to gather a calm vividness like flowers at evening." And then at the end she said: " Dear Friends, brothers and sisters, whom I love as those for whom my Lord has died, believe me, I know what this great blessedness is; and because I know it, I want you to have it too. I am poor, like you; I have to get my living with my hands; but no lord nor lady can be so happy as me, if they haven't got the love of God in their souls." Dinah is a great creation.

"Adam Bede" was a tale that its author really loved. Hetty's piteous search for her betrayer was written from her heart. There was only one way for that tragic object to go—all her little vanities and egotism had disappeared and she was a rudderless barque in a cold, cruel sea. "Poor wandering Hetty, with the round, childish face, and the hard, unloving, despairing soul looking out of it." The ending of the book is the weak spot in it and here Lewes's advice was wrong. George Eliot was ostensibly setting forth not an ordinary story but a great idea and it was clear that with her conception of sin and its consequences there could have been no happy ending such as was beloved and almost demanded of Victorian writers. As to Dinah, George Eliot, herself the most dependent of women, never really believed that a single woman could find full satisfaction in her solitary life, and she felt bound to find a husband for one who had renounced the world as truly as any nun. Then poor little Hetty should have suffered the pains of death for she was left to weep out her eyes in Botany Bay, and that being so, there came the difficult question of what was Arthur's duty. Should he not wait for her release and marry her? That appeared in those days to be too much to expect of the heir to a great property, and yet when we come to ideas and not facts something of the sort is demanded. Is it that we have stepped beyond the limits of dramatic representation and reached a rarefied region that we associate with religion ? And do we fall between two stools and satisfy neither of the two ideals ? This is the sort of problem that torments us.

Our reflections on the subject inevitably turn back to a corresponding drama treated in a different way by an artist as great or even greater. George Eliot was all the time in her own particular surroundings and amongst the people she knew. She looked back on former days, not as the romantic school did as something to be delighted in just because it is the past and has a glamour of olden days about it. To her the old world was her own world, and a lovable one. She knew its dark spots but she also knew and showed to us the bright ones. Sir Walter Scott's " Heart of Midlothian " is a romance, and a splendid romance, with all the quick movement and broad touches and sharply defined characters that a great romantic writer can give. We are left little time to reflect on the inwardness of what is occurring, but are carried on almost breathlessly from event to event, each marvellously described. The trial scene and Jeannie's truthfulness even to her sister's hurt is dramatically told, and undoubtedly Jeannie is a more forcible character than Dinah, though, given the necessity, we believe Dinah would have acted similarly. We are not however sure that she would have been capable of the speech before Queen Caroline.

But Effie is not as pathetic a figure as Hetty, though there is a certain resemblance between the two in their weakness and their vanity. Still, though we are full of admiration for Scott's treatment of a great subject, the latter part of the novel and Effie's part in it is so far-fetched and unconvincing, that as a study of weak womanhood George Eliot's tale excels possibly because it is written by a woman. Jeannie Deans is Scott's great success in women characters, and the combination of strength and gentleness makes her immortal. Perhaps we should not compare the two novels, each with transcendent, if different, merits, but it would be interesting to know whether George Eliot, who had so great an admiration for Scott, had the other story in view when she wrote " Adam Bede." Perhaps, too, in the end, we may be forced to acknowledge that human nature treated psychologically grows old as ideas and manners change, whereas human nature treated in its more universal aspects endures. So that pure romance would appear to have the best hope of permanent endurance if it is only true to nature. But even this is speculation.

CHAPTER VII

AN AUTOBIOGRAPHICAL NOVEL: "THE MILL ON THE FLOSS" (1858-1860)

THE two who had joined their lives together in so unconventional a way were finding the outward circumstances of their lives uncannily happy. The man was as conscious of it as the woman. " Life has been a new birth," he exclaims. " I owe to her all my prosperity and my happiness." But though we may admire the domestic life of the pair as they sallied forth together with the wonderful cheque for " Adam Bede " converted into money, and bought the china, glass and other domestic necessities for a new and larger house in Wandsworth called Holly Lodge, we have the feeling that this atmosphere was almost too free from the dust of life, so far as the woman was concerned. No doubt the " friend at her elbow " as she termed Lewes, read aloud to her the reviews and letters which poured in upon them, but always with discretion ; the unpleasing things were kept away.

No authoress was more essentially a woman in her taste and inclination. She had the true country-woman's ideal of a home, which included " endless fields and hedgerow paths and rough grass," and even now had a vision of future possibilities in these directions. She hated dust and disorder and never

forgot the housewifely lessons learned long ago at
Griff. She had also the typical country-woman's
recognition of family claims, and the death of her
half-sister " ploughed up her heart." Then she
loved her pets ; Rough, her dog, was her constant
companion and it was later succeeded by " Pug,"
sent her by Mr. Blackwood. The letter of thanks
to the donor of " Pug " is characteristic. " Pug
is come !—come to fill up the void left by false or
narrow-hearted friends. I see already that he is
without envy, hatred or malice—that he will betray
no secrets, and feel neither pain at my success nor
pleasure in my chagrin. I hope the photograph
does justice to his physiognomy. It is expressive ;
full of gentleness and affection, and radiant with
intelligence when there is a savoury morsel in
question—a hopeful indication of his mental
capacity. I distrust all intellectual pretension that
announces itself by obtuseness of the palate ! "

There were only passing troubles to annoy the
pair of literary folk. The author of them was
annoyed when it was said that Mr. Poyser's sayings
were not fresh from her mint, but derived from an
existing store of proverbs. Then a certain Mr.
Liggins, a native of Warwickshire like herself,
actually claimed the authorship of her books. How
the Liggins myth arose it is difficult to divine, but
it became credited, and a deputation of ministers
went to the gentleman to ask him to write for the
Eclectic Review and found him washing his slop-
basin at a pump. Whether this seemed to them
too incongruous to make the authorship credible,

history does not relate ; but finally a letter was written by the real author to *The Times* to show up the unfortunate Liggins.

It seemed now to be making itself clear that the author's name had to be revealed. Her great friends at Wandsworth were the Richard Congreves ; it was not they, however, but an older friend, Barbara Bodichon, who was the first to recognise " Adam Bede " as hers—" the first heart," she says, " that has recognised me in a book that has come from my heart of hearts." Now she was fain to confess that however it might be in fact, she ought to be glad that she had lived, for without being a self-satisfied author who took popular success to be everything that mattered, she could not but have some satisfaction in the public appreciation of her work. The private appreciation of the " dear, dear husband, the prime blessing that has made all the rest possible to me, giving me a response to everything I have written," she was sure of.

All the same, now that she was coming into the open, the usual self-conscious dreads and doubts were ever present with her. She belonged to a class that did not reveal itself with the freedom that we have now come to expect as normal. People in middle-class England did not commonly talk of their inmost feelings and religious sentiments in these days, and this sort of self-revelation was so distasteful to George Eliot that long years afterwards it was disallowed in the drawing-room at the Priory. And yet here she was in every line of her writings openly avowing her religion, openly making known to the world the deepest part of her nature ; for in her case there was no superficial side in the great endeavour of life. Each story was founded on no chance plot, but one selected as the medium whereby the important message that was always before her could best be conveyed. Whether this detracted from her value as a writer of fiction it is for the reader to decide. In the present day there are those who would scout it as affectation.

Prophets and seers are not usually happy people in themselves. They see too far into the realities and are not content to lead the cheerful lives of ordinary souls who are satisfied with the world as it appears and can afford to turn away from its sorrows and tragedies. The tragic was never far away from George Eliot however happiness might seem to reign, and this, along with her intense self-consciousness, took away from much of the pleasure that should have come from her great success. It made her look sad when she told herself she was happy. She kept before her the anxieties of the future—could she ever meet the demands that were being made upon her—the demands of personal duty and intellectual production—would her nature stand the strain upon it ? These constant questionings took from her much of the joy she might have had in her accomplished work. She thought about her girlhood's dreams and her longing for fame and the happiness it was to bring—and she told herself that fame brought *no* happiness. Why did not she feel strong in thankfulness that her life had vindicated itself and given her reason for gladness that she had been born into the world ?   The sad thing was that she did not have this gladness.

Then again home worries troubled her—anxieties, perhaps exaggerated, about Mr. Lewes's health. She had on her hands also cares for the three sons, to whom she wrote with real maternal solicitude about their voyage through the difficulties of life and the necessity of forming good habits and living good lives.

The following letter is addressed to Charles Lewes, the eldest of the three : " The sun is shining with us too, and your pleasant letter made it seem to shine more brightly. I am not going to be expansive in this appendix to your father's chapter of love and news, for my head is tired with writing this morning—it is not so young as yours, you know, and, besides, is a feminine head, supported with weaker muscles and a weaker digestive apparatus than that of a young gentleman with a broad chest and hopeful whiskers. I don't wonder at your being more conscious of your attachment to Hofwyl now the time of leaving is so near. I fear you will miss a great many things in exchanging Hofwyl, with its snowy mountains and glorious spaces, for a very moderate home in the neighbourhood of London. You will have a less varied and more arduous life : but the time of *Entbehrung* or *Entsagung* must begin, you know, for every mortal of us—and let us hope that we shall all—father and mother and sons—help one another with love."   In those days women seemed to take domestic problems very solemnly and also to write themselves down as old at a time at which they never would think of doing so now ; and yet it would appear to us that they showed a lack of elementary knowledge about how to order their lives, as youth passed to middle age. The Leweses thought nothing of travelling through the night to save time, even although it involved arriving at their destination at 3 a.m., and wandering about till some place was open to receive them. All their expeditions, whether house-hunting or scene-hunting for the novel in prospect, were conducted on these odd lines.

A new novel was now on its way and provisionally it was christened " The Tullivers " or " St. Oggs on the Floss " ; though the title " Sister Maggie " was the one eventually preferred. Unfortunately the publisher for some reason did not care for the name, and selected that of " The Mill on the Floss," which was really less suitable. The trouble taken over the staging of the book was immense, and Mr. Lewes, in spite of his other work on the dissection of insects and other animals which he was carrying out for his new book on the Physiology of Common Life, nobly seconded all Mrs. Lewes's efforts.

Since " Adam " had been so great a success, others, like Dickens, tried to get the periodical rights of this coming book. But George Eliot did not like this form of publication. She was, she explains in rather pontifical language, intent on doing good and true work, writing only what she loved and believed, and that from her inward promptings and not from any form of external compulsion such as periodical production seemed to imply. If she could have taken the events of life simply, all might have been well; but she had ever the striving of the moth for the star, and never could she throw off the sense of incompetence that this striving brought with it. Maggie Tulliver and Mary Ann Evans were not made for serenity : and even when the latter declares she is perfectly happy in her work and in the love of her dear one, we feel that she was protesting overmuch.

The " Prisoner in the Castle of Giant Despair " as she called herself, who had made up her mind that her work was detestable and (with a sort of premonition) that the end was the climax of detest-ableness, at last got back her proofs with the most encouraging words from Blackwood, and her book was finished on March 21st, 1860.

*   *   *   *   *

" The Mill on the Floss " will go down to posterity as a woman's autobiography and be set beside those of Charlotte Brontë when she wrote of herself in the guise of her heroines, and of Marie Bashkirtseff in acknowledged autobiography ; for the heroine of " The Mill on the Floss " was none other than Mary Ann Evans as she was in childhood and young womanhood, though this she never would publicly acknowledge. Privately it was different, for those who knew her intimately were told that the experiences recorded in the Mill were her own, and even that instead of being exaggerated they were softened. Mary Ann Evans would fain have written a real autobiography, a form of literature for

which she had great regard, but as she felt this was
out of her power, she did the next best thing, which
was to write under the protective guise of fiction.
Thus the work is a psychological study of a quite
different kind from any that preceded it, and the
reason is that it is developing the life history of a
remarkably sensible and sensitive girl, instead of
telling the story of peasant lives, or lives of what
might be called the ordinary run of parsons, squires
or lawyers.　Maggie Tulliver has become immortal ;
and nothing could be more attractive than the account
of the early part of her life.　But it is all a reflection
of what we read of the writer's own thoughts
and feelings, with the necessary differences in the
surroundings, in the parentage of the heroine, and
in the fact that Maggie, in maturity at least, had
bestowed upon her personal grace and beauty
which were never Mary Ann's.

Tom and Maggie Tulliver are like Isaac and Mary
Ann, happy brother and sister, living in their home
at the Mill, which has been in their father's family
for five generations.　Maggie is an affectionate,
impulsive and passionate girl, devoted to her brother
Tom, who is much less clever at books than she,
and thoroughly material and self-sufficient, loving
to lord it over the little sister whose heart is often
broken by her apparently unrequited affection.
And Maggie *lived* for affection and recognition.
Tom, on the other hand, though only thirteen,
" had no decided views on grammar and arithmetic,
regarding them for the most part as open questions,
but he was particularly .clear on one point—namely,

that he would punish everybody who deserved it ;
why, he wouldn't have minded being punished himself, if he deserved it : but, then, he never *did* deserve
it." So Maggie had to suffer when she forgot to
feed his rabbits—just as when Mary Ann entered
into a union disregarded by Church or State her name
ceased to exist for the upright brother Isaac.

When things went well, all was cheerful, and
the poem " Brother and Sister " tells what happy
life meant. There are few—perhaps no—faithful
accounts of child life, because we always distort
our recollections by magnifying or over-emphasising
special incidents. The injustices of childhood are
apt unduly to rankle in our minds. Matters that
are accepted as part of the normal condition of things
at the time, are reflected on later with a different
standard of values, and made to appear dispropor-
tionately important. Then, again, the happy days
of sunshine are sometimes made to appear as if the
sun always shone and we were always happy.
The impression really depends largely on the idiosyncrasies of the child, and Mary Ann was an introspective child, in whom every minor happening to
herself was intensified till it appeared of the deepest
import. If her brother Isaac had had the power
of writing an account of the selfsame happenings,
we can imagine how different the account of them
would have been. He, like Tom, was sent to a
private school that he probably disliked as much
as Tom did his. But he would never, like Maggie,
have retired to mourn over his sorrows in a garret,
or kept a fetish on which to inflict vicarious

punishment. To Tom, all came in the day's work. On the other hand, when Maggie was not angry, " she was as dependent on a kind or cold word as a daisy on the sunshine or the cloud ; the need of being loved would always subdue her."

Thus Maggie always had a life of ups and downs, bliss and sorrow. She ran away to the gipsies in a fit of jealousy, and then found what a mistake she had made. Her father fails, owing to an expensive lawsuit with a neighbouring lawyer named Wakem, in which the decision is given against him ; and after an angry encounter with Wakem he has a " stroke " which leaves him helpless, in addition to which he was bankrupt. The practical Tom comes back from school and sets to work to redeem the family fortunes, while Maggie has three years of poverty and misery at home. In her sorrow Maggie seeks solace in self-sacrifice, and, like Mary Ann Evans, finds comfort in reading Thomas à Kempis. The son of the hated Wakem, a deformed lad called Philip, who was a fellow-pupil with Tom, formed a strong affection for Maggie, and she in her craving for affection, had constant meetings with Philip, unknown to her brother, who, when he discovers this, forces her to break with him. By Tom's diligence, the creditors are paid, but the father dies after another altercation with Wakem. Maggie goes out to teach, but she returns to pay a visit to her cousin, Lucy Deane ; and, as she has developed into a beautiful and attractive woman, a young man named Stephen Guest, who was paying his addresses to Lucy, becomes infatuated with her.

Maggie fought against her love, but finally goes off
with him, though, before she had gone far she re-
pents and returns. Public opinion goes against
her, and though Stephen, who is a coxcomb, still
wishes to marry her, she will not consent. The climax
is a terrible flood (such as once really occurred in
Lincolnshire) in which Maggie attempts to rescue
Tom at the Mill ; they understand one another
once more, but only in the moment of death.

The first part of the tale is universally admired.
The description of the Tulliver family could not be
excelled. The father was the conventional man " of
safe traditional opinions " ; but on one or two points
he had trusted to his unassisted intellect, and had
arrived at several questionable conclusions ; among
the rest that " rats, weasels and lawyers were
created by Old Harry." He was indeed very different
from the sane and sensible Robert Evans, the writer's
father. The mother was the handsomest and stupid-
est of the Dodson sisters, utterly without a sense
of humour, and with no courage to face adversity.
She was " fair, plump and dull-witted, and all would
have gone well had prosperity always reigned. . . .
But milk and mildness are not the best things for
keeping." Mrs. Tulliver was thankful to have been
a Dodson, and to have one child (Tom) who " took
after her own family." The Dodsons had particular
ways of doing everything, " of bleaching the linen,
of making the cowslip wine, curing the hams, and
keeping the bottled gooseberries ; so that no daughter
of that home could be indifferent to the privilege
of having been born a Dodson rather than a Gibson

or a Watson. . . . Its vices and virtues alike were phases of a proud, honest egoism, which had a hearty dislike to whatever made against its own credit and interest, and would be frankly hard of speech to inconvenient ' kin,' but would never forsake or ignore them—would not let them want bread—but only require them to eat it with bitter herbs."

In reading the Dodsons' incisive remarks when the Tullivers were in deep water, we are inclined to feel that they are indeed too much given to administering bitter herbs to be quite natural ; at least while many of their prototypes deal in bitter speech, they yet do kindly deeds, even if in a trying way. The characters are, however, supposed to be derived from Mrs. Evans's three Pearson sisters ; and if the child's early dislike to her aunts did not prejudice her to their better sides, we may assume them to have been faithful transcripts. George Eliot went so far as to defend them and to say that they were really very nice people to whom we owe much for keeping up that religion of respectability, the only one then possible to the mass of the English people. Carlyle's deadly blows against the respectability of middle-class England had not as yet borne their effect and it still held an honoured place. Even in these days, however, one can never quite believe that rich Aunt Pullet would refuse to buy in the checked linen " spun, bleached and marked " by Mrs. Tulliver's hands because " she's got more checks a'ready than she can do with " ; and would only buy " the sprigs " from her weeping sister because " she's never had so many as she wanted of that pattern"; nor again that the sisters would reject the precious " chaney " because, as Mrs. Tulliver said : " they all found fault with them when I bought 'em, 'cause o' the small gold sprig all over 'em, between the flowers." Could callous disregard go any further ? Nor can we put such action down to the lack of imagination in post-Reformation education, as George Eliot was inclined to do.

Perhaps there was the same hereditary hardness in Tom Tulliver, who takes such a hard and almost brutal attitude to Maggie when he meets her with his enemy Philip Wakem in the " Red Deeps." Of course in real life, Maggie, even in those far-off days before women had gained their liberty, would have fought for her rights to choose her friends more fiercely, now she was a full-fledged young woman and no longer just a little sister. And that is a weak point in the narrative with which, when it was pointed out by Edward Bulwer Lytton, the author fully agreed. Had her book been still in manuscript she would, she says, have expanded the scene. Also the final tragedy, she agrees, is not adequately prepared. " This is a defect which I felt even while writing the third volume, and have felt ever since the MS. left me. *The Epische Breite* into which I was beguiled by love of my subject in the first two volumes, caused a want of proportionate fullness in the treatment of the third, which I shall always regret." But we can better understand the brutal frankness of the domineering Tom, who, after all, is working day and night to redeem the honour of his father's name, and fears the frustration

of his work by his sister's conduct, than follow
the later phase when Maggie is carried away by the
attraction of Stephen Guest, the admirer, and
almost betrothed of her dear cousin, Lucy Deane.
How, we ask, could the sensible and understanding
Maggie be attracted by a man " whose diamond
ring, attar of roses, and air of nonchalant leisure
at twelve o'clock in the day are the graceful and
odoriferous result of the largest oil-mill and the most
extensive wharf in St. Ogg's " ?　And what of
the moral side of stealing away a lover from a
beloved cousin, let there be doubts and qualms of
conscience as many as are stated ?　For anyone else
we should say that no one can tell where love and
infatuation may appear ;　and that the country-
bred Maggie may have taken appearances for reality
and even been flattered by the attentions of the
beau of St. Oggs.　But we all believe in Maggie,
and disbelieve that she could have been so extraordinarily mistaken.　We think of her warm affections for father and brother, of her nobility of
character all through the years of trouble, and we
refuse to believe that this high-minded soul could
fall to so mediocre a plane.　And yet the author of
her being says that Maggie's position towards
Stephen " is too vital a part of my whole conception and purpose, for me to be converted to the
condemnation of it.　If I am wrong there—if I
did not really know what my heroine would feel
and do under the circumstances in which I deliberately placed her—I ought not to have written this
book at all, but quite a different book, if any.　If

the ethics of art do not admit the truthful presentation of a character essentially noble, but liable to
great error—error that is anguish to its own noble-
ness—then it seems to me the ethics of art are too
narrow and must be widened to correspond with
a widening psychology.' The heart knoweth its
own bitterness, and the writer knew what temptation
was, and how hard it was to meet it. She should
conceive of a soul essentially noble, succumbing.
But she should not have made us adore our Maggie,
so as to disbelieve that she could have committed
so heinous a sin against propriety.

There have been many criticisms of the latter
part of the life Mill on the Floss, but Swinburne's
is the most trenchant. He thought the 'Mill '
on the whole at once the highest and the purest
and the fullest example of her magnificent and matchless powers—for matchless altogether they undoubtedly are in their own wide and fruitful field of
work. The first two-thirds of the book suffice to
compose perhaps the very noblest of tragic as well
of humorous prose idylls in the language, com-
prising, they likewise do, some of the sweetest as
well as saddest and tenderest as well as subtlest
examples of dramatic analysis—a study in that
kind as soft and true as Rousseau's, as keen and
true as Browning's, as full as either's of the fiery and
bittersweetness of a pungent and fiery fidelity.
But who can forget the horror of inward collapse,
the sickness of spiritual reaction, the reluctant in-
credulous rage of disenchantment and disgust with
which he came upon the brief incredibly pitiful part ? "

And he goes on to say that if we are really to think it conceivable that a " woman of Maggie Tulliver's kind can be moved to any sense but that of bitter disgust and sickening disdain by a thing—I will not write a man—like Stephen Guest ; if we are to accept as truth and fact, however astounding and revolting, so shameful an avowal, so vile a revelation as this ; in that ugly and lamentable case, our only remark, as our only comfort, must be that now at least the last word of realism has surely been spoken, the last abyss of cynicism has surely been sounded and laid bare."*

Swinburne's diatribe (there is more of it) is exaggerated : the case was not as bad as he describes it, and his further suggestion that the whole story owed much to " Mrs. Gaskell's beautiful story of ' The Moorland Cottage ' " and wonders at " the reticence which reserves all acknowledgment " is absurd, and was indignantly resented by George Eliot. The difference between the two tales is so immense, that we can hardly conceive of the comparison being made ; much less any indebtedness to the admirable but less well-equipped writer being thought of.

As a matter of fact there is all through this remarkable book the struggle between the two ideals— that of renunciation and the other—the tempting one of pleasantness. Sometimes, as happens in life, one gets the upper hand, sometimes the other. " Often," Maggie said to Philip Wakem when he

* " A Note on Charlotte Brontë," by Algernon C. Swinburne, p. 28 *et seq.*

was pressing her to be his friend despite her brother's
feelings, "when I have been angry and discontented,
it has seemed to me that I was not bound to give
up anything ; and I have gone on thinking till it
has seemed to me that I could think away all my
duty. But no good has ever come of that—it was
an evil state of mind." And yet she knew too well
the force of Philip's argument that " there are
certain thing we feel to be beautiful and good,
and *must* hunger after them. How can we ever be
satisfied without them until our feelings are
deadened ? " And the theme once more recurs
in the final tragedy, when she feels she must renounce
Stephen Guest, though for her own happiness, alas,
too late, as well as for her cousin's : " We can only
choose whether we will indulge ourselves in the
present moment, or whether we will renounce that
for the sake of obeying the divine voice within us,
for the sake of being true to all the motives that
sanctify our lives."

Leslie Stephen, who, as we have seen, had serious
misgivings about George Eliot's interpretation of
male characters, is inclined to think that she did
not realise the impression she was making upon her
readers in her portrayal of Stephen Guest, nor that
she was aware that she was depicting a " mere
hairdresser's block." He would have liked the
third volume of the book to have been suppressed.
But that is not borne out by the writer's own
strongly expressed views, and the final happenings
evidently formed part of her conception of what
Maggie *might* do when her feelings carried her

M

away. We are bound to argue that she did many foolish things before that, from the time that she cut off her long black locks and ran off to the gipsies; and repentance always came too late. Maggie's life could never have been a happy one, and it was not meant to be so. Stephen is not an attractive character and perhaps he is not drawn as he might have been drawn had the task been allotted to a man. But he is not intended to be an attractive character, of that one is very certain, and many women fall in love with men of an ignoble sort, and yet themselves remain noble. Mr. Watts-Dunton applies the dictum sometimes attributed to Thackeray that "no woman could ever really distinguish a cad from a gentleman." That, too, would appear to be a most debatable point. Besides, the far from attractive Stephen was not as bad as his detractors made out; he passionately loved Maggie and with all his faults he never gave her away; he was not a "cad," if not a gentleman.

The fact is that the ending of this great novel will always be a matter of debate, and there are not many who wholly defend it. The concluding chapters give one the impression of hurry; the flood and its results are quite unconvincing, and we go back with pleasure to the early part, where the author lingers over the old scenes and the people she loved so well. She knew as well as any of her readers that this was the part in which she had given of her best, and one wishes that she had had the chance to rewrite the last. When she deals with the relations of the broad, ordinary life of the country people and relates its action to the deep springs of the philosophy of existence, she reaches her highest point.

The success of the book was immense. Six thousand copies were soon sold ; others were being prepared, and most people preferred " The Mill " to "Adam Bede." A French translation was made by George Eliot's old friend, M. d'Albert of Geneva, but Edouard Scherer says in his Essay upon her, written in 1885, that " the name of George Eliot might serve as a measure of the distance which separates France from England. The very name of this writer, whom our neighbours regard with so much admiration, is hardly known among ourselves and arouses neither memory nor interest." Still the book appears to have had some sale even in France. Mr. Helps, who was Clerk to the Privy Council, and who came a good deal into touch with Queen Victoria, told George Eliot that the Queen had been speaking to him in great admiration of her books, and especially of " The Mill on the Floss," and this gave her pleasure as always did any royal recognition.

*　　　*　　　*　　　*　　　*

There were two short stories written about this time that have always been a little surprising to readers of George Eliot, as their style is very different from anything she wrote before or after. The first was written in 1859, after " Adam Bede " but before " The Mill," and it was called " The

Lifted Veil." Of it she writes : " Finished a story
—' The Lifted Veil ' which I began one morning at
Richmond as a resource when my head was too
stupid for more important work." The tale is a
strange and eerie one, about a man endowed with
a power of seeing into the future, whose life was
rendered miserable owing in great measure to these
supernatural powers. It is a disagreeable story,
for there are no pleasant characters and no sense
of humour. The subject who writes about himself is mysteriously attracted by a most unattractive
woman, the affianced bride of his brother. The
brother is accidentally killed, and he marries her.
The marriage is a failure, and the wife's maid
and she conspire to poison him. The maid apparently dies of peritonitis, but is sufficiently brought
to life again by means of artificial respiration and
the transfusion of blood, to confess the attempted
crime, after which she expires. In the end the man
lives solitary, " the curse of insight "—of his double
consciousness—never having left him. We can see
a sort of reason for so strange a subject presenting
itself at a time when artificial respiration and
apparent restoration of life was being discussed,
and when people considered that there were curious
possibilities in connexion with the exercise of
scientific experiment. And for the rest, probably
George Eliot wished to drive home the lesson that,
as she herself says : " the soul needs something
hidden and uncertain for the maintenance of that
doubt and hope and effort which are the breath of
its life : " and that if all were revealed to us the

result would be disastrous.   In 1873 she writes to
John Blackwood that she does not think it will
be judicious to reprint it at the time and alone,
but " I care for the idea which it embodies, and which
justifies its painfulness.   A motto which I wrote on
it yesterday is a sufficient indication of that idea :

> " Give me no light, great heavens, but such as turns
> To energy of human fellowship :
> No powers save the growing heritage
> That makes completer manhood."

" And," she adds, " there are many things which
I would willingly say over again, and I shall never
put them in any other form.   But we must wait
a little."

The other story—" a slight tale," she calls it—
was " Mr. David Faux, Confectioner " (Brother
Jacob) which Mr. Lewes thought " worth printing."
But it is dubious whether he was right.   It was
published in the *Cornhill Magazine*, to which it
was given as a solatium, when " Romola," which
was produced in it serially and for which the author
received seven thousand pounds, had not proved a
commercial success.

*   *   *   *   *

George Eliot was now at the height of her powers,
but though she had another short novel of a similar
type to produce—and that one of her best—she
felt that possibly the vein might have been worked
out, and that it was time that she should, as she
says, " go and absorb some new life, and gather fresh
ideas."   It was certainly a time of new ideas, for

Darwin's " Origin of Species " had just appeared,
and though to George Eliot his " theory of development and all other explanations of processes by
which things came to be, produce a feeble impression compared with the mystery that lies under
the processes," she saw at once that it marked an
epoch. But she wanted more than ideas, whether
philosophical or scientific. She required a change
of scene, and she and Mr. Lewes started for Italy
on March 22nd, 1860. On the manuscript of " The
Mill on the Floss " she inscribed: " To my
beloved husband, George Henry Lewes, I give the
MS. of my third book, written in the sixth year of
our life together at Holly Lodge, South Field,
Wandsworth, and finished 21st March, 1860."

CHAPTER VIII

An Idyll and a History
(1860–1863)
"Silas Marner"

A journey to Italy has an extraordinary effect on the traveller, if it comes at the moment in life when impressions are formed on impressionable natures. Of this the outstanding example is that of Goethe, whom it influenced almost more than any external event in his life ; in George Eliot's case it also marked an important era in her work, and caused her to turn from one subject to another and completely different one. The Italian journey was one that had been looked forward to for years with what the traveller called : " the anticipation of the new elements it would bring to my culture rather than with the hope of immediate pleasure." She felt that " travelling could hardly be without a continual current of disappointment, if the main object is not the enlargement of one's general life, so as to make even weariness and annoyance enter into the sum of benefit." Thus she started off in the orthodox fashion of those days, seeking, like her great predecessor, not only enjoyment as does the present day voyager abroad, but above all what was intellectually to be gained from the expedition. Enjoyment pure and simple was indeed looked on somewhat askance in those times, and the immense effort to profit from experiences, and remember every detail must have been oppressive, one would have said, to the traveller ; and yet he would not have demanded less of himself.

Despite the demands upon her, George Eliot loved her travels, and forgot her headaches and other ailments in her enjoyment. Her only anxiety— " the only crow that flew in heaven's sweetest air " was as usual anxiety about her dear companion's health. They talked Italian, admired Count Cavour, but above all, George Eliot adored the common people as she always did. " Oh, the beautiful men and women and children here ! " she exclaims. " Such wonderful babies with wise eyes ! Such grand-featured mothers nursing them ! As one drives along the streets sometimes, one sees a Madonna and child at every third or fourth upper window ; and on Monday a little crippled girl seated at the door of a church looked up at us with a face of such pathetic sweetness and beauty, that I think it can hardly leave me again." No woman writer ever had a deeper sense of motherhood than George Eliot, the childless, and we know well where the future Lillo found his origin as did all the beloved little immortals of whom she wrote.

The journey included Florence, and there, amidst its overwhelmingly vivid interests, historical and artistic, George Eliot was stimulated to entertain an ambitious project which was so ambitious that she kept it a secret from all excepting her publisher and his brother. To write an historical novel of another country and age for one who had entirely confined her efforts in fiction to scenes of domestic life at home, was indeed a bold step, and one that required great consideration. However, the occasion was not immediate, for another home story came across the other plan by a sort of inspiration. It had somehow, in that strange and mysterious manner in which such things occur, unfolded itself in her mind and forced her to write it. It was a story of old-fashioned village life which had developed from the tiniest seed. As she put it : " the millet-seed indeed was small, for it was but the sight in early childhood of a linen-weaver with a bag on his back "—surely the slightest foundation possible for the building up of a tale. George Eliot was, however, at all times impressionable, and this one simple fact so impressed itself upon her brain, that she wove out of it all sorts of possibilities. This work, like all the rest, represents one particular mental phase. The author used to say that she never desired to delay the publication of any one of her writings, because when once they were past and done with she lost all sense of identification with them, and felt that, however much she liked them, it was with an external sort of liking. They had to her no more real or personal interest.

Why the impulse to write the tale came just at a time when she was somewhat overwhelmed with worries at home and in travelling, it is difficult to tell. For these worries as a rule affected her writing, and made her timid in regard to it. A removal from Wandsworth to 16, Blandford Square* entailed

* She occupied 10, Harewood Square temporarily.

a great deal of work, and she had been induced to
sit for her portrait to Samuel Lawrence, and the
sittings took up time. The two old folks, as they
called themselves (though George Eliot was only
forty-one years of age) felt that they should give up
roving and have a quiet settled home for the young
people. Charles, the eldest of the Leweses, aged
seventeen, had come home from his school in
Switzerland to settle with them ; and his step-
mother loved having him and enjoyed playing
Beethoven duets on the new grand piano with one
who was a passionate musician. The sonatas of
Beethoven and the songs of Schubert were her
favourites, and the love of music made a common
bond with the boy. Charles was a clever lad, who
took a top place in the Post Office examination and
was thus launched in life while the other two boys
were studying elsewhere. Her letter to Charles—
" her dearest Grub " or " dear Top-knotted Chick "
—are natural and charming. " When anything
pleasant happens when you are away I feel that
the joy is not quite complete until our ' Grub '
knows it," she writes to him at school ; and again,
" ' God bless our boy.' Mütter sums up all her
wishes for him in that little sentence."

The weary business of settling into the new
house, the " time-frittering " business of furnishing
and arranging was at last completed. The woman
is never free of such shackles, and in her heart she
usually loves them, however she pretends to crave for
freedom, because they are part of her nature. This
was doubtless so with George Eliot, for though

relieved as she was of material anxieties since the vulgar matters of money were no longer the source of trouble, she was not relieved of the smaller worries of daily life ; for instance, her pen was lost —her favourite pen—that with which she had written for eight long years—it had disappeared. This, indeed, was a culmination of her woes !

However, in the end of 1860 she was safely in her new home, " a paradise of greenness," where for two days at least she " thought she looked splendid in the glass," and on March 10th, 1861, her new book was finished.

The book was called " Silas Marner, the Weaver of Raveloe." It is a beautiful idyll of country life as it was about the year 1820, and it came to its author as a sort of legendary tale that might best have been dealt with in metrical form ; but as her mind dwelt on the subject, she became inclined to a more realistic treatment. " I don't wonder at your finding my story as far as you have read it, rather sombre," she writes to John Blackwood, " indeed I should not have believed that anyone would have been interested in it but myself (since Wordsworth is dead) if Mr. Lewes had not been strongly arrested by it. But I hope you will not find it all a sad story as a whole, since it sets—or is intended to set—in a strong light the remedial influences of pure, natural, human relations. The Nemesis is a very mild one." The book has a spontaneity which makes it a little different from her other novels ; and consequently it is with many people their favourite. Those who see mannerisms in her writings, and who complain of a didactic style, have nothing to annoy them here. It is singularly direct and free of moral reflection, unless it be that of the purifying effect of family life spoken of above ; and is almost the only book George Eliot wrote without any of the fits of agonising struggle which usually occurred in actually bringing her progeny to birth.

Raveloe was a village in a Midland town, in Warwickshire no doubt, though the actual spot is not identified. Silas Marner, the hero, was a hand-loom weaver who fifteen years before the story begins had been a valued and earnest member of a dissenting chapel which met in Lantern Yard in a north country manufacturing town. He found his whole interest and soul in his church connection, and had a special friend amongst the members who unjustly accused him of theft—a theft committed by himself. It was decided to try the case by the casting of lots according to the custom of the Body, and the unfortunate Silas was found guilty and cast off, not only by the church members, but also by the woman he loved, who married his rival. Silas was utterly shattered and lost all the faith he formerly had in God and man. He left the place and wandered into the country, finally settling near some deserted stone-pits at Raveloe. He had always been subject to cataleptic fits which made him suspect both at Lantern Yard and in his new home, so that he lived a solitary life and did not wish to mingle with his neighbours, though he carried on his work of weaving their linen. Gradu-

ally he amassed money by so doing, and by carrying
on his work Sunday and Saturday alike, he managed
to acquire a store of gold; and he found his only
pleasure in counting it over when his work for the
day was done. Then it befell that on a winter's
night when he entered his cottage he found the
gold gone. In desperation he rushed to the
Rainbow Inn and told the band of village worthies
who were assembled there of his loss. What had
happened—though it was not known till long
after—was that a good-for-nothing younger son of
the village squire named Dunstan Cass had committed the theft. Godfrey Cass, the elder son,
though in love with an eligible daughter of a neighbour called Nancy Lammeter, had recently married
a barmaid in a neighbouring town who took drugs.
Dunstan, in desperation for money, stole Silas's
gold and disappeared. Godfrey's wife was on New
Year's Eve making her way to declare her marriage
to his father at Raveloe, when she was overcome
by the drugs she had taken, and died in the snow,
allowing her child to creep into Silas's cottage
unseen by him. When he recovered from one of his
fits and opened his eyes, he saw the child's golden
hair, and thought at first that his gold had been
returned to him. The child touches his heart, and
with the help of a good neighbour, Dolly Winthrop,
he brings her up, calling her " Eppie." Eppie's
presence brings him back to his former cheerfulness
and humanity, and he forgets the loss of his money.
Sixteen years later the draining of the stone-pits
reveals Dunstan's body and Marner's money.

Godfrey had now married his bride, Nancy Lammeter, and he tells her Eppie is his daughter, which he had hitherto concealed, and they determine to adopt the girl as their own, since they have no children. But Eppie cleaves to Silas, and will not leave him, preferring to remain a simple village girl.

Certainly " Silas Marner " is more of a poem than any of George Eliot's other prose works, and more poetical possibly than any of her verse. But there is plenty of realism in the description of the characters, especially in those of the squire and his neglected wild sons; and any amount of humour in the conversations at the village inn, and those of the delightful Dolly Winthrop, the very practical good angel of Silas and the child. This is the last of George Eliot's tales with just the atmosphere of rural life as she herself knew it. Lantern Yard and its little Bethel she must have come across—perhaps in Coventry—for in those days there were many such all over Midland and manufacturing England, where men and women sought relief from their sordid and trying surroundings in an idealism which, however narrow and unsatisfying it may seem to us, did provide that outlet for their emotions which they so sorely required. " The whitewashed walls ; the little pews where first one well-known voice and then another, pitched in a peculiar key of petition, uttered phrases at once occult and familiar, like the amulets worn on the heart ; the pulpit where the minister delivered unquestioned doctrine, and swayed to and fro, and handled the book in a long accustomed manner, the very pauses

between the couplets of the hymn, as it was given
out, and the recurrent swell of voices in song :
these things had been the channel of divine influence
to Marner—they were the fostering home of his
religious emotions—they were Christianity and
God's Kingdom upon earth." As to the casting of
lots no one who realised the simple acceptance by
such plain folk of Old Testament customs would
wonder ; nor would they wonder at the terrible
upset in Silas's mind when the methods in which
he had trusted with all his soul, failed him. Off he
went with his sack on his back, as the weaver
whom George Eliot saw as a child, to seek a different
resting-place ; and he found one in the country,
where the old associations were gone, and where
the religion was something quite different and
incomprehensible.

There have been stories with a certain resemblance to this—there was, for instance, a Polish
one called " Jermola " which was thought to have
a special resemblance to it. But it is not the idea
which is so interesting, as the working of it out.
Silas is the typical man living for himself, caring
for nothing but the wealth he was gradually accu-
mulating. " Marner's face and figure shrank and
bent themselves into a constant and mechanical
relation to the objects of his life, so that he produced the same sort of impression as a handle or a
crooked tube, which has no meaning standing apart.
The prominent eyes that used to look trusting and
dreamy, now looked as if they had been made to
see only one kind of thing that was very small, like

tiny grain, for which they hunted everywhere : and he was so withered and yellow, that though he was not yet forty, the children always called him ' Old Master Marner.' Silas worked away in his cottage as a linen weaver. . . . The questionable sound of his loom, so unlike the natural, cheerful trotting of the winnowing machine, or the simple rhythm of the flail, had a half fearful fascination for the Raveloe boys, who would often leave off their nutting or bird-nesting to peep in at the window of the stone cottage, counterbalancing a certain awe at the mysterious action of the loom by a pleasant sense of scornful superiority, drawn from the mocking of its alternating noises, along with the bent, tread-mill attitude of the weaver." The desolate miser weaver is described with much vividness, and we do not wonder at the mingled awe and fear with which the country folk looked on the " pallid, undersized men who sometimes came from mysterious, far-away lands, and who looked like the remnants of a disinherited race."

Once the terrible discovery had been made that the hidden gold was gone, Marner hurried off to the " Rainbow," to him a place of luxurious resort for " rich and stout husbands, whose women had superfluous stores of linen," where he could best make his loss public ; and here he found the conversation at a high pitch of animation, though it had been slow and intermittent when the company first assembled. " The pipes began to be puffed in a silence which had an air of serenity ; the more important customers, who drank spirits and sat nearest the fire, staring at each other as if a bet were depending on the first man who winked ; while the beer-drinkers, chiefly men in fustian jackets and smock-frocks, kept their eyelids down and rubbed their hands across their mouths, as if their draughts of beer were a funeral duty attended with embarrassing sadness." Then comes an incomparable conversation between Mr. Snell, the landlord, " accustomed to stand aloof from human differences as those of beings who were all alike in need of liquor," the butcher, the farmer, Mr. Tookey, the deputy-clerk, and above all, Mr. Macey, tailor and parish clerk. It was he who, when Tookey, being criticised for his voice, protested that there might be two opinions, made the memorable remark : " You're right there, Tookey ; there's allays two 'pinions ; there's the 'pinion a man has of himsen, and there's the 'pinion other folk have on him. There'd be two 'pinions about a cracked bell, if the bell could hear itself."

When the question of who was to act as constable arose, after Silas broke in on the company, Macey objected to the farrier so doing, since his father had told him no doctor could be a constable. " And you're a doctor, I reckon, though only a cow-doctor—for a fly's a fly, though it may be a hoss-fly."

One wonders whether the conversation in the " Rainbow " was ever excelled by a modern writer. Dickens's conversations in the inns of olden days were as good, but hardly better ; and certainly it is a feat on the part of a woman to produce such natural talk when it is hardly conceivable that she could ever herself have heard it.

People became kinder to Silas after his troubles, and tried in their rough way to comfort him. One of the few reflections of the author in this tale concerns that fact : " I suppose one reason why we are seldom able to comfort our neighbours with our words, is that our good-will gets adulterated, in spite of ourselves, before it can pass our lips. We can send black puddings and pettitoes without giving them a flavour of our egoism ; but language is a stream that is almost sure to smack of a mingled soil." Mrs. Winthrop was the real helper—" a comfortable woman." It seemed surprising that Ben Winthrop, who loved his quart-pot and his joke, got along so well with Dolly ; but she took her husband's jokes and joviality as patiently as everything else, considering that " men *would* be so," and viewing the stronger sex in the light of animals whom it had pleased Heaven " to make naturally troublesome, like bulls and turkey-cocks." Her theology was simple : " if we'n done our part, it 'unt to be believed as Them that are above us 'ull be worse nor we are, and come short o' Their'n." And her little Aaron is another of the galaxy of beloved little children.

The Squire's family is not quite as convincing as the delightful Dolly Winthrop, or as Silas himself, and this perhaps once more bears out Leslie Stephen's criticism on George Eliot's men. The Squire himself is true to life, but the sons are not so impressive—the elder one is rather uninteresting,

and the younger too definitely and brutally bad
for us to have a real belief in or care for him. The
colour is laid on too thickly. The villain of the
piece, whether he be Dunstan Cass, Stephen Guest,
or Gwendolen Harleth's husband, Grandcourt, is apt
to recall to the modern reader the villain of the
films. But the countrymen like old Mr. Tulliver,
or Adam Bede and innumerable others, not of the
" gentleman " class, are different, and so of course
are the clergymen and professional men like Lydgate. So that it is the *type* rather than the genus
in which George Eliot seems to fail. In addition
to this her characters require time to develop. Her
method is different from Scott's, for instance, for
it is carried out through delicate touches rather
than by broad effects. Dunsey, for instance, has
to be got out of the way hastily or the story would
not have developed : had there been time to draw
him he might have been a different being.

It may be said that Providence has made its
hand too conspicuous in the book ; but this, in
any complete story ending happily, is difficult to
avoid. And the *deus ex machina* is less conspicu-
ously evident than in many other novels of the
time—certainly than those of adventure. If it
were not for Providence in some guise or other,
hardly any novel would reach the ending such as
in those days at least, hearts desired. And the
finding of the child is not wholly incredible, though
such occurrences are more usually dealt with by the
poets than matter-of-fact prose writers. Anyhow
there is real pathos in the account of Silas

finding the golden-curled child on his hearth, and his insistence on holding to his newly-found possession. And then his initiation into the mysteries of the child's clothing in their " due order of succession " as supplied by Mrs. Winthrop, is delightful. " The men are awk'ard and contrairy mostly, God help 'em—but when the drink's out of 'em, they aren't unsensible, though they're bad for leeching and bandaging—so fiery and impatient. . . But I can teach this little 'un, Master Marner, when she grows old enough," says Dolly. " But she'll be my little un," said the already jealous Marner, rather hastily. " She'll be nobody else's."

Next to Dolly Winthrop the talk of the Miss Lammeters at the Squire's party shows George Eliot's powers of humour at their best. " For I *am* ugly—there's no denying that," says Miss Priscilla. " I feature my father's family. But, law, I don't mind, do you ? " Priscilla here turned to the Miss Gunns rattling on in too much preoccupation with the delight of talking, to notice that her candour was not appreciated. " The pretty uns do for fly-catchers—they keep the men off us. I've no opinion of the men, Miss Gunn, and I don't know what *you* have. And as for fretting and stewing about what *they'll* think of you from morning till night, and making your life uneasy about what they're doing when they're out o' your sight—as I tell Nancy, it's a folly no woman need be guilty of, if she's got a good father and a good home : let her leave it to them as have got no fortin, and can't help themselves."

The idyll once finished, the serious work of fiction had to be attacked, and the attack meant the prospect of long and weary work.   First of all Florence must be visited and in a different spirit from the last delightful stay in it.   The " paradisaic " journey by the Cornice Road was made, and despite a really serious attack of illness hope and happiness returned—hope for what was before her.   " We have been industriously foraging in old streets and old books.   I feel very brave just now, and enjoy the thought of work—but don't set your minds on my doing just what I have dreamed.   It may turn out that I can't work freely and fully enough in the medium I have chosen, and in that case I must give it up : for I will never write anything to which my whole heart, mind and conscience don't consent, so that I may feel that it was something—however small—which wanted to be done in this world, and that I am just the organ for that small bit of work." The two had a busy time going to the Magliabecchian library, and poking about everywhere in the town—she " having very little self-help of the pushing and inquiring kind."   Thirty-four days were so spent : " Will it all be in vain ? . . . Alas, I could have done much more if I had been well ; but that regret applies to most years of my life."

Home was reached on June 16th, 1861.   " I am in excellent health," says her Journal, " and long to work speedily and effectively.   If it were possible that I should produce *better* work than I have yet done !   At least there is a possibility that I may make greater efforts against indolence and

despondency that comes from too egotistic a dread
of failure." As to indolence not the severest
critic could tax the writer with indulgence in it,
but the despondency was the dark cloud in her
life. "It was," she writes, "that sort of despair
that sucked away the sap of life of the hours which
might have been filled by energetic, youthful
activity; and the same demon tries to get hold of
me again whenever an old work is dismissed and
a new one is being meditated." It was this growing
physical depression that was to cloud her latter
years, and in some degree to affect her powers.
Even Mr. Lewes's buoyant spirits did not serve
to dispel it. This time the account of the bringing
to birth of the new novel is exceptionally painful :
a point was reached at which she got into such a
state of wretchedness in attempting to concentrate
her thoughts on the construction of her story that
she became desperate, and suddenly burst her
bonds saying, "I will not think of writing." A
few days later the plot developed itself more distinctly; music gave her pleasure and relief, and
finally there was a visit to Malvern to take the
new "hydropathic" treatment. The hills at
Malvern, first despised, became respected, and "we
creep about them with due humility."

Things were thus so bad that for a time
"Romola" had to be left alone and the less arduous
task attacked of correcting the earlier books for a
cheap edition; but once the first chapter was
written, matters grew a little more cheerful. The
ups and downs in life, with those endowed with the

artistic temperament are amazing ! After complain-
ing of her bad health and depression George Eliot
would walk five miles on Hampstead Heath with
Lewes and Herbert Spencer, and say she was in the
happiest, most contented mood, with only good news
to tell. " Imagine me always cheerful, and infer
the altered condition of my mucous membrane,"
she exclaims to her dear friend Mrs. Congreve.
But of course these same friends well knew that
next month there would be the familiar cry : " So
utterly dejected, that in walking with G. in the
Park, I almost resolved to give up my Italian
novel." So it goes, up and down, reading in the
British Museum or looking over costumes there.
" Flashes of hope are succeeded by long intervals
of dim distrust." Visitors came in especially on
Saturday evenings—Wilkie Collins, Huxley, Pigott
and others—Sir Frederic Burton (then Mr. Burton)
and W. S. Clark of Cambridge. But the main and
overwhelming business was the serious work that
had to be undertaken for the great historical novel,
and the studies of topography that must accompany
the reading. Mr. Cross, in his Life of George Eliot,
gives a list, a page long, of the books read during
the latter half of the year, 1861, and we marvel
not only at the length of it, but even more at its
comprehensiveness. There are works by all the
great Italian historical writers who dealt with the
period of Savonarola and in addition those of English
writers such as T. A. Trollope, Hallam and Gibbon ;
even Latin books are included. To one who has
been allowed to see some of these books and the

careful annotations, it is amazing to think of the manner in which George Eliot conceived it to be necessary to equip herself for her great task.* One would have imagined that she was about to write a complete Florentine history.

It was indeed a heavy task that the author had undertaken, and if only there had been no visible results of the labour in the book we might not have regretted her labours. In the beginning of 1862 the whole had been scrapped and a new start made on the plot, all apparently different. Then came discoveries about historical mistakes, questions as to the possible retardation of Easter and so on, and fits of black depression worse than any that had come before if that were possible. As a matter of fact no one but a professional historian could have made such a complicated tale correct in detail and then it would have been a history, not a novel.

And now the invaluable Mr. Lewes, to whom admirers of George Eliot can never be sufficiently grateful, came to the rescue. Had it not been for his constant help and encouragement " Romola " would probably have been on the dust heap instead of on our bookshelves. And his astuteness is as remarkable as his sympathy, for he took his suffering partner in life not only to the theatre, but even to the pantomime ; and wiser still, to hear the notes of the blackbird in the country.

At last the almost superhuman effort ended and the last stroke was put to the book on the 9th June,

* The long " Istoria Florentine de Sabrone Ammirato" (1826), now in the possession of Mrs. Maurice, is specially interesting as being fully annotated.

1863, eighteen months after the second beginning of it, and very much longer after the first start. On this one occasion the author deserted her faithful publisher who took her desertion in the best possible spirit, but who perhaps had some reason to congratulate himself later on the financial side. The *Cornhill*, from whose editorship Thackeray was just retiring, procured its serial rights for seven thousand pounds, the first suggestion being that ten thousand (then an unprecedented sum) should be paid for serial rights and copyright as well.

CHAPTER IX

A GREAT RELIGIOUS NOVEL
" ROMOLA "
(1863)

GEORGE ELIOT was now embarking on a double effort. Not only was she attempting to write an historical novel of more than four hundred years ago, but she was attempting also to write a religious story which centred on the spiritual experiences of a beautiful young woman. To tell the truth the heroine represents to us one with the outlook of a Puritan girl rather than of a maiden of the fifteenth century in Italy, which shows how impossible it was for the writer to escape from herself and her own thoughts and views of life.

Throughout her life George Eliot was always a woman despite her self-possession and broad, masculine intelligence. She had the woman's dependence on external support and sympathy from the time she was the little sister to her cold, self-reliant brother Isaac, to the time when all her powers of facing her life-work depended on another, intellectually her inferior. And she was also a woman in respect of her intense assertion of personality. This was useful to her in her tales of home life, all of which had a certain biographical trend. In them she looks at life from the point of view of one taking part in it, who can sympathise with every phase. But when her flight carries her to another age and country far removed from what can be personally known and loved, she loses her certain touch. Or rather, when she concerns herself with the new surroundings, we may get an enormously interesting study of character and action, but it is given us from the standpoint of the woman who, while she knew middle-class English life to the core, carried its problems into uncharted seas.

At this particular time George Eliot had religion and its problems much on her mind, and she struggled through this religious novel to prove that there was something real beyond the forms and ceremonies which sympathetically and emotionally she enjoyed. She wanted to show her faith in the working out of higher possibilities than the Catholic or any other Church has presented, and that, as she puts it, " those who have strength to wait and endure are bound to accept no formula which their whole souls—their intellect as well as their emotions —do not embrace with entire reverence." Hers was fundamentally no emotional religion. As a real stoic she wished to prove that the highest calling and election is to live through all our pain with conscious clear-eyed endurance, and she trusted that great facts might be able to find a voice—brokenly perhaps—through her means.

Intellectually George Eliot rejected the forms which she thought out of date and unnecessary to the time in which she was living. But just as she clung to the social traditions of days gone by,

and divested herself of the old conventions only
to long for them in the depths of her soul when
they were once discarded, so with the forms of an
old religion that had served the purposes of count-
less generations ; she rejected them with her reason,
and yet had a yearning for them in her heart.
Thus she writes, after going to James Martineau's
chapel, as she sometimes did, " I enjoyed the
fine selection of Collects he read from the Liturgy.
What an age of earnest faith, grasping a noble conception of life and determined to bring all things
into harmony with it, had recorded itself in this
simple, pregnant, rhythmical English of those
Collects and of the Bible ! " Then, again, after
hearing the " Messiah " at Her Majesty's Theatre :
" What pitiable people those are who feel no poetry
in Christianity ! Surely the acme of poetry hitherto
is the conception of the suffering Messiah, and
the final triumph. ' He shall reign for ever and ever.'
The Prometheus is a very imperfect foreshadowing
of that symbol, wrought out in the long history of
the Jewish and Christian ages." Indeed, she so
much believed in the hold that the outward form
of religion had on the country, that she told a young
undergraduate at Balliol, who was to be Prime
Minister of England,* that she fully expected a
great Revival in the Roman Catholic religion.

There was thus the perpetual struggle between
the very human woman who could not live without
the idea of a personal Christ influencing His time
and symbolising its best ideals, and her reason,

* The Earl of Oxford and Asquith.

which seemed to give no satisfactory basis for the history of the Man Christ Jesus. The Bible she adored, not as a manual of fine literature, but in and for itself ; and Lewes, who could not understand this strange obsession, any more than he understood much of the ideal side of Mrs. Lewes's nature, presented her with a large typed Bible as a provision for her old age, and with the benevolent assurance that he " saw no harm " in her reading it, though he himself had no inclination that way. Again, George Eliot loved Newman's " Apologia," which she felt breathed new life into her when she read it. Especially did she love the passage where Newman thanks his friend Ambrose St. John, and she longed to make a pilgrimage to Birmingham to see the Cardinal ; but this visit, unfortunately, never came to pass. One wishes it had.

All this makes it evident that the old religious forms had a deep hold on George Eliot's mind, despite her deliberate and reasoned break with them. It was so with most of her generation and upbringing, though there were of course those, like Lewes, to whom the ancient traditions meant nothing. It was this that made a religious struggle such as that in the time of Savonarola so intensely interesting to her. The whole problem caused by the fresh living spirit bursting forth from the dead tradition of the past—a problem which recurs over and over again in history—appealed to her much as the same problem did when it was confined to the life-story of the individual human being. Now she felt that she was taking out a larger canvas and dealing with the events of history as they appear, not only in this particular, but in their universal significance ; and hence it was worth while to make herself mistress of the historical situation. Unfortunately she found that this cannot be done alone by study, hard as it may be. There was within Romola, her heroine, nearly as much of George Eliot herself as there was in Maggie Tulliver, however differently she was drawn ; and we seem to have already met the weak and, vacillating unmoral Tito as well as Romola's father, Bardo de' Bardi, the blind scholar who was bound up in his books. To some of us, however, this anachronism, if so it may be called, is not altogether a drawback ; and at least the lesson that selfishness and egotism defeats its own end, is one that is immortal.

In any case George Eliot made a tremendous struggle to put new wine into old bottles and exhausted herself in the effort. But :

> " Even the weariest river
> Winds somewhere safe to sea,"

and she did arrive, though not exactly in the way she hoped. Stoicism as a philosophy is not to be set aside as irreligious and unsatisfying. It has profound faith in a divine Reason ordering all things aright, without the support that the belief in a personal Christ and personal immortality give. It is a hard doctrine but not a hopeless one. " Beholding the sun, moon and stars, enjoying earth and sea a man is neither helpless nor alone." The inward freedom and peace is reached, as Epictetus says, through the thought of " that great community which consists of God and man."

Now we must try to understand why the novel had so intense a meaning for its writer. It is far from being merely a novel of action. It is easy to condemn it, as it has often been condemned, as too reflective and introspective, or else as inaccurate in details while it professes accuracy. There is no ideal for historical fiction. We love our Scott though we may not take our history from him—we know that he is thinking always of his action and never of himself, even when his own character and life is evidently at the back of his mind. Probably he is our ideal historical writer of fiction just because he forgets himself in his task and makes it paramount. Disraeli, Kingsley, Lytton, Charles Reade, all have their merit in different ways, though many of us go so far as to prefer Harrison Ainsworth, slipshod as he often was, to any of them. He at least came nearer to that immortal writer of romance, Dumas, whose great novel " The Three Musketeers," like Tolstoy's " Peace and War," is not of one country but of all. George Eliot writes in quite a different vein and does not try to emulate her predecessors. She is the philosopher almost more than the novelist, the seeker after truths in the religious and ethical world as well as the narrator of historical events. It is as such that she must be judged.

*   *   *   *   *

Romola was a beautiful Florentine girl living at the

end of the fifteenth century—a notable time in the
history of Florence. The story, that is to say, is
placed in the Renaissance period, one of the great
periods of history—æsthetic, religious and political.
The events of the tale take place from about 1492 to
1498. Romola lived with her father, Bardo de' Bardi,
a blind and somewhat selfish scholar, whose consuming desire is to be assured that the library he has
collected will be preserved to Florence after his death.
His fortune has been spent in collecting it, and as
to his infinite grief his son had left him to become
a monk, he trains his daughter to undertake his
duties and become his amanuensis. There appears
however upon the scene Tito Melema, who ingrati-
ates himself with the scholar, and apparently takes
the place of the son, while he falls in love with the
daughter. Tito had a curious history. He was
the adopted son of a rich scholar Baldassere Calvo,
who, when the two were shipwrecked, was captured
by pirates. Tito saved himself by swimming and
carried off gems belonging to his father to Florence.
He sells the gems for his own benefit, forgets about
his father, assuaging his conscience by assuming
him to be dead, though a monk brings him a letter
from his parent begging him to use the gems to
ransom him from slavery. The monk turns out
to be Romola's brother, and Tito endures great
anxiety till he dies without revealing his knowledge.
Tito does nothing for his adopted father, but,
being attractive in person, gentle and charming in
manner, becomes engaged to, and finally marries
Romola. Meantime he has had another love affair

with a pretty contadina called Tessa, with whom he goes through a mock marriage at the Peasants' Fair. Tito, the worldling, prospers after his father-in-law's death, and when in 1494 the French King Charles VIII enters Florence, he takes great part in his reception. Some of the prisoners escape, and one lays hold of him, and he finds it is his father Baldassere, but refuses to recognise him ; therefore Baldassere, though his mind has partially given way through suffering, concentrates what powers are left on vengeance. On the death of Romola's father, Bardo de' Bardi, Tito sells his library, which Romola looked on as a sacred trust left for the people of Florence. This and other things open Romola's eyes to the baseness of her husband, Tito, and she decides to leave him. She starts for Bologna, but meets and is turned back by Savonarola, whose sermons are stirring Florence. Thus, from being an unbeliever, she becomes a devoted follower of the great Dominican preacher. Tito keeps in touch with both sides, the Medician and that of Savonarola, and prospers greatly. When a Medician plot is discovered, Romola's godfather, Bernardo, is condemned and executed, notwithstanding Romola's appeal to Savonarola, and she hears of Tessa's existence as her husband's mistress from Baldassere, who, however, is cast into prison for two years owing to his having made a public charge against Tito which the latter denies. Romola, in despair, at last leaves Florence and gets to a plague-stricken village where she is an angel of mercy. Meantime Savonarola is arrested, and there are riots in Florence.

o

Tito becomes an object of hatred and leaps into the Arno to escape the mob. He is found on the bank by Baldassere who strangles him and dies himself. Romola returns to Florence, hears of this tragedy, seeks out Tessa and her children, deserted and miserable, and takes them to live with her.

The tale is thus a somewhat complicated one with different threads all representing different influences and qualities. Savonarola, the central figure so far as the moving force is concerned, is clearly and sympathetically drawn from the biography of Pasquale Villari, and the accuracy of the portrait is not questioned. His was just the sort of figure that was attractive to George Eliot, and we need not wonder that she chose him as her subject. He represented the man who puts the high things before him, and who moulded his life in accordance with those ideals, and yet who was not free from human weaknesses with which he had to do battle, not always successfully. " There was nothing transcendent in Savonarola's face," the author writes. " It was not beautiful. It was strong-featured, and owed all its refinements to habits of mind and rigid discipline of the body." One wonders whether the physical resemblance that her friends often saw between George Eliot and her great subject ever came before her mind. In any case she understood him more than most. " The objects towards which he felt himself working had always the same moral significance. He had no private malice—he sought no petty gratification. Even in the last terrible days when ignominy, torture, and the fear of torture, had laid bare every hidden weakness of his soul, he could say to his importunate judges : ' Do not wonder if it seems to you that I have told but few things, for my purposes were few and great.' "

Savonarola was, however, depicted as subject to all the difficulties that beset the ordinary troubled soul, and none so greatly as the writer herself. When the distressed and perplexed Romola pleaded earnestly and eagerly with him, then at the height of his power, for her godfather Bernardo's life, he said : " Be thankful, my daughter, if your own soul has been spared perplexity, and judge not those to whom a harder lot has been given. *You* see one ground of action in this matter, I see many. I have to choose that which will further the work entrusted to me."   To Romola this was heresy : there was but one road of rightness and that was to save the lives that were in dire jeopardy in the name of justice as well as mercy, and she taxed the Father with making the furtherance of God's Kingdom the furtherance of his own party.   And then the Father boldly declared that the cause of his party was the cause of God.   " I do not believe it ! " said Romola, her whole frame shaking with passionate repugnance. " God's Kingdom is something wider—else let me stand outside it with the beings I love."   This was one of the tests in which the great preacher failed. Later on comes Savonarola's terrible shrinking from the Ordeal by Fire, and when it was obviated, and he walked off as he had come, " there seemed no glory in the light that fell on him now, no smile of heaven." And then, when he was at length dragged forth by the tumultuous crowd, he thought " the worst drop of bitterness can never be wrung on to our lips from without : the lowest depth of resignation is not to be found in martyrdom ; it is only to be found when we have covered our heads in silence." It was then that he felt he was not worthy to be a martyr ; " the Truth shall prosper, but not by me." Again there was the so-called confession under torture, when the old vehement self-assertion had gone and the voice of sadness and sorrow followed : " Thou hast taught others and failed to learn thyself." There was none of the martyr's joy for Savonarola. " But therefore he may the more fitly be called a martyr by his fellow-men for all time. For power rose against him, not because of his sins, but because of his greatness—not because he sought to deceive the world, but because he sought to make it noble." He sunk in shadow, and yet he had the light. He was ready to suffer, yet when the awful suffering came he shrank from it physically. Still his words remained true, as uttered in his great sermon : " O Lord, Thou knowest I am willing— I am ready. Take me, stretch me on Thy Cross ; let the wicked who delight in blood, and rob the poor, and defile the temple of their bodies, and harden themselves against Thy mercy—let them wag their heads and shoot out the lip at me ; let the thorns press upon my brow, and let my sweat be anguish. I desire to be made like Thee in Thy great love. But let me see the fruit of my travail—let this people be saved ! "

Perhaps no other novelist could have entered into the inwardness of this great tragedy like George Eliot, though a poet like Browning might. For it was a real tragedy. In true tragedy there must be valid moral power on both sides which come into collision ; and here we have the collision in a form which it took one who looked deeply into the realities of things to fathom.

But if Savonarola is the central figure in this book, the most interesting one in other ways is the heroine, Romola, who passes through the story like a beautiful but cold statue. There is a wonderful account in the early part of it of the girl caring for her blind father who " sat with head uplifted and turned a little aside towards his daughter, as if he were looking at her. There was the same refinement of brow and nostril in both, counterbalanced by a full, though firm mouth and powerful chin, which gave an expression of proud tenacity and latent impetuousness. . . . It was a type of face of which one could not venture to say whether it would inspire love or only that unwilling admiration which is mixed with dread." Thus Romola was no easily won, susceptible beauty. She was a proud woman endowed only with tenderness when the occasion required : she could ask for a return for what she gave, and expect to receive it. Therefore, when she found she had been deceived in her husband's character, she considers herself released from her marriage vows, and is the rebel we know so well in George Eliot's writings, as well as in fact. When rebellion is justified, and when it is not, is one of those never ending problems which baffle the wisest men and women, and one that she continually dwells on. It is the moral question that interests her in this novel of political turmoil.

This moral dilemma is best portrayed in the impressive scene when, sitting under the cypress, after her departure from Florence, Romola is accosted by Savonarola and bidden to turn back to her husband and home. Hitherto she had not acknowledged any right of priests or monks to interfere with her actions, and this interview put the religious view of the duty of self-sacrifice in the clear light in which it always presented itself to George Eliot herself from the old days of youth when she pored over the " Imitation." " You assert your freedom proudly, my daughter," says the monk : " But who is so base as the debtor that thinks himself free ? . . . And you are flying from your debts : the debt of a Florentine woman ; the debt of a wife. You are turning your back on the lot that has been appointed for you, and you are going to choose another. But can man or woman choose duties ? No more than they can choose their birthplace or their father or mother. My daughter, you are fleeing from the presence of God into the wilderness. . . . Make your marriage sorrows an offering too, my daughter : an offering to the great work by which sin and sorrow are being made to cease. . . . It may be our blessedness to die for it : to die daily by the crucifixion of our selfish will—to die at last by laying our bodies on the Altar. My daughter, you are a child of Florence : fulfil the duties of that great inheritance." At last the proud Romola succumbs and says : " Father, I will be guided. Teach me. I will go back." And she goes back to work for her own distressed people since she can do so little for her husband.

Though this will never be the most popular of George Eliot's writings, it will always count as a great historical novel and have its keen admirers amongst those to whom the deep lessons it has to convey signify more than the actual occurrences. Tito is not an attractive character, and in the end his evil doings are so deliberately cruel as to make him altogether repellent ; but we trace his gradual downfall from his deliberate choice of the pleasant and wrong thing rather than the unpleasant and good, with a sense of the inevitable. A great critic says : " He is thoroughly and to his fingers' ends a woman," but if this is true—if his misdeeds are of the feline sort that are usually ascribed to woman-kind—they are drawn, as is his whole character, with consummate art, and seem to the reader to be such as might belong to one sex as much as the other. We see the beautiful, wily, insinuating Greek laid bare ; we see him gradually succumbing to the corroding effect of self-indulgence, and falling lower and lower in the moral plane, while materially he prospers marvellously. His beauty is vividly described—his dark curls, agate-like eyes, his sunny brightness of expression ; and yet there is the canker at the root which comes from his first false step when he decides that it is not necessary for him to search for his father by adoption. " Tito was experiencing," says George Eliot, "that inexorable law of human souls, that we prepare ourselves for sudden deeds by the reiterated choice of good or evil which gradually determines character." Could the situation have been saved had Romola been of a more pliant disposition and tried harder to keep her love and gain a confession from her husband? Such questions are often put in real life, but the interest of the story is that she was *not* of that nature, and that she held herself apart in conscious virtue, loathing the prevarication and lies in which he dealt. Romola has been greatly criticised as a character and even her author was not fully satisfied that she had overcome the many difficulties belonging to the treatment of such a nature, but she believed that she had not used a phrase in her work that did not gather its value to her from its supposed subservience to her main artistic object.

George Eliot's other novels were relieved by humorous characters and conversations, but there is not a great deal of this in "Romola." We are kept in a tense atmosphere nearly all the time thinking of the tragedies of souls rather than the entertainment of the mind. It has been said of her writing that " What George Eliot's characters *do* is subordinate to what they *are*," and this is specially true of "Romola," for we are all the time carrying on an introspective examination of the various characters, and are only interested in their actions in so far as they throw light upon them. " Romola " was the favourite novel of Richard Holt Hutton, a competent critic, and . he appreciated just this

quality—the capacity of delineating human character, while tracing the constant conflict between
liberal culture and passionate Christian faith.

If, however, we are bent on looking for relief in
the humour that makes so delightful a part of many
of George Eliot's writings, we have to find it, not
in Tessa, Tito's rather too stupid young mistress
with the charming children, but in Monna Brigida,
the garrulous, good-hearted old cousin of Romola,
with the black velvet berretta under which surpris-
ingly massive black braids fell in rich plaited curves
over the ears, and with an equally surprising carmine
tint appearing in the upper region of the fat cheeks.
There is an amusing account of her " conversion "
at the " Bonfire of Vanities " when she was made per-
force to abandon her rouge and false hair, and then,
though half persuaded of its right, was overcome
by her subsequent appearance. She was comforted
by Romola, who (in much too plainly nineteenth
century language), said : " I think all lines of the
human face have something either touching or grand,
unless they seem to come from low passions. How
fine old men are, like my godfather ! Why should
not old women look grand and simple ? " " Yes,"
replied Brigida, " when one gets to be sixty, my
Romola, but I am only fifty-five ! "

The Epilogue to " Romola " when Romola is
talking of old days to Lillo, the son of her husband
and Tessa, his mistress, whom she had adopted, is
one of the most beautiful passages in the whole
book, and amongst the most beautiful of its kind
in literature. It sums up and estimates the whole

lesson to be learned of the value of life. Lillo would, boy-like, look forward to happiness and pleasure in his future life, as well as greatness. Romola says : " That is not easy, my Lillo. It is only a poor sort of happiness that could ever come by caring very much about our own narrow pleasures. We can only have the highest happiness, such as goes along with being a great man, by having wide thought, and much feeling for the rest of the world as well as ourselves ; and this sort of happiness often brings so much pain with it, that we can only tell it from pain by its being what we would choose before everything else, because our souls see it is good. There are so many things wrong and difficult in this world, that no man can be great—he can hardly keep himself from wickedness—unless he gives up thinking much about pleasure or reward, and gets strength to endure what is hard and painful. . . . And so, my Lillo, if you mean to act nobly and seek to know the best things God has put within reach of man, you must learn to fix your mind on that end, and not on what will happen to you because of it. And remember, if you would choose something lower, and make it the rule of your life to seek your own pleasure and escape from what is disagreeable, calamity might come just the same ; and it would be calamity falling on a base mind, which is the one form of sorrow that has no balm in it, and that may well make a man say : ' It would have been better for me if I had never been born.' "

Thus a wonderful novel concludes with a confession of faith put in a few short sentences. Its
faults are obvious, and perhaps become more so
as time goes on. It is often called artificial and
mannered : it is true that Romola belongs more to
our own time than to that of the Renaissance, that
too much midnight oil has been expended on the
study of the history of the period while the spirit
of that age of violence and treachery and human
passion let loose has not been caught. The book.
may even merit the attribute " academic "—for in
suggesting too careful a study of authorities, and
too little of realities, it moves heavily and lacks
the directness and swiftness of our greatest authors.
Still it will remain a classic in our literature ; and
it is also the one its author loved most of all her
works. She says, long after, in 1877, after reading
it again : " There is no book of mine about which
I more thoroughly feel I could swear by every
sentence as having been written with my best
blood, such as it is, and with the most ardent care
for veracity of which my nature is capable."

Romola was finished, but as the author herself
exclaims : " I began it a young woman—I finished
it an old woman." It ploughed into her more than
any of her books, as Mr. Lewes remarks, and one
is apt to ask, was it worth while ? It was worth
while if she were enabled to say what she could
not otherwise have had the chance of saying ; as
to this it is not for us to judge, though we cannot
forbear to express the obvious desire that the
expression had come in an easier form, and that the

intellectual agony of writing the book had not taxed so deeply the writer's mental and physical powers. For ever after the effort seems to have influenced her work. The deep philosophical reflection that we find in Romola made inroads even into the account of ordinary English life that she was able to put before us so well, and we never get quite the same spontaneity and freshness of vision again.

CHAPTER X

George Eliot as a Poet
(1863–1867)

THE strenuous labours at length concluded, a holiday was imperative. There is a delicious account of a journey to the Isle of Wight where there were cows (George Eliot always adored cows) which provided the " quintessence of cream," and a young lady waiter attired in the crinoline of the day. And then the boys at home were beneficial in their cheerfulness though they sometimes disturbed the equable tenor of their seniors' lives.* But a move was made—the last of so many by the couple who were difficult to please—to the house that was so well known as George Eliot's residence during her later days at The Priory, 21, North Bank, Regent's Park. Now it has wholly disappeared.

Moving was like a nightmare, but the new house was altogether charming and comfortable and much better than any of the preceding residences. Mr. Owen Jones undertook its decoration, and not only the decoration of the house but the beautifying of its mistress, who was to be made to look her part ; for taste as to dress was never George Eliot's strong

---

* The eldest, Charles, to their pleasure, engaged himself to Miss Gertrude Hill, " a very handsome girl with a contralto voice," and sister of one who was to become famous in work for the poor as Octavia Hill.

point. " You would have been amused," she writes
to her friend, Mrs. Congreve, who, after the young
people, always seemed to receive the most natural
of her letters, " to see an affectionate but dowdy
friend of yours, splendid in a grey moiré antique—
the consequence of a severe lecture from Owen
Jones on her general neglect of personal adornment."
It seemed difficult for the writer to escape the
pontifical in her epistles. Even to Mrs. Congreve
she adds: " My soul never flourishes in attention
to details which others can manage quite gracefully
without any conscious loss of power for wider
thought and cares. Before we began to move I
was swimming in Comte and Euripides and Latin
Christianity. Now I am sitting among puddles."

George Eliot really envied the other type of
person—the person who was born to make things
pretty. She loved her music and enjoyed practising
with the violin, and felt it did her good. She would
even have liked to have been able to " garden," for
the cult was now beginning. But she knew too
well that she could enjoy outside things but could
not create them.

So there she was, happy in the surroundings
made for her by others, reading voraciously ; and
now that she had an attractive house within easy
call, visitors did their best to crowd in upon her.
Not that it was an easy thing to obtain access to
what was now becoming so much desired a circle,
for it was kept a strictly limited circle. There were
the old friends who had been friends in cloud and
sunshine, and a few—not very many—women ; for

the writer who seemed so strong and self-reliant to others had a curious sensitiveness about her domestic relations which one might have thought would long since have vanished. Hence in addition to the faithful friends of past days, she welcomed the addition of one of the quality of Julia Hare, the wife of the Archdeacon, whose " sweet woman's tenderness " was very pleasant to the older woman, in addition to which she seemed to be able to bestow upon her moral strength. Mrs. Hare, to her friend's great grief, died early from consumption. We shall see later on how the simple gatherings at the Priory developed into Sunday *Salons*.

This life at home was of course varied by travel. After visiting Scotland, the two went once more to the beloved Italy whither they were accompanied by an agreeable companion in the shape of Frederick Burton who was then drawing the portrait we know so well. This experience did not, however, check the impulse to write again; and if George Eliot had chosen a difficult medium before, she selected a yet more difficult one now, for she wished to put her ideas into verse. Now verse was a very unwieldy medium for this great writer of prose fiction, and though she had a craving for writing poetry, it did not come naturally or spontaneously to her. She always got an idea—some great idea–that laid hold of her, and then she felt that it should be put into poetic form. This, perhaps, was true ; but that is not supposed to be the way in which most poets set to work, and it was hardly successful in her case.

The subject was one which had fascinated George Eliot in reading Spanish history, and she set to work in her systematic way to learn more of it, even going so far as to acquire the Spanish language in order to do so better. " I feel it is so much easier to learn anything," she exclaims, " than to feel I have anything worth teaching." She was to write a drama, and it was her first effort in blank verse and on a considerable scale ; but though as ever encouraged by her faithful friend, she soon " stuck in the mud." This was a none too promising beginning ; but as she went on the troubles also went on, until at last Mr. Lewes himself was convinced that something was wrong, and that the time had come to cry a halt ; her conceptions, he felt with her, had gone beyond her medium. In February of 1865 she utters the cry : " Ill and very miserable, George has taken the drama away from me." Could any venture of the kind have a less promising beginning ! Meantime she set her hand to one or two short poems.

It was not till a year later (1866) and after her next novel, " Felix Holt," was written, that she tells Mr. Frederic Harrison as a great secret between the two, that she was going to take up the task again. The work indeed was one that she could not easily abandon, though she realised, as she told her correspondent, that the idea of the characters had come to predominate over the incarnation. Now she looked at her work again ; she found how deeply the conceptions moved her, and how completely they had taken hold of her mind.

The idea was truly a great one, but it was one that had to be worked out with infinite pains instead of being so to speak a drama ready to hand. So the writer, as before with " Romola," set to to prepare what she called her " quarry," that is the collection of material necessary before a serious historical or critical work was begun. She " swam " in Spanish history and literature, and the end of the year was melancholy enough, for " the days seemed to have made a muddy flood, sweeping away all labour and all growth." Once more the case was desperate, and at length the usual anodyne was taken and a journey to Spain projected and carried out.

The journey had the desired result of restoring the author's health and spirits. The two companions visited Mme. Mohl at Paris, and met Renan (" something between the Catholic priest and the dissenting minister," she says) as well as Scherer, the critic George Eliot admired so much. They practised the Spanish tongue together by question and answer, and wandered through the East and Centre of Spain, all with the work that lay so near its author's heart in view. In March, 1867, George Eliot could return to work and confess the nature of her scheme to her publisher. Some of it was written during a summer visit to Ilmenau and Dresden ; and when the poem which she named " The Spanish Gypsy " was at last completed, the considerate John Blackwood kept it in type for months for purposes of revision, and cheered the once more depressed author with his words of encouragement. The

P

faithful Lewes who had been daunted by nothing in this long course of strenuous preparation, played his part nobly, and at length in May, 1868, the poem was published, after having occupied more or less completely two years of its author's life.

It has always surprised the world that there should have been in so perfect a prose writer the passion for expressing herself in verse. But the writer herself was obsessed with the idea that she had to express her great ideas in the fashion of the great Greek tragedians and she had ideas which are worthy of being so expressed ; only in her case one cannot see why they should be put in verse rather than prose which would have appeared to be the better medium. Possibly, however, it might have been difficult to make the story chosen reasonably probable in prose form.

George Eliot herself left Notes on this tragedy which enable us to understand how it came into existence. The idea came to her from a picture of the Annunciation by Titian which she saw in Venice. The way in which the scene presented itself to her was that of a great dramatic motive of the same class as those used by the Greek dramatists, and yet essentially differing from them. A young maiden, believing herself to be on the eve of the chief event of her life—marriage—and full of young hope, has it suddenly announced to her that she is chosen to fulfil a great destiny entailing a terribly different experience from that of ordinary womanhood. She is chosen, not by any momentary arbitrariness, but as the result of foregone hereditary conditions, and

she obeys. This is certainly a great idea, and it
is one which, in one form or other, never left George
Eliot's mind. We have it in many of her novels
more or less developed ; the only essential difference
that exists in regard to the momentous choice
between the Pleasant and the Best, as it presented
itself to Esther Lyon or Romola, and then to
Fedalma the Gypsy, is that in the former cases
the " call " is that of the individual who has to
save her own soul, rather than of the individual
who has to be true to her race ; and yet with
Romola, the Florentine, the racial call was also in
a measure there.

Having got her idea, and a subject which she
considered grander than that of Iphigenia, George
Eliot proceeds to clothe it and give it historical
and local conditions. This brought her to the
period in Spanish history when the struggle with
the Moors was attaining its climax, and when there
was the gypsy race existing under such conditions
as would enable her heroine to have an hereditary
claim upon her among the gypsies. Fedalma, a
gypsy by birth, stolen from her tribe when an infant,
has been educated as a high-born Spanish girl, in
the family of Duchess Diana, Duke Silva's mother.
Silva is deeply in love with Fedalma, and the two
are betrothed. Prior Isidor, the Inquisitor, wishes,
however, to stop the marriage on the ground that
Fedalma is really a gypsy heretic. While Fedalma
is dancing, her real father, Zarca, recognises her,
and exhorts her to place her duty to her people
before her personal happiness. This is the crucial

test. Fedalma feels the call of the blood, and escapes with her father, sacrificing her hopes of happiness with Silva. Eventually Silva follows her, but again she stands by her race, and Silva, seeing no other way, takes the gypsy oath. Zarca allies himself with the Moors against the Spaniards and Silva's friends are attacked and killed : as the Prior is led out to execution he curses Silva as a traitor, and Silva in desperation stabs Zarca. Zarca magnanimously spares Silva's life, and dies after laying on Fedalma the duty of taking his place as leader of the gypsies. She takes up the burden, leads her people to Africa, while Silva seeks pardon at Rome in the habit of a pilgrim.

Thus, in George Eliot's eyes, the whole drift of the poem is to show the part played in human life by hereditary conditions ; and duty finds itself in these conditions. " In Silva is present the claim of fidelity to social pledges ; in Fedalma the claim constituted by an hereditary lot less consciously shared." In the essay which the writer left behind her, and in which she works out her conception not only of the poem but of tragedy in general, these points are developed. " A good tragic subject," she says, " must represent a possible, sufficiently probable, not a common action ; and to be really tragic, it must represent irreparable collision between the individual and the general (in different degrees of generality). It is the individual with whom we sympathise, and the general of which we recognise the irresistible power." In Greek tragedy the collision is, she holds, . often that between the hereditary, entailed Nemesis, and the peculiar individual lot.

All this is interesting ; but we have the sense that the essay runs too much into the poem, and the poem into the essay. Instead of starting her work with an inspiration that carries her away with it and *makes* her write, the writer starts with an abstract conception, and proceeds to fill it in with agonising labour. That is to say she is a philosopher first, and a poet afterwards. A somewhat cruel critic has called George Eliot's poems " imitation poems," like forged ancient masters. " We see not so much poetic passion as a passionate yearning after poetic passions." And there is truth in the criticism, as also in the assertion that she never really had that exquisite sense of the value of words that may transmute common speech into poetry. Of all her critics and admirers hardly any maintain that she is a genuine poet, or has the true poetic *flair*. There are some fine passages in her work, but many that are discords to the poet's ear.*

With George Eliot poetry has to be regarded as a fetter, not a stimulus, and the criticism that her characters betray the intellectual analysis to which they have been subjected, and to illustrate which they have been created, is too just. Her poetry may indeed owe something to Wordsworth, as far as her poetic theory goes, because in both we have the poem which is to illustrate belief ; but beyond that point there is little or no true similitude. No doubt

* She told Tennyson in 1871 that Professor Sylvester's " Laws for Verse-Making " had been useful to her, and Tennyson made the terse reply : " I can't understand that."

there were other poets of the same calibre at this time, but the one who most resembles her in regard to their " high seriousness " and ideals, is Matthew Arnold. Arnold always had the conception that poetry is a criticism of life, and hence his poems are often called academic or self-conscious. Like his contemporaries he often failed in lightness of touch and was apt to express himself in language almost identical with his prose. But though the same intellectualism may have affected both, Arnold had a simplicity and melody that was unfortunately denied to George Eliot.

Despite all critics, however—and there were many even at the first appearance of the poem, who were some of them disturbing to the author's stoicism —the work soon passed into a second and a third edition and it is impossible to forget that a great task was attempted, and that, as far as conception went, it was accomplished. If imagination, noble conception, and noble language, could have made a great poem, George Eliot would have succeeded, but it was *not* sufficient, and consequently she failed. And if this is so in the " Gypsy " it is equally or more so in many of her other poems. In all, she wrote fourteen shorter poems, published in one volume in 1874, but many of these were written several years before, though none before she had reached the age of forty-four. " The Legend of Jubal," published in a magazine in 1869, is one of the best known, and perhaps actually the best of her poems. It is the tale of the patriarch who invented music. He wanders about, for many years, seeking higher music and greater songs, and returns to find his original discovery is being celebrated in great festivals, but he himself is forgotten, jeered at, and finally thrust out to die. Dying, he is consoled by a vision of the greatness of his gift to man in the discovery of song. The idea here is a fine one, and it expresses the doctrine George Eliot was so fond of enunciating, that the important thing is to have the consciousness that we have tried to do our duty in life, and that reward or fame as such are of little or no account.

> " For with thy coming Melody was come.
>   This was thy lot, to feel, create, bestow,
>   And that immeasurable life to know
>   From which the fleshly self falls shrivelled, dead,
>   A seed primeval that has forests bred."

Though Jubal was to lie tombless on the ground he would shine in man's soul, " a god who found and gave new passions and new joy." We have the sense that the writer's inherent love of music introduced a greater sense of reality into the reflections here, and also that we have a better medium for developing them in this legendary tale. " Armgart," another poem, is the story of a beautiful young singer who suddenly loses her voice by an attack of throat disease. When at the height of her fame a noble wishes to marry her, but after she has lost her powers he does not renew his offer ; she is in despair, until through her old music teacher and her cousin she learns that one must " bury one's dead joys and live above them with a living world." There are other poems including " The College Breakfast Party," which is a tremendous philosophical discussion hardly suited to verse. The charming " Brother and Sister," describing in simple language the writer's early life, rings true, but it has been spoken of before ; and finally there is the poem that has more than any other made George Eliot's reputation as a poet, " O may I join the choir invisible."

This poem is quite short, but it expresses in its few lines, written in 1867, an epitome of its writer's religious and philosophical tenets. It is probable that many people bought the book of poems when they first appeared, for the sake of this one poem which had a phenomenal success. It gives the only lines which are remembered and quoted freely as representing George Eliot's highest poetical aspirations. It was published at a time when the orthodoxy of early Victorianism had been somewhat shattered by the attacks of the scientific world, but when, as we have seen, there was an almost overwhelming seriousness amongst the thoughtful young people of the day. They were desperately looking around for some rock to which to cling, and they believed they had got it here :

> " This is life to come,
> Which martyred men have made more glorious
> For us who strive to follow. May I reach
> That purest heaven, be to other souls
> The cup of strength in some great agony,
> Enkindle generous ardour, feed pure love,
> Beget the smiles that have no cruelty—
> Be the sweet presence of a good diffused,
> And in diffusion more intense,
> So shall I join the choir invisible
> Where music is the gladness of the world."

It was not that these young people were Posi-
tivists, though Dr. Congreve thought the Poems a
" mass of Positivism," but they had no sure hope of
heaven, or fear of hell such as they had been taught
to believe in ; and yet they had the passion to make
their lives somehow one not only with all that was
best on earth, but with the " immortal dead who live
again in minds made better by their presence." At
least this gave unity to their distraught lives, and an
object worth suffering for. In the seventies and
eighties nearly every " Mutual Improvement Society "
had a lecture on " George Eliot and her moral and
religious teaching," and the religion was mostly
founded on this poem.

We have spoken of most of George Eliot's published poems, but there are still the verses to be considered which head her chapters, and which, though
unsigned, are many of them by herself, and not
quotations from others. They, like much of her
other work, are apt to savour of that kind of ethical
rhetoric masked by rather pompous imagery, which
characterises her acknowledged poetry. She is
(like Hobbes and the other seventeenth century
writers) the very type of the person of commanding
intellectual power who thinks that the temple of
the Muses can be stormed by mere strategy and
force.

But, while we cannot defend her poems as poetry,
we may say that she did a great work in raising the
thoughts of men and women to the highest things,
and concentrating on them. She was never content
to take the fleeting or casual events of time as her

subjects, but always made for the greatest. Her poems are not read now, because our attitude to these great questions has altered, and we are not interested in them in the same way ; nor is there anything in the beauty of their form and sweetness of their cadence to attract us to them for themselves. Still, we have to thank their author for raising her eyes to the stars even if, like the old philosopher, her footsteps sometimes stumbled on the ground.

CHAPTER XI

George Eliot as a Political Novelist:
"Felix Holt"
(1865-1866).

Before the "Spanish Gypsy" came to maturity another book was written of a very different sort. It dates from the time when the poem was first discarded, and when George Eliot's only hope seemed to be to turn to something entirely different. It is possible that what brought the political side of things so definitely before her mind, was not that she was thrown into personal contact with the political questions of the day, but that Lewes had undertaken the editorship of the *Fortnightly Review*, a new Review which was designed to follow the lines of the *Revue des Deux Mondes*. Owing to this fact, the author felt that she must lend a hand and revert somewhat to her journalist days. She likewise contributed some short articles to the *Pall Mall Gazette*—also a new venture. Of course the very fact that this work was being done, brought the two into touch with a number of eminent men, some literary and scientific, such as Browning, Huxley, Warren, and the economist, Bagehot. The collaborators worked together in this as in all other matters in entire sympathy, Lewes taking all the physical trouble of finding books and carrying out the details of a busy literary life.

Books, indeed, were needed in abundance for the new political novel. Again, as in the case of " Romola " and the " Spanish Gypsy," the work of investigation was almost overwhelming, and apt to stifle the imagination that was struggling for expression. Fawcett, Mill, Neale, Hallam and Blackstone were all being perused ; while, as the scene was laid in the days of the Reform Bill, a period slightly later than that hitherto studied, the brave author went through the file of *The Times* for the years concerned. Hence once again the book grew but slowly " like a sickly child," owing to general depression bringing about ill-health. It was completed " after days and nights of throbbing palpitation " on May 31st, 1866 (two years before the " Spanish Gypsy "), when the Leweses immediately dashed off to Schwalbach to recuperate. They returned to find the " handsome volumes " published and Blackwood's cheque for £5,000.

In " Felix Holt " George Eliot went back to the scenes of her native land—the Midlands she loved and understood so well. The introduction to the book gives an account of the happy days of coaching, " the days of unrepealed corn-laws, three-and-sixpenny letters, a brawny and many-breeding pauperism " with its other and more cheerful side. " The tube journey," she says, in curious anticipation of the future, " can never lend much to picture and narrative ; it is as barren as an exclamatory O ! Whereas the happy outside passenger seated on the box from the dawn to the gloaming gathered enough stories of English life, enough of English labours in town and country, enough aspects of earth and sky, to make episodes for a modern

Odyssey." And as she describes it all we seem to feel she is right. " It was worth the journey only to see those hedgerows, the liberal homes of unmarketable beauty—of the purple-blossomed ruby-berried nightshade, of the wild convolvulus climbing and spreading in tendrilled strength till it made a great curtain of pale-green hearts and white trumpets, of the many-tubed honeysuckle which, in its most delicate fragrance, hid a charm more subtle and penetrating than beauty. Even if it were winter the hedgerows showed their coral, the scarlet haws, the deep-crimson hips, with lingering brown leaves to make a resting-place for the jewels of the hoarfrost." This is the scenery she loved, and the country which was her spiritual home.

But the book was not to be a simple account of country life and country surroundings with all their interests, their loves and warfares. Or rather it was to be that and a good deal more. The scene was laid at a time of political unrest and turmoil—the year that immediately succeeded the passing of the Reform Bill of 1832, and it was to show us how the new spirit of revolt and struggle for liberty was making its way into the pleasant country-side that must always be conservative so long as its conditions are tolerably good. In those days they were not good, and there were coal-pits near where " powerful men walked queerly with knees bent outward from squatting in the mine, going home to throw themselves down in blackened flannel and sleep through the daylight, then rise and spend most of their high wages at the ale-house." In the crowded centres, at least, there was a population not convinced that old England was as good as she could be, and even the country-side was affected by the same ideas. It was a wonderful time to choose as the subject of a novel, and with the writer's knowledge the book ought to have been a greater success than it was. There are admirable descriptions of places and people, and some of the characters, like Rufus Lyon, are drawn with perfect skill and insight ; but though George Eliot was in a certain sense a rebel, she was never a political rebel, and rebellious times did not suit her. She sympathised too intensely with the old ways to understand the new. The new was upsetting and alarming to the Victorians of her day, when put quite crudely as it was by the successors of Cobbett and the precursors of the Chartists ; and the hero does not live up to his part as an iconoclast. We do not wonder that he failed to engender much enthusiasm amongst the supporters of his party.

The story is a difficult one—too difficult to follow quite easily—but it is well thought out into a real plot in a way George Eliot had never so far attempted. In 1832 Harold Transome returns from Smyrna to England, as on the death of his brother he has become the heir to Transome Court. He finds a weak-minded invalid father, and a mother handsome and imperious, but under the domination of Jermyn, the lawyer who has been fleecing the estate. Harold is rich and treats his mother generously, but he takes the reins into his own hands, and to her dismay announces that he is to stand for the representation of the county as a Radical. In his canvass he comes into touch with Felix Holt, a Radical watchmaker, who has induced his mother to give up the sale of worthless medicines, and has relinquished his study of medicine himself because he wished to serve, and live with, his own class. Felix, on his part, comes into relation with his mother's Independent minister, Rufus Lyon, the reputed father of a beautiful and fastidious girl named Esther, who cares for the refinements of life, and who has been educated abroad in order to become a governess. Felix is at first frankly rude to this girl, so different from what he conceives as his ideal of womanhood ; but gradually he is attracted by her, and she by him, in spite of his outspoken, hectoring ways, and extreme opinions. Esther is not really Mr. Lyon's daughter, but the child of a young French widow whom he befriended and subsequently married ; and Rufus at last lets this be known to her and is immensely relieved to find that it only draws her more closely to him. By a curious concatenation of accidents it is discovered that Esther's real father was a certain Bycliffe, and that consequently she herself is now the rightful owner of Transome Court, about which there had been much previous litigation. Harold Transome, when he learns of this, tells his mother, and she wishes Esther to come and stay with them at Transome Court with a view to getting matters amicably settled. Transome is defeated in his election, but falls in love with Esther, and it seems as if the succession might be settled by their opportune marriage. However, on the election day there was a terrible riot in which Felix had got involved, and while really trying to quell the rioters he accidentally killed a constable. Hence he is arrested and accused of manslaughter. There is a remarkable trial scene in which Esther gives evidence in favour of Felix, and learns that she loves him. Felix is convicted and sentenced to imprisonment, but a petition is got up in his favour and he is pardoned. Eventually Esther gives up her claim to the property, and to all the pleasantness of life that has so greatly attracted her, and chooses to marry Felix, the working man.

This is a very slight and quite incomplete sketch of the tale, for it is complicated by endless legal and other intricacies. The wicked lawyer Jermyn turns out to be Harold's father ; the history of how Bycliffe came to be heir to the Transomes is so complicated as almost to require a legal training to follow it. Anyhow, few who read novels do take the trouble to follow such complexities. It seemed to be necessary to George Eliot's conception of the story that these complexities should exist, and she got the help of Frederic Harrison in getting her law correct. Possibly a young lawyer enjoyed working out a complicated legal plot and others may equally enjoy unravelling it.* The interest of the book is not here, but in the representation of the new forces that were working in the nation, and affecting the young people of the day in different ways. Each one of the male characters primarily concerned had his different ideal marking him off from the reaction of the generation before him. Harold Transome, though standing as a Radical, certainly does not show many signs of advanced opinions ; but though self-sufficient and self-loving, he had a general idea of getting things out of the hands of purse-proud tradesmen where the Whigs would have left them by limiting the franchise to the ten-pound householders. His

---

* Frederic Harrison told the author that he would always be able to say that he had written at least a sentence which was embodied in English literature. Later on he had to defend his law from criticisms made on it in the *Edinburgh Review*.

idea was to be a good landlord and retrieve the honour of his family, and he behaved honourably in his great difficulties at the end. Philip Debarry, the Conservative canditate, was a high-minded and generous man, who, when the dissenting minister did him a service, insisted on treating him as one gentleman would another, repelling his father's suggestion to do no more than send a present of game to the " quibbling, meddlesome Radical." Instead of this he wrote a letter which does him credit. He was what was later called a Tory Democrat.

Rufus Lyon is taken from life and represents his class far more accurately than does a Stiggins or Chadband, neither of whom ever had a prototype, entertaining as they are. George Eliot's knowledge of the father of her schoolmistress of old days in Coventry, taught her the beauty of a character which to the outside observer was simply absurd. For forty-four years had the original, the Rev. Francis Franklin, laboured as pastor of the Cow Lane Chapel at Coventry, and this is said to be a faithful portrait. " At the first glance everyone thought him a very odd-looking, rusty old man ; the freeschool boys often hooted after him and called him ' Revelations ' ; and to many respectable church people old Lyon's little legs and large head seemed to make Dissent additionally preposterous. But he was too short-sighted to notice those who tittered at him—too absent from the world of small facts and paltry impulses in which titterers live." In truth, whatever failures there may be in this, perhaps the least popular of George Eliot's books, it was well worth writing for the sake of its representation of this noble type of political dissenting minister—he

Q

made a special point of being political—who was
faithful in season and out of season to what he felt
to be his sacred calling. And his relations to his
adopted daughter Esther, the child of such different
traditions and different outlook, are very touching.
Esther longed for ladyhood, and George Eliot never
forgot what that girlish longing meant. When she
was left in the parlour amidst the lingering odours
of the early dinner, not easily got rid of in the small
house, she rebelled against it. " Rich people, who
know nothing of these vulgar details, can hardly
imagine their significance in the history of multitudes of human lives in which the sensibilities are
never adjusted to the external conditions." And, as
George Eliot says, it was to the ultra refined and
beautiful girl's credit that she got the " vision "
about which the pedagogic Felix told her, and chose
the poor man's lot rather than the rich. The
renunciation to her was not easy.

There are other delightful characters. Felix's
mother, the loquacious Mrs. Holt, who was such a
terribly large thorn in her pastor's side, is one of
them. " She was a tall elderly woman dressed in
black, with a light-brown front and a black band
over her forehead," and when she goes to her
minister to complain of her son's conduct in putting
an end to the sale of the quack medicine she pours
out her woes in no measured words, for " not her
greatest enemy can say she deserved this trouble."
" And when everybody gets their due," she goes on,
" and people's doings are spoke of on the house-
tops, as the Bible says they will be, it'll be known
what I've gone through with those medicines—the
pounding and the pouring and the letting stand,

and the weighing—up early and down late, there's nobody knows yet but One that's worthy to know ; and the pasting o' the printed labels right side up. There's few women would have gone through wi' it ; and it's reasonable to think it'll be made up to me ; for if there's promised and purchased blessings, I should think this trouble's purchasing 'em." And then, as almost always, there is a delightful and comical child, little Job with his " germinal nose, large round blue eyes, and red hair that curled close to his head like the wool on the back of an infantine lamb."

The characters in " Felix Holt " are most of them interesting, and of some we long to know more ; in this book there is not, except in legal matters, the same outward evidence of midnight oil as in " Romola," and the author describes what she knows and has seen. The trouble is with the hero Felix himself. He had plenty of material to work on in the slow-going rather sordid people of Treby Magna, the county town. The inhabitants must have been awakening to a sense of their political rights and power ; Felix came from Glasgow deeply impressed by the new ideas and ready to preach them ; and yet he is a failure. He might have been the apostle of the dispossessed rural labourer just as Cobbett was of the industrialist ; but much more likely he would have been with Thomas Cooper, the Chartist poet, who was imprisoned for participation in a Chartist riot in 1842, and had been roused to white heat by finding the Leicester stocking-weavers working for four-and-sixpence a week, *with deductions*. And that was not all, for six unfortunate Dorchester labourers were in 1834 sentenced to transportation for the dreadful crime of administering illegal oaths, i.e. forming a Labourers' Trade Union, and the Whig reformed Government refused to interfere. Or else he would have joined hands with Richard Carlisle who, also a freethinker, brought out Paine's books, refused to pay church rates, and consequently spent nine years of his life in prison. These were the people who would have been likely to influence Holt, and when we read of his mildly expressed views—views that might come from a reactionary of that or any day who was trying to preach high ideals without violent change, we fail to be interested in him. And when ultimately he marries the charming Esther, we are not surprised that, in spite of protests, a small annuity is accepted—only, of course, as she explains, a fraction of what she is entitled to—from the money that is her due ; and that he " grumbles a little that she has made his life too easy, and that, if it was not for much walking, he should be a sleek dog." George Eliot liked to leave her heroes and heroines comfortable and happy—it was demanded in her day—but that is not the stuff the heroes of the time of the Reform Bill or " hungry forties " were made of.

The truth is that it was almost impossible for one living as George Eliot was living in a sheltered life of comparative comfort, and in the midst of the happy illusions of Victorian respectability and optimism, to realise the heartbreak and the misery that were going on around her. Even in her time, such cries as Disestablishment, manhood suffrage, abolition of religious disabilities were considered wild excesses. She herself had no belief in voting

by ballot, believing that no external arrangement
could put an end to bribery.   There were still the
old-fashioned middle-class fetishes regarding certain
ossified established institutions, and probably Felix
would in the thirties have been a Republican and
possibly an Atheist.   Therefore all was toned down
to suit the later age, and Holt hardly even reached
the " muscular Christian " type of socialism identified with the names of Maurice and Kingsley.   It
is a pity, for the age was a great one, and deserved
a great artist to depict it on the political side.
" Alton Locke " and " Sybil " give us parts of it,
and George Eliot's powers would have been well
diverted to another aspect of the same subject.
It is not necessary to be a radical to preach, as
against universal suffrage and the other points of
the Charter the excellent doctrine that these are
but engines, and that the force to drive them must
come from men's passions, and that they must be
regenerated—public opinion must be reformed.   We
all hear that *ad nauseam*, and require more solid
food if we are to be labelled Reformers and to
struggle for Reform with genuine passion.   Still, the
book has a certain fascination in spite of its faults,
and Henry James, after reading it in illness, wrote
that though it was not altogether warmly greeted :
" I was to hold fast to the charm I had thankfully
suffered it to work."   And others have felt the
same.

CHAPTER XII

A Middle-Class Novel
" Middlemarch "
(1869–1872)

A FRESH project was soon in view which concerned
not visionaries but ordinary people as they lived
ordinary middle-class lives, in an ordinary middle-
class country town. This was to be no flight into
the realms of poetry, or of history, or even politics ;
but a tale which was to reveal the tragedies and
comedies that existed in the most unexpected places,
dubbed not only unromantic but also uninteresting.
No extremities of wealth or poverty were to be
described, no depths of wickedness or heights of
virtue, but just the sort of life that is carried on
every day by the greater portion of the inhabitants
of this island.

Somehow the domestic side of life was now specially appealing to one who was happy in her domestic
relationships and who felt that her work was prosper-
ing. She was, despite her anxieties, enjoying her
home life, attending glorious concerts, and talking
of versification with Browning. Lewes and she went
to Leeds as the guests of Dr. Allbutt (Sir Clifford
Allbutt) to study a new hospital which was to play
an important part in the coming book. The great
ironworks of Sheffield were also visited, and Matlock,
the rushing River Derwent, and the Arkwright mills,

among which Mary Ann Evans had driven with her
father while a girl in her teens.

Yet another visit to Italy, also made at this time,
had a remarkable, though unforeseen, result; for in
Rome Mr. Cross first met his future wife, and he gives
an interesting account of how she then appeared to
him. " I still seem to hear, as I first heard them,
the low, earnest, deep, musical tones of her voice :
I still seem to see the fine brows with the abundant
auburn-brown hair framing them, the long head
broadening at the back, the grey-blue eyes, but
always with a very loving almost deprecating look
at my mother ; the finely formed thin transparent
hands, a whole *Wesen*, that seemed in complete
harmony with everything one expected to find in
the author of ' Romola.' " Very soon the acquaintanceship was to ripen, because the two were to meet
at Weybridge when both were anxious and troubled.
the Leweses about their " boy," and Cross about his
sister. " A day did the work of a year," he says,
" our visitors came to the house as acquaintances,
they left it as lifelong friends."

Trouble had indeed now come in a personal way,
for the second son, " Thornie," came home from
Natal to die. The account of his illness and subsequent death is very touching, for no mother could
have been more devoted than the one who had taken
the place of a mother—as she said, his death seemed
to her the beginning of her own. There is nothing
more beautiful in George Eliot's life than the love
she lavished on the three boys, not her own, and
the consideration she had, when serious illness came,
for the real mother, who had meant so little to
them, but whom in this case she asked to come and

see the dying boy. And when she did come, George Eliot herself was careful to keep away. She had the real mother-instinct, and in a long and beautiful letter to Mrs. Beecher Stowe she addresses her as her dear friend and fellow-labourer who has not only had longer experience as a writer, but fuller experience as a woman, " since you," she says, " have borne children and known the mother's history from the beginning." Her childlessness left her life incomplete, and she could but fill it as best she might with those not her " children after the flesh."

For a book in which medical matters were to play a considerable part, it was necessary to read many treatises on medicine and medical teaching. Also, when the two went to Berlin, as they did in 1870, Lewes was working at psychiatry at the Charité Hospital. Then there was a visit to the Mark Pattisons at Oxford,* where George Eliot saw a brain dissected at the laboratories, and where the acquaintance with Jowett developed. It is difficult to say that this last passed beyond an ordinary acquaintanceship ; but Jowett sent her the sheets of a volume of his Plato on its publication, and offered a return visit to her in London ; and there are those who tell us of the impression she made on the undergraduates 'at Balliol. When she was Jowett's guest, Sir Almeric Fitzroy relates that though she was, of course, the most conspicuous figure in the company, she displayed a gentleness and accessibility, as well as a genuine hopefulness of outlook, for which he was not prepared. Another

* Mark Pattison was usually held to have suggested the character Casaubon.

young Balliol man (Lord Oxford and Asquith) narrates
that on one occasion when the Master inquired of
Lewes whether he considered that there was any
sign by which the sex of the author should have
been recognised, the reply was given after some
hesitation : " I should say that the sign was to be
found in the almost entire omission of any reference
to field sports in the country," an acute and pertinent
criticism. In quite late life George Eliot recorded
with no little pride that she had attended a Meet.

We have reached the eventful year 1870 when
the Franco-German War was raging and when the
world was in a state of tension. The brutality of it
all shocked George Eliot, as it was sure to do. It
pained her that educated people whose ideas ought
to have been lofty did not take a higher moral line
respecting national and international duty.

All this time the Leweses were sometimes residing
at Shottermill, where Tennyson was one of the
" hill-folk " who found them out, and more often
in London. George Eliot was working away at her
long novel, which was to be christened " Middlemarch." The length of it was concerning her
publisher, and we cannot wonder at his view. But,
as usual, its author was firm under criticism.
" There was nothing in the book, she believed, that
could be omitted as irrelevant to her design of
showing the gradual action of ordinary rather than
exceptional causes, and that in directions outside the
beaten track." Her success was her justification.

The first part of the novel was published on
December 1st, 1871, and the book was concluded
next year, 1872. It was certainly a great testimony
to the reputation of the writer that a four-volume

novel first issued in eight parts, should be received in the way it was. The parts were watched for with excited interest. The two stories—that of Dorothea Brooke and her two marriages, and that of Dr. Lydgate and the Vincy family, are quite distinct, or capable of being regarded so. But the interest of the book is in a manner in its loose construction, for the whole gives one the impression of real life as it is lived in an ordinary small provincial town backed by a surrounding of county gentry of the class George Eliot could describe so well. In reality people's lives are something of a tangle, as they appear here : one influences the other in a curious mixed way ; and there was a certain novelty in a book that represented this sort of life in detail— a life in which, from the mere fact of their physical proximity and common business, different classes of people and people of different outlooks are brought into close contact with one another. It may be said of the life depicted (which is that of the time just before the Reform Bill) that though its accuracy is undisputed, it is long ago passed and is of little but historical importance. But those who know provincial life best are. well aware that the sort of life described is not essentially different now. No doubt the county families have lost the importance they then had in affairs, and no doubt the provincial professional man may be more enlightened, and the minor manners and customs, dress and demeanour have altered : but the proof of the great quality of the book is that we have in it the essentials of men's and women's relationship to one another, such as they are for all time. Not very many, perhaps, wander through six hundred pages of closely-printed

matter in these days ; but those who are not put off
by the length, and by certain obvious blemishes,
recognise this to be true.

Dorothea is the character who most approaches
that of a heroine in the story, and she is the character that her maker loves—the woman of high
aspirations—one who would have chosen the saintly
life in other days or under another religion, and who
in endeavouring to realise her aspirations, comes
into terrible difficulties. She is the niece of Mr.
Brooke, a bachelor landowner who is the guardian
of herself and her sister Celia, " a man, nearly sixty,
of acquiescent temper, miscellaneous opinions, and
uncertain vote." He had travelled in his younger
days, and took great credit to himself for that,
had a rambling manner of speech, wished to plunge
into politics, for which he thought himself specially
qualified, and desired to be advanced without
" going too far," just as he desired to be benevolent
without spending too much. He is the typical Whig
squire of Victorian and pre-Victorian days. Dorothea
herself is a noble-minded girl with an almost quixotic
desire to do great deeds and prove herself worthy,
disdaining dress and the frivolities of life that delighted Celia. She " had that kind of beauty which
seems to be thrown into relief by poor dress . . .
her stature and bearing seemed to gain the more
dignity from her plain garments, which by the side
of provincial fashion gave her the impressiveness of
a fine quotation from the Bible—or from one of
our elder poets—in a paragraph of to-day's newspaper. . . . Sometimes when Dorothea was in company there seemed to be as complete an air of repose
about her as if she had been a picture of Santa

Barbara." All she lacked was a sense of humour and proportion, as her attractive but ordinary commonsense sister felt. Not seldom she reminds the reader of the authoress herself, who appears in so many of her tales in different guises.

At nineteen Dorothea rejects the addresses of a young baronet, Sir James Chettam, whom her sister Celia eventually marries, and who endeavours to ingratiate himself with her by his interest, real or assumed, in the cottages which she plans. She subsequently marries the middle-aged and pedantic clergyman, Mr. Casaubon, not because she is really in love with him, but because she is intent on making herself of use to him in the great work on " Comparative Mythology " in which he is supposed to be engaged, and puts this call before her as a call to high service. He, on his side, is attracted by her, but being cold and selfish at heart, he looks on her as one who will be a helper to him as age advances, and thinks little of the sacrifice she is making. The two go to Rome for their honeymoon, and Mrs. Casaubon soon came to realise that her husband was not what she thought, and that his work was unfruitful and arid.* She is helped to come to know this by meeting a young relative of her husband's, Will Ladislaw, to whom her husband has given assistance, but of whom he becomes jealous. Dorothea's loyalty to her husband in spite of her attraction to young Ladislaw, the Bohemian artist, till the untimely death of the former at their home

* Ladislaw said that Casaubon did not study German, and therefore he did not know the work that had been done, but Lord Acton states that Germany was as behindhand in the study of Comparative Mythology as anywhere else, and that Ladislaw did not know what he was speaking about.

near Middlemarch, is finely drawn. Her moral rectitude is great, but it exists with a certain self-consciousness that must have been irritating to the equally self-centred but self-satisfied man, and we have a sneaking sympathy with him, as had George Eliot herself. When he dies, it is found that he has made an insulting provision in his will, that Dorothea shall forfeit the property he leaves her if she marries Ladislaw. Her sister and brother-in-law, the Chettams, wish to get rid of Ladislaw, but he remains to help Mr. Brooke in his candidature for Parliament. Eventually Dorothea gives up her money and social position to marry him, and this is a disappointing part of the story, for it is difficult to believe that the result will be satisfactory. Will Ladislaw was a favourite of the writer, but he is too irresponsible a being to attract the reader. He may bear some resemblance to George Lewes in his youth ; at any rate he is thought to have done so.

From the country we come to the town of Middle-march, where the central figure is Dr. Lydgate, a young doctor of good family who settles there without money, but with immense enthusiasm for the scientific part of his profession. He is building up a practice, and is helped by a Mr. Bulstrode, a rich man who is trying by his philanthropy to atone for past misdeeds ; and Mr. Bulstrode appoints him physician to the new fever hospital. Lydgate thereby comes into opposition with the old practitioners, who disapprove of his new-fangled ways. Unfortunately for Lydgate's high ideals, while still a struggling doctor he falls in love with Rosamond Vincy, the pretty and ambitious daughter of the Mayor. Rosamond is impressed by Lydgate's being

nephew of a baronet, and, hoping for social position
and with no idea of any higher aim, becomes his
wife. Then it gradually appears that Lydgate
cannot afford to support an expensive household ;
Rosamond will be a fine lady and will not adapt
herself to any humbler mode of life, and the results
are disastrous, especially as Mr. Bulstrode becomes
involved in a scandal, and seeing that he has lent
money to Lydgate, the latter is unjustly implicated
in it. Dorothea, with whom Lydgate has come into
touch over Mr. Casaubon's illness, and who has
generously helped the hospital, now comes to his
aid ; and not only does she stand by him almost
alone, but she talks to Rosamond, and tries to
persuade her to do the right by her husband, despite
the fact that she thinks she has been flirting with
Ladislaw.

In the end the unfortunate Lydgate has to give
up his ideas of scientific distinction and high-minded
practice, and he goes to London, where he becomes
a fashionable physician. The struggle between
Lydgate and Rosamond is developed with great
subtlety. Rosamond " had an excellent taste in
costume, with that nymph-like figure and pure
blondeness which gives the largest range to choice
in the flow and colour of drapery. She was ad-
mitted to be the flower of Mrs. Lemon's school. . . .
No pupil exceeded that young lady for mental
acquisition, and propriety of speech, while her
musical execution was quite exceptional. . . . Rosamond never showed any unbecoming knowledge, and
was always that combination of correct sentiments,
music, dancing, drawing, elegant note-writing, private album for extracted verse, and perfect blonde

loveliness, which made the irresistible woman for the doomed man of that date." She opposed to her husband a gentle inflexible obstinacy, before which he was helpless. She looked upon him, indeed, as a being of curious and mistaken ideas who required to be brought out into the correct conventional paths of life by one like herself, who had all the recognised virtues and common sense besides. It would not be "lady-like" to quarrel, so she never used rough language ; she got her way by far more subtle and certain methods. The contrast between Dorothea and Rosamond when they meet is the contrast between a high-minded woman who does not understand the small things of life, and the would-be smart woman who suddenly sees in the light of the other how small her outlook really is ; though she does not really understand Dorothea's greatness. Rosamond Vincy is too common a type to be easily forgotten, and her doings and sayings in relation to her husband will be quoted long after " Middlemarch " as a whole ceases to be read. Theirs is the sort of tragedy that makes life tragic to very many.

There is curiously enough another little story, quite a gem in itself, intertwined in the whole novel, and that is the tale of poor connections of the prosperous Vincys, the Garths. Fred Vincy, Rosamond's brother, rather a wild lad, falls in love with the sensible, good-natured, humorous Mary Garth, the daughter of Caleb Garth, builder and land-agent. Mary was plain and short. " Advancing womanhood had tempered her plainness, which was of a good, human sort, such as the mothers of our race have very commonly worn in all altitudes under a more or less becoming headgear. Rembrandt would have painted her with pleasure, and would have made her broad features look out of the canvas with intelligent honesty. For honesty and truth-telling fairness was Mary's reigning virtue." The plain Mary is wooed also by a more eligible suitor, the Rev. Mr. Farebrother ; but despite all Fred's tiresomeness and other failings, about which she had no illusions, she clings to him, and after he has made a mess of his life by his own foolishness, she gets him to give up the Church, for which he had been educated and was quite unsuited, and become a steady-going farmer ; and thereafter she marries him.

A great deal of " Middlemarch " is attuned to a low pitch. The *Spectator* called it a " sad book " and many have felt the same, though there are no very tragic happenings in it. But the account of the Garth family is delightful. Here the writer is at home, for Caleb Garth, the father, is clearly drawn from her own father, Robert Evans, and a good deal of the family life evidently comes from the old Griff days. Garth was " one of those rare men who are rigid to themselves and indulgent to others. He had a certain shame about his neigh-bour's errors and never spoke of them willingly. . . . His virtual divinities were good, practical schemes, accurate work, and the faithful com-pletion of undertakings : his prince of darkness was a slack workman. . . . He was one of those precious men within his own district whom every-body would choose to work for them, because he did his work well, charged very little, and often declined to charge at all." Therefore the Garths were poor, but did not mind it. George Eliot loved to dwell on a character such as Caleb's, which represented her ideal of the honest workman. And the very way in which she constantly treats of money and the lack of it comes straight from the writer's own experience. Caleb's wife admired her husband's virtues, but soon realised his incapacity for minding his own interests, and " renounced the pride of her sex in ' tea-pots and children's frillings,' " and sometimes " took pupils in a peripatetic fashion, making them follow her about in the kitchen with their book or slate. . . . Mrs. Garth in a general wreck of society would have held her ' Lindley Murray ' above the waves." Her own children are the jolly children that George Eliot never fails to give us in each of her books, and altogether in this rather poor household there is an atmosphere of joyousness that we fail to find in the more sophisticated circles.

Humour of another and more caustic kind is however found in the account of old Peter Featherstone's funeral—the funeral of the uncle from whom many—and especially the Vincys—had " expectations," and who disappointed them all. " When the animals entered the Ark in pairs, one may imagine that allied species made much private remark on each other, and were tempted to think that so many forms feeding on the same store of fodder were eminently superfluous, as tending to diminish the rations . . . the same sort of temptation befell the Christian carnivora who formed Peter Featherstone's funeral procession ; most of them having their minds bent on a limited store which each would have liked to get the most of."

R

The bulky and asthmatic Mrs. Crach, the woolly-toned Mrs. Waule with her crape-shadowed bonnet—all the mourners are described with realistic touches that make them stand clearly before us. No one can describe a funeral or the reading of a will better than George Eliot who had probably at one time had the scene before her.

Other effective characters are the Bulstrodes—he, " the pious banker whose present piety blotted out a lurid past and who had a deferential bending attitude in listening, and an apparently fixed attentiveness in his eyes, which made those persons who thought themselves worth hearing infer that he was seeking the utmost improvement from their discourse," and who had " taken his selfish passions into discipline and clad them in severe robes, so that he had walked with them as a devout cloak." But when Bulstrode's professions are found out and he leaves Middlemarch as a disgraced man, Mrs. Bulstrode stands fast to him. She was not a woman of education or ideals, but she was loyal-hearted and true in spite of the suggestions of Mrs. Hackbutt—evidently a character from old days in Warwickshire—" that it was an encouragement to crime if such men are to be taken care of and waited on by good women."

We have seen that the writer took pains to arrive at knowledge of medical matters and hospital management : Lydgate, on his best side, has even been supposed to have had his prototype in the eminent medical man whom the Leweses visited at Leeds. But though this is simply conjecture, it is the case that George Eliot undoubtedly derived from her talks at Leeds the new views on hospital construction, and the idea of having a separate fever hospital in addition to the old infirmary, and thus making a local medical school and obviating the rush to London on the part of those who wished to study medicine. The scientific point of view was in the air and it influenced George Eliot as it was influencing others. Lydgate was but seven and twenty—" an age at which many men are not common—at which they are hopeful of achievement, resolute in avoidance, thinking that Mammon shall never put a bit in their mouths," and he had been drawn to the study of medicine—a study then considered unworthy of his class—by accidentally reading an article in a Cyclopædia on Anatomy; this gave him his first vivid notion of the finely-adjusted mechanism of the human frame. From that time on he felt the growth of an intellectual passion. He studied in London, Edinburgh and Paris after his 'prentice days were over, and he saw that his profession wanted reform and believed that he would win celebrity away from London intrigues and quackery. He refused either to dispense drugs or take percentage from druggists. George Eliot takes a real joy in describing the state of medical knowledge at the time and what was being attempted to improve it, and one is quite sure that George Lewes was equally interested in this unusual section of a novel. We can easily tell that the matter was dominating the writer's mind at the time, just as was Octavia Hill's scheme for improving the housing of the people, of which we can see evidence in Dorothea's plans.

But on the whole this book may be said to be a study in egotism. " Your pier-glass or extensive

surface of polished steel made to be rubbed by a
housemaid, will be minutely and multitudinously
scratched in all directions ; but place now against
it a lighted candle as a centre of illumination, and
lo ! the scratches will seem to arrange themselves in
a fine series of circles round that little sun." This
is how George Eliot explains the egotism of her
characters—of Miss Vincy, for instance, who believed
that she had a special Providence of her own.
What undoubtedly makes the book depressing is
the sadness of the fate of the two principal
characters—a fate that seems inevitable. To Mr.
Casaubon, Providence had, he believed, provided
the wife he needed, modest and useful as a secretary,
and sure to think her husband's mind all-powerful.
But he did not consider whether Providence had
taken equal care of Miss Brooke, and hence the
tragedy when she found not only his " Key to all
the Mythologies," but himself to be wanting. As to
Rosamond Vincy it was Lydgate who made the
same discovery, and as death did not intervene to
save him as it saved Dorothea, he gradually
succumbed to the constantly exercised pressure
from without.

Is there anything sadder than the paragraph that
tells the end of this high-spirited, ambitious young
man ? " Lydgate's hair never became white. He
died when he was only fifty, leaving his wife and
children provided for by a heavy insurance on his
life. He had gained an excellent practice, alternating, according to the season, between London and
a Continental bathing-place ; having written a
treatise on gout, a disease which has a good deal of
wealth on its side. His skill was relied on by many

paying patients, but he always regarded himself as a failure ; he had not done what he once meant to do. . . . As the years went on he opposed her less and less, whence Rosamond concluded that he had learned the value of her opinion ; on the other hand, she had a more thorough conviction of his talents now that he had gained a good income, and instead of the threatened cage in Bride Street, provided one all flowers and gilding, fit for the bird of paradise that she resembled."

" Middlemarch," indeed, is essentially, not only a middle-class but also a " middle-age novel," one in which the illusions of youth are lost, but deep knowledge of character is gained. We get little information as to the political state of the country, for instance, though the scene is set in a time of violent political upheaval and there are a certain number of characters in it occupied with politics. But we have a true picture of life in its more lasting attributes.

CHAPTER XIII

THE LAST NOVEL: "DANIEL DERONDA"
(1872–1876)

THE usual journey after the completion of a book was in this case to Homburg, where the scene of a young girl gambling with " hags and brutally stupid men around her " was to produce its result in a coming novel. On the return home came the reviews of " Middlemarch," though all the work connected with correspondence and " weeding out " was as before performed by the " sublime husband " who presented to his wife only those criticisms which he thought she ought to see. To this decision she, one is almost sorry to say, never demurred. The book in its complete form was received with more enthusiasm than any of George Eliot's novels had before obtained ; even " Adam Bede " paled before it, and the New Year's Day entry in her journal testifies to the happiness that this result gave her. The price of the book was two guineas— a large price even with the usual discount—but a guinea edition also appeared very soon and by the end of 1874 nearly 20,000 copies had sold.

A visit to Frederick Myers at Cambridge, ostensibly to see the boat-races, resulted in George Eliot's acquaintanceship with a " hopeful group of Trinity men." Among those she met were " young Balfour," " young Lyttelton," Henry Jackson,

Edmund Gurney, Henry Sidgwick and R. C. Jebb.
This visit was also helpful in her future work, as
possibly was another summer visit paid to Jowett
at Oxford, where she met Professor T. H. Green,
Max Muller and other notabilities. Mr. W. L.
Courtney* gives an account of this visit, and
describes how he was a youthful spectator of the
group of eager undergraduates clustering round
their distinguished visitor in the Common Room at
Balliol. " The face was that of a tired woman,"
he says, " the large features being remarkable for
only occasional flashes of inspiration. . . . But her
eyes were a different matter. They were wonderful
eyes--eyes that now and again seemed to flash a
message or analyse a personality." George Eliot
appears to have paid little attention to the tutors
and dons. She had come to study the characters
of the young undergraduates and the result of her
studies is seen in her account of Daniel Deronda
and his friend Meyrick.

Another journey abroad included a visit to her
friend of old days, Mme. d'Albert, at Geneva, but
for the most part the two travellers had no definite
plans but wandered about as they listed. After
their return they retreated to a house at Blackbrook
near Chislehurst, once thought of as a possible
permanent country home. George Eliot writes :
" In the country the days have broad spaces, and
the very stillness seems to give a delightful roomi-
ness to the hours." Or as she expresses it in the
book she was soon to produce : " A human life, I
think, should be well rooted in some spot of a native
land, where it may get the love of tender kinship for

* " The Passing Hour," by W. L. Courtney. London. 1925.

the feel of the earth, for the labour men go forth to, for the sounds and accents that haunt it, for whatever will give that early love a familiar unmistakable difference amidst the future widening of knowledge."

That country life combined with the domestic life at home, where there was a beloved grandchild —" a ravishing child," she is called—gave the sort of setting George Eliot thought so essential to her kind. " If all personal joy were to go from me as it has gone from you," she writes to a friend who had lost her husband, " I could perhaps find some energy from that interest, and try to teach the young." The tragedy was that this could not have been a successful attempt, since small children never really took to her, being possibly repelled by her serious and somewhat formidable manners and appearance. One must hope she never knew this.

The new book spoken of above was " Daniel Deronda," and this, which was to be her last work of fiction, was now coming into being. " I am slowly swimming towards another big book, but people seem so bent on giving supremacy to ' Middlemarch ' that they all seem not to like any future book so well," she says to John Blackwood. And now she was at the height of her fame and ought, indeed, to have been satisfied ; but she was never free from a strange self-conscious dread. In her review of the past year (1873) she says: " Our children are prosperous and happy—we have abundant wealth for more than our actual needs ; and our unspeakable joy in each other has no other alloy than the sense that it must one day end in parting." That fear always haunted her, characteristically causing her frequent tears in anticipation and preventing her from enjoying the present happiness that ought to have been hers.

Another temporary home was found at Rickmansworth in an old Georgian red-brick house. From thence she writes to her sympathetic publisher about " Deronda " : " I can't say that I am at all satisfied with the book, or that I have a comfortable sense of doing in it what I want to do ; but Mr. Lewes is satisfied with it, and insists that since he is as anxious as possible for it to be fine, I ought to accept his impression as trustworthy." The only comfort in the depression from which she suffered was that it was not for the first or second time that she experienced it in publishing a novel. The issue began on February 1st, 1876, and in April the author was able to say that the success of the work was greater than up to the corresponding point of the publication of " Middlemarch." " What will be the feeling of the public as the story advances ? " she says, with considerable discrimination, " I am entirely doubtful. The Jewish element seems to me likely to satisfy nobody." The book was finished on June 3rd, 1876.

The last of George Eliot's novels is one regarding which there is great difference of opinion. There are one or two, like Oscar Browning, who class it as her best ; others—most others—think that it shows a failing imagination and more of the didactic and psychological element than any that had preceded it. But all agree that there are certain characters extraordinarily well drawn, and of these the heroine, Gwendolen Harleth, is the most outstanding. It is doubtful whether in any of George Eliot's novels we have a woman's character so

carefully and justly analysed. And a remarkable
point about it is that nowhere else in her writings
is there any character resembling her, although
there may be a certain similarity in some of the
crucial problems that are set before her. Henry
James, no mean critic, says : " I was to remain a
very Deronda of Derondists, for my own wanton
joy : which amounts to saying that I found the
figured, coloured tapestry always vivid enough to
brave no matter what complications of the stitch."

Like " Middlemarch," the book is a long one,
and it is also, like " Middlemarch," composed of
two stories which only interlace at certain points.
It is a curious, and rather original mode of writing,
but it gives one a sense of naturalness that is very
often lacking in the ordinary set plot. The one tale
may again be called a study in egotism or selfishness
on the part of an attractive young woman; but
though this same study has appeared before us in
the writer's delineation of female characters, the
egotism is of a different sort. Gwendolen is one
who does not succumb to her failing like Rosamond
Vincy, for example, since in the end she is saved
through suffering. The other parallel narrative
gives a vivid account of Jewish life and ideals, as
well as inherited aspirations, such as have never
come into George Eliot's canvas before, unless it
may be said to have done so in the tale of the
" Spanish Gypsy."

Gwendolen Harleth—George Eliot took great
pains with her names—was a beautiful girl who
had been thoroughly spoiled by an admiring family,
and who craved for and claimed a distinguished
position. Her mother is dominated by her, and so

are her half-sisters and former governess. The family is not rich, and Gwendolen has, she feels, to make her own way to the distinction to which she aspires. Sir Hugo Mallinger's nephew, the rich Henleigh Grandcourt, descends on the country where the Harleths live, and evidently admires her. He is a blasé autocrat, and Gwendolen at first holds herself aloof from him in her proud way, and hence, unused to such treatment, he is the more attracted to her. He has a mistress named Mrs. Glasher, who makes herself known to Gwendolen, and the latter promises not to marry Grandcourt because of her claims, and because it is clearly Grandcourt's duty to legitimatise his children. Gwendolen goes off to the Continent to avoid Grandcourt's attentions, and while gambling at Leubronn, Daniel Deronda sees her and is able to be of assistance to her without making this known. Deronda is a handsome man with unusually noble moral qualities, who is much attached to Sir Hugo Mallinger, who brought him up, and whom he believes to be his real father. From Leubronn, Gwendolen is suddenly called home by learning that her mother's small fortune is gone, and that she herself must earn her bread. This so upsets the proud girl that she breaks her promise to Mrs. Glasher, and accepts Grandcourt's offer of marriage, as she makes herself believe, for her mother's sake. Mrs. Glasher conveys a letter to her rival on her wedding-day, which greatly distresses her, and the marriage begins badly : it goes from worse to worse, for Grandcourt is a selfish tyrant, winding his coils around her like a snake. While visiting Sir Hugo Mallinger, Gwendolen meets Deronda again, and

takes him as a sort of spiritual guide. Grandcourt
is jealous, and disagreeable scenes follow. Deronda
is not in love with Gwendolen though he admires
her, for he is immersed in his own life in London in
which another woman is involved. While rowing
on the Thames, he rescues a girl called Mirah Cohen
or Lapideth from suicide, and takes her to the
home of his friend Hans Meyrick, whose mother and
sisters befriend her. He sets out to search for the
girl's lost brother Ezra, and meets Mordecai, a
consumptive Jewish mystic. From Mordecai he
learns much about Jewish history and ideals, more
particularly about the dream of a restored Jewish
nationality. It is finally discovered that Mordecai
is Mirah's lost brother, and he and Mirah come
together while Deronda's love for Mirah gradually
increases.

All this time Gwendolen becomes more and more
unhappy, and she feels the need of spiritual comfort and longs for Deronda's advice. Grandcourt
goes on a yachting expedition to the Mediterranean
and forces his wife to accompany him. At Geneva
he is indignant at finding Deronda, who had been
summoned to meet his unknown mother. She
proves to be the Princess Halm-Eberstein, once a
prima donna, a Jewess who hated her race and had
sent her little son to be brought up in England in
ignorance of his birth. Grandcourt takes Gwendolen
out in a sailing boat and accidentally falls over-
board. Gwendolen, who has been driven frantic by
his cruelty, delays a moment in throwing the rope,
and though she afterwards jumps in after him, is
overwhelmed with remorse when she is rescued and
finds her husband dead. To Deronda she un-

burdens herself, and he gives her wise counsel. Gwendolen discovers that Mrs. Glasher's son is made Grandcourt's heir and she herself has only a small provision. Deronda is delighted to discover that he is a Jew, and is received with joy by Mordecai and Mirah. He and Mirah marry, and when Mordecai dies they go to Palestine to try to carry out their dream of a restored Jewish nation.

The latter part of the story is, as can be seen, too improbable to carry conviction ; the finding of the brother and indeed the whole Jewish part of the tale, is curiously unreal. Daniel Deronda is in personal appearance taken from the Christ in Titian's " Tribute Money," which haunted George Eliot for years after she saw it in the Dresden Gallery, just as she was haunted by another Titian in Venice in relation to the story of the " Spanish Gypsy." It is perhaps dangerous to develop characters in fiction from pictures. In any case, Deronda is not a typical young Englishman, though his parentage may explain many of his un-English qualities. " Deronda would have been first-rate if he had more ambition was a frequent remark about him. . . . Certainly Deronda's ambition, even in his springtime, lay exceptionally aloof from the conspicuous, vulgar triumph, and from other ugly forms of boyish energy; perhaps because he was early impassioned by ideas, and burned his fire on those heights. . . . The impression made at Cambridge corresponded to his position at Eton. Everyone interested in him agreed that he might have taken a high place if his motives had been of a more pushing sort, and if he had not, instead of regarding studies as instruments of success, hampered himself with the notion that they were to feed motive and opinion, a notion which set him criticising methods and arguing against his freight and harness, when he should have been using all his might to pull." He was discontented with the futility of examinations which demanded retentive memory and dexterity without any insight into the principles of things. He characteristically helped his poor friend Meyrick, who was suffering from inflammation of the eyes, to gain his scholarship, and failed in his own examination.*

All this we can accept, but we cannot rise to the account of his personal appearance. " Rowing in his ' dark-blue shirt and skull-cap ' " (one would have expected a Cambridge man to wear light blue) " his curls closely clipped, his mouth beset with abundant soft waves of beard, he bore only disguised traces of the seraphic boy ' trailing clouds of glory.' . . . Look at his hands ; they are not soft and dimpled, with tapering fingers that seem to have only a deprecating touch ; they are long, flexible, firmly grasping hands, such as Titian has painted in a picture when he wanted to show the combination of refinement with force. . . . His eyes had a peculiarity which has drawn many men into trouble ; they were of a dark yet mild intensity, which seemed to express a special interest in everyone on whom he fixed them," and so on. It is not surprising that every woman he met was impressed by this dazzling creature, but he is what is called a woman's man more than a man's. The rough and

* Hans was originally to have been rusticated, but on inquiry this was considered unlikely and his mishap was altered to eye trouble arising from cold caught in the then draughty third-class carriages. George Eliot took immense trouble in getting her facts accurate.

tumble of life did not attract him ; he did not feel disposed to work at politics or at the ordinary philanthropic schemes of the day. With his self-repressed exterior he found his romance among the things of everyday life, but not his work.

Gwendolen Harleth was made of very different stuff. She was a real flesh and blood human being, and no paragon of conscious virtue. It is on the whole true that George Eliot's women are more real than her men, who tend to be either stage villains like Grandcourt, or rather tiresomely high-minded like Deronda. Felix Holt is not interesting, which means that he is not true, and certainly Deronda bores us. We may criticise even Adam Bede, but then we must remember the absolute successes such as Lydgate, Tom Tulliver, Amos Barton and many others. But we may go as far as to allow that there are hardly any real failures amongst George Eliot's women, and this is as it should be in the case of a great woman writer. George Meredith prided himself on his women characters, but most women critics do not entirely accede to this particular claim. Clara Middleton is a fine creation, but to most of us Gwendolen Harleth is a truer woman. And there is not much variety in Meredith's female characters any more than in the majority of Scott's.

The novel opens with this question about Gwendolen. " Was she beautiful ? and what was the secret of form or expression which gave the dynamic quality to her glance ? Was the good or the evil genius dominant in those beams ? Probably the evil ; else why was the effect that of unrest rather than of undisturbed charm ? Why was the wish to look again felt as coercion, and not as a longing in which the whole being consents ? " This was the question asked about the gambling girl. " Having always been the pet and pride of the household, waited on by mother, sisters, governess and maids, as if she had been a princess in exile, she naturally found it difficult to think her own pleasure less important than others made it, and when it was positively thwarted, felt an astonished resentment apt, in her cruder days, to vent itself in one of those passionate acts which look like a contradiction of habitual tendencies. Though never even as a child thoughtlessly cruel, nay, delighting to rescue drowning insects and watch their recovery, there was a disagreeable silent remembrance of her having strangled her sister's canary-bird in a final fit of exasperation at its shrill singing which had again and again jarringly interrupted her own. She had taken pains to buy a white mouse for her sister in retribution ; and though inwardly excusing herself on the ground of a peculiar sensitiveness which was a mark of her general superiority, the thought of that infelonious murder had always made her wince."

It is evident that the queen-like girl who wished to have all the good things of life and none of the evil, would suffer badly if the good things did not come to her as she expected, and when poverty came, her first idea of going on the stage was blighted by the painfully truthful artist, Herr Klesmer. Marriage seemed the only way out : and to marry Grandcourt was to sin against her better nature—for a better nature she had. And when she married, and the concentrated brutality of her husband showed itself, she instinctively turned to Deronda who seemed to be looking at life from a higher and more detached standpoint. Deronda certainly is playing with fire in taking the part of a mentor, when Gwendolen tells him that a time may come when she can bear her position no more ; but good man as he was, he held his ground, and gave her admirable advice in somewhat sententious form. If he had been of ordinary flesh and blood and less immaculate, we might have condemned, but still sympathised more truly with him.

In this book the reflective analysis of character and sentiment is more marked than in any other. It lacks the freshness of the early novels and gives the feeling of having been worked out with infinite pains and labour. Grandcourt in his wickedness might have been an element of reality, but in his conversations and dealings with Lush, his agent and toady who preferred a life of sycophancy and luxury to doing an honest day's work, we are given a sense of repulsion without a corresponding sense of truth. Lewes related that a critic had maintained that these scenes were not *vrai semblable,* and were of the imperious *feminine,* not masculine order : he was, however, comforted just afterwards by hearing that Bernal Osborne had declared them the best parts of the book ; for he considered that Osborne had seen more of the sort of life depicted than had the unnamed critic. George Eliot, who was unwittingly becoming somewhat receptive of adulation of this kind, was also greatly satisfied with the testimony of " men of experience." However that may be, the world has decided that the writer had not the power of describing brutal or mean-minded men that the two solitary girls on the Yorkshire

s

moors, in their less protected lives, possessed so thoroughly.

The part of the book that deals with Mordecai and his aspirations, and the intense interest that these arouse in Deronda, and his final joy in discovering that he himself belongs to the Chosen Race has always been a difficulty to English readers. George Eliot herself was keenly interested in the Semitic race, and studied Hebrew, as we have seen, even in the old Coventry days. The attitude of Christians to the race from which their religion was derived always annoyed her. And its Spanish form attracted her specially, so Deronda was proved to be of the line of Spanish Jews that has borne many students and men of practical power. But the prosaic Briton felt that Deronda's hopes of restoring a political existence to his race would prove disappointing. The design would not, however, as things turned out, have seemed Utopian fifty years later.

As to poor Gwendolen who had clearly loved Deronda, all that was left to her was to acknowledge that it was better for her that she had known him. " Do not think of me sorrowfully on your wedding-day. I have remembered your words—that I may live to be one of the best of women, who make others glad that they were born."

So that the story ends happily, only as far as it is happy to have hearts renewed and lives refined even through fire. There is nothing joyous about the novel—little humour and none of the delightful characters like Mrs. Poyser, to make us forget the troubles of everyday life. And so many people read novels with this object, that this novel did not have the same chance of being permanently popular as some of the others. But if we want to study character of an unusual sort, and to reflect on the inward meanings of action as we see it, and if we do not mind an introspective and didactic style, then we have something to learn from " Daniel Deronda."

* * * * *

The journey after the completion of this last novel ended at Ragatz after a pilgrimage to Les Charmettes. On the travellers' return, plenty of letters were found from Jews and Christians, but more especially from the former. It was a real disappointment to the author that her ideas in regard to the relations between the Jewish element and those of English social life had not been fully appreciated even by the race she was most concerned to vindicate. She considers that the attitude of English people to all Orientals is a national disgrace, and there was nothing she would more gladly do than to rouse the imagination of men and women to their claims. " To the Hebrews we have a special debt," she says, " and it is a sign of intellectual narrowness and stupidity that our attitude to them and others is as it is."

CHAPTER XIV

The Last Years

(1878–1880)

At length the long sought for country home was found in a charming house—The Heights, Witley, near Godalming—with beautiful scenery all around, and enchanting walks and drives and eight or nine acres of pleasure ground—just the place George Eliot had always longed for. She only regretted its not being snug enough for occupation winter and summer alike. She actually played lawn tennis by the hour together and seemed younger than since she reached her fifties. As she writes on New Year's Day, 1878: "All is happiness, perfect love, and undiminished intellectual interest." And again to James Sully: "I don't think I ever heard anybody use the word 'Meliorist' except myself," and she terms it an unfashionable confession in the face of the fashionable extremes. This word expresses just her "moderate" outlook on life in middle age—the outlook that came to her when the storms of her youth were over and depression was kept at bay.

There is little now to tell about the superlatively happy but uneventful life, to which all things that had ever been desired seemed to have come, whether of a material, intellectual, or moral sort. The letters show a quiet old age—for the Leweses liked to consider themselves old despite their youthful penchant

for lawn tennis which became battledore and shuttle-
cock when tennis out of doors was impracticable.
Lewes was in truth one of those never-grow-olds
who not only play games but sometimes do indiscreet things, as when he asked the young Burne-
Joneses to spend Christmas at the Priory. George
Eliot's letter about this is so characteristic that it is
worth quoting. She writes : " I have been made
rather unhappy by my husband's impulsive proposal
about Christmas. We are dull old persons, and your
two sweet young ones ought to find each Christmas a
new bright bead on their memory, whereas to spend
the time with us would be to string on a dark shrivelled berry. They ought to have a group of young
creatures to be joyful with ; I was conscious of this
lack in the very moment of the proposal, and the
consciousness has been pressing on me more and more
painfully ever since. Even my husband's affectionate hopefulness cannot withstand my melancholy de-
monstration, so pray consider the kill-joy proposition
as entirely retracted and give us something of your-
selves only on simple black-letter days, when the Herald
Angels have not been raising expectations early in the
morning." Hostesses of modern days who may have
had to write the same sort of letters, will admire
without being able to emulate this intellectual effort
with its underlying good sense and humour.

But it was not that the two would-be elderly
persons were recluses. They dined at Mr. (Lord)
Goschen's with a " picked party " to meet the Crown
Prince and Princess of Germany—Dean Stanley,
Kinglake, Froude and various other celebrated
people were there. Perhaps this was the symbol
that past unconventionalities were now forgotten.

Another was the visit of an emissary from the Royal Palace to inquire about George Eliot's health. Mr. J. W. Cross was a constant visitor, and between his trouble about the illness and subsequent death of his mother, and the anxiety which grew about Mr. Lewes's health, the friendship developed. In 1878 Mr. Lewes suffered from cramping pains which made him suspect that there might be something seriously amiss, though this did not damp his imperturbable good spirits. " Even on his worst days he had always a good story to tell, and I remember," says Cross, " on one occasion, in the drawing-room at Witley, between two bouts of pain, he sang through with great *brio*, though without much voice, the greater portion of the tenor part of the ' Barber of Seville ' —George Eliot playing his accompaniment, and both of them thoroughly enjoying the fun."

Mr. Cross gives us an informing account of the life at Witley which was very secluded though there were some pleasant neighbours like the Tennysons, Du Mauriers and Allinghams. He also tells us of the corresponding life in London, where the increasing number of friends and acquaintances made growing demands on George Eliot's time and energy. The Sunday receptions had in the sixties been confined to a small number of intimate friends, but now they had enlarged so as to embrace a great many interesting people. He writes : " These receptions have been so often and so well described, that they have hitherto occupied rather a disproportionate place in the prevalent conception of George Eliot's life. It will have been noticed that there is very little allusion to them in the letters; but, owing to the seclusion of her life, it happened that the large majority of people who knew George Eliot as an author never met her elsewhere. Her *salon* was important as a meeting place for many friends whom she cared greatly to see, but it was not otherwise important in her own life—for she was eminently *not* a typical mistress of a *salon*. It was difficult for her, mentally, to move from one person to another. Playing around many disconnected subjects, in talk, neither interested her nor amused her much. She took things too seriously, and seldom found the effort of entertaining compensated by the gains. Fortunately, Mr. Lewes supplied any qualities lacking in his hostess. A brilliant talker, a delightful raconteur, versatile, full of resource in difficulties of amalgamating diverse groups, and bridging over awkward pauses—he managed to secure for these gatherings most of the social success which they obtained." Then he goes on to explain that the larger the company grew the more difficult it was to manage as there was a fatal tendency to break up into groups which made conversation difficult.

Most people came to the Priory not to hear music when it was forthcoming, as it often was, but for the chance of a few words with their hostess alone. " When the drawing-room door opened, a first glance revealed her always in the same low arm-chair, on the left hand side of the fire. On entering, a visitor's eye was at once arrested by the massive head. The abundant hair, streaked with grey now, was draped with lace arranged mantilla-fashion, coming to a point at the top of the forehead. If she were engaged in conversation, her body was usually bent forward with eager, anxious desire to get as close as possible to the person with whom she talked. She had a great dislike to raising her voice, and often became so wholly absorbed in conversation, that the announcement of an incoming visitor sometimes failed to attract her attention ; but the moment the eyes were lifted up, and recognised a friend, they smiled a rare welcome—sincere, cordial, grave—a welcome that was felt to come straight from the heart." The conversation was best when the company was small—best if *à deux*—but whatever number was present Mr. Lewes was always equal to the occasion. George Eliot was likewise always ready to give of her best, and was intent on the one person with whose conversation she was engaged. There were a certain number of evening entertainments in earlier days and occasional dinners that never exceeded six in number; on one notable evening Tennyson read aloud " Maud," the " Northern Farmer " and parts of other poems.

Mrs. W. K. Clifford, the young wife of a celebrated husband, who was soon to become known as a novelist herself, was one of the favoured women to visit at the Priory. It seemed as if Mr. Clifford, hitherto a constant visitor, was expected to come unaccompanied as in former days ; but to this he demurred till it was explained to him by a mutual friend that he must ask leave to bring his wife. It was an awe-inspiring experience for a young girl to break into the galaxy of talent to be found in the quiet little house hidden away behind its dark-painted fence, but luckily Lewes broke the ice for her by giving her a merry greeting. " He was a wonderful being in his way," she says. " He was considered to be a very ugly man ; why, I cannot think, for his expression was so pleasant, so kindly, that it disguised

his features—if they were bad. I don't think they were;
he certainly had a good forehead, and bright alert grey
eyes like a dog's. He made one think of a dog in many
ways—a rather small, active, very intelligent dog.''

George Eliot never allowed a man to come to her
receptions without good reason, and often refused
it ; women were never invited unless they asked for
it. Thus there were many of the great men of the
time but few of their wives. Indeed it was rather
an ordeal for most women to be called on to speak in
a company so critical in nature, though the hostess
saw them through with the kindest expression on her
face. And her sympathy in trouble was immense.
Mrs. Clifford tells us how in a time of grief the older
woman held her hand and " had the most wonderful and soothing touch of any woman I ever
knew." She also describes how the Leweses were
seen in the Concert Hall : " He happy and alert, a
little way ahead of her as they went along the gang-
way ; she in black or soft grey, with a lace veil
hanging low in front of her bonnet, or thrown back
and making a sort of halo about her head.''*

Sir Edmund Gosse gives a vivid account of how
several times he met driving slowly along a victoria
which contained a strange pair. " The man pre-
maturely ageing, was hirsute, rugged, satyr-like,
gazing vivaciously to left or right ; this was George
Henry Lewes. His companion was a large, thick-set
sybil, dreamy and immobile, whose massive features,
somewhat grim when seen in profile, were incon-
gruously bordered by a hat, always in the height of
the Paris fashion, which in those days commonly
included an immense ostrich feather ; this was

* *Nineteenth Century*, July, 1913.

George Eliot. The contrast between the solemnity of the face and the frivolity of the head-gear had something pathetic and provincial about it."*

As time went on George Eliot's style tended to stiffen and her tone to become more artificial. For that there are various reasons. The main one is the time in which she lived, and the nature of her intimate surroundings. For women as a rule are much more under the influence of their time than men. They are—or were—brought up from infancy to respect it and all its implications. George Eliot was a rebel in girlhood, but a rebel bound hand and foot. She tried to escape from her bonds, and did so, as we have seen, to what her contemporaries thought a dangerous extent. But though she got into a precarious position for a period, and finally took one of the boldest steps a woman can take, she inwardly longed for the old bonds that once seemed so irksome, because she saw, or thought she saw, that they pointed to the truly happy and honoured life for which she craved. And here we have an extraordinary happening. Mary Ann Evans went with Lewes, knowing that she could not be his lawful wife : Lewes was one who had at least the reputation of having lived the life of a free lance and enjoying it—and yet once the two were united, contrary to all belief and expectations, they settled down to be Darby and Joan of the most respectable and conventional of mid-Victorian type. This was truly amazing and calls for some discussion.

What was Lewes's real character ? Such was the question put by that world to whom the union was an astonishment. Whatever his early career he had

* " Aspects and Impressions," by Edmund Gosse.

probity and she to whom he had allied himself promised, if given time, to refute the criticisms made upon the step she took : " If I live five years longer," George Eliot says, " the positive result of my exist ence on the side of truth and goodness will outweigh the small negative good that would have counted in my not doing anything to shock others, and I can conceive no consequence that will make me repent the past." Lord Acton in an article in the *Nineteenth Century* states that George Eliot gave up more than she knew, and that what she really sacrificed was " freedom of speech, the first place among the women of her time, and a tomb in Westminster Abbey." The last only seems justified, and perhaps George Eliot did not yearn for it. Indeed the possibility may not have occurred to her.

We have many accounts of Lewes's appearance besides those mentioned above. We hear of his long hair and ugly clothing, his quiet way of pattering along as though in list slippers, and of his good humour and kindness and constant readiness to encourage young writers. " There was something almost mercurial in him, like a perpetual current of youth among the many years to which the grey hair and wrinkled face bore witness that he had accumulated." But there was along with his mercurial spirit and his bright, happy way of relating amusing anecdotes, a certain strength of character hidden below his boyish vivacity. If he had been other than he was, George Eliot's life would have stood a good chance of being wrecked. He supplied just what she needed. She was deficient in vitality and he gave it ; she was deficient in courage to do the tasks of everyday life, and he did them for her. He was a devoted and admiring servitor who must have given up much for her sake, and suffered many interruptions in his work. " She " was a sort of divinity to him. He poured out tea at the receptions and Mrs. Lewes was reverently served ; if Lewes unwittingly stayed too long with friends talking about music, he would suddenly rush off at a gallop with the words : " We were talking about music— but *She* is waiting to hear it." And the excellence of it was that all was sincere. He had, again, a thorough belief in himself, but yet he was not above confessing himself to be in the wrong if he was so, instead of shifting his ground. " Differences of opinion rouse no egotistic irritation in him," George Eliot writes, and the happiness of their union came much from the " perfect freedom with which we each follow and declare our own impressions."

Let us try to picture the scene at one of the weekly receptions : George Eliot with her back to the window in the comfortable bookish room with a chair beside her on which the favoured visitor was placed. Most of the visitors were scholars and thinkers and a circle of them sat down after greeting their hostess : when six o'clock struck a motion was made to indicate that they must depart. It was significant that the hostess's works were not to be even mentioned, and a truly Victorian rebuke fell on any indiscreet person who did so. Frederick Locker-Lampson describes the famous gatherings vividly—the homely form, the somewhat equine head as though intended for a longer body, hair in loops hiding the ears, and without the waist then fashionable—the measured but impressive speech which might have been pedantic, but was not. Indeed, he declares her speech to have been excellent, and though not possessed of the abandon of the woman of the world, far more interesting. Her earnestness and evident sense of responsibility prevented her from being captivating, but she was a good listener, extremely sensitive, and although intellectually self-contained, dependent on the emotional side of nature.

Still Locker-Lampson considered the atmosphere unhealthy and the reunions too solemn, and he did not care for Lewes, admiring neither his ill-fitting garments nor his ridicule of the dogmas of revealed religion. He was of course not likely to find much in common with a man of his views, and he had a grievance against George Eliot in that he presented her with a valuable Rembrandt etching and did not receive the gratitude he expected. Thus he judged that art did not much appeal to her. But latterly she received many gifts, and possibly was weary!

Henry James, again, gives an amusing account of a visit to her country house at Witley, taken thither as he was in a storm by his adventurous friend Mrs. Greville. He was unfortunate in finding the authoress suffering peculiarly from the fury of the elements in a " chill desert of a room " with a minimum of the paraphernalia of reading and writing, not to speak of a complete deficiency of what he most desired, which was tea! And he also had the misfortune, after presenting one of his books, to have it feverishly returned on his hands as he was parting by the careful help-meet who did not wish George Eliot troubled with more. In spite of this unfortunate experience he says in his Letters: " The Leweses were very urbane and friendly and I think I shall have the right *dorénavant* to consider myself a Sunday habitué.

The great G. E. herself is both sweet and superior, and has a delightful expression in her large, liny, pale, equine face. I had my turn in sitting beside her and being conversed with in a low, but most harmonious tone ; and bating a tendency to *aborder* only the highest themes I have no fault to find with her."

Of course all these accounts concern later days, but in a less degree conditions were always the same. Lewes resolved himself into the ideal husband who did for George Eliot what the Prince Consort did for Queen Victoria, excepting that we read of hardly any criticism such as the Prince occasionally gave his august spouse. Perhaps the devotion which she enjoyed was hardly in every way good for George Eliot's work and life, wonderful as it was. Without it she certainly might never have written fiction at all, and Lewes's never failing encouragement carried her through her constant depression and weariness, for he never lost patience as some men would have done, with her constant nervous crises. The process was just carried too far, for the cold blasts of criticism were kept too securely away from her. As Lord Morley says " To stop every draught with sandbags, screens and curtains, and to limit one's exercise to a drive in a well-warmed brougham with the windows drawn up, may save a few annoying colds in the head, but the end of the process will be the manufacture of an invalid." It is rather true that latterly George Eliot lived in a forcing-house atmosphere of adulation in which she ceased to be an ordinary citizen of the world and tended to become a sacred Lama.

As another friend, Mr. Kegan Paul, points out, there was very little stimulation between the two. Life was happy and settled, but terribly artificial and attention was concentrated on making the surroundings as agreeable as they could be in consideration of the health and well-being of the main individual concerned. This matter of health and comfort was indeed continually being discussed and constant changes of air and scene were deemed necessary : surely this, too, was typical of the age. The time was a wonderful one, but there was a curious way of dwelling on the trivialities of life and glossing over its realities. In orthodox middle-class households it was overtly held that everything was as it should be ; and the Leweses, with all their genius, were somewhat under the domination of their age ; what was going on out in the world was of little moment if all was made to look right in the sacred inner circle. In their case, it is true, we find a quite extraordinary intelligence and intellectual curiosity over matters of the mind : every sort of literature was perused so long as it was of the best, and perused with the utmost care : but as to politics, reform, poverty —of all these burning questions there is comparatively no mention. The allusions to bad times, bad harvests and political crises are perfectly casual. This shows us why outside happenings never were depicted in George Eliot's works as part of life important enough to move men's hearts and souls. Her own politics were mildly conservative, but there was no drive in them of any sort— no true radicalism or young Tory zeal.

As regards the marriage question it was somewhat the same. Both of the Leweses had gone through deep experiences on this side ; but those too, seemed in George Eliot's novels smoothed away.

And now we possibly come to the real reason why the books are not more popular than they are in the present day. This generation looks at life quite differently. It does not allow artificial barriers to hold it from probing to the bottom of whatever problem it takes up, however difficult it may be. No one dug deeper than George Eliot, but there were regions which she left untouched. The story of Hetty would now be treated possibly in a much less delicate but certainly in a much more realistic fashion. It would not be so "beautiful" or idealistic a tale, but it might be more true to life. There is not much reverence in the present generation, we are accustomed to say; but in its mind the reverence of the Victorian days was a sort of false convention that set up a hedge to protect shams. The same is the case with the sacredness of the family which George Eliot was never tired of emphasising. "The possibility of a constantly growing blessedness in marriage," she says, "is to me the very basis of good in our mortal life." There is a freer view of what that relationship involves in these times, and not the same haunting fear of losing the blessedness of the relationship by extending one's interests beyond the narrow limits which family life supplies. Then, again, the moderate demand for university education and such other outlets for the young womanhood of the time, though in theory she approved them, were ever somewhat alarming to this true Victorian who herself, as well as her royal contemporary, might have been thought to have shown the way to larger conceptions of duty by the value of the services they rendered to the community. The new views may have their drawbacks, but there is perhaps more intellectual honesty than in the old days.

Hence the younger generation thinks George Eliot's characters move in a somewhat unreal atmosphere, and they are bored by the constant reflections on the development of the drama. They do not sufficiently recognise the great truths that lie embedded in the somewhat clogged material, nor the idealism that breathes through all her writings. Such fiction is not light reading : unless a good deal is skipped over, as is apt to happen. George Eliot, on the other hand, liked her books to be taken in slow doses and to be read slowly ; and to appreciate them fully this is necessary.

In the autumn of 1878 both had had rather a trying time in point of health, but the country life was happy in spite of the threatened illness of Mr. Lewes. He was, however, able to discuss the coming book of essays, and do the business that he had always helped to carry out. They were back in London when the illness became much more severe and the book was deferred. He, her beloved companion and support, died on November 28th, 1878.

The blow of Lewes's death was terrible to one who had been so absolutely and entirely devoted. George Eliot saw no one except Charles Lewes and the very few whom she had to see on business ; and occupied herself with Mr. Lewes's unfinished MSS., with which work Charles Lewes helped her. When the usual New Year's entry is made in 1879 the only words are : " Here I and sorrow sit." The desolation and the life she led told on her health. The mourning was of the kind that now is no more—the mourning of a widow who feels her

T

life is over. We have it in the widowhood of Queen Victoria. The life had been such that it seemed as if it were no use thinking of happiness without her devoted helper and lover. She could not read her letters at first, but sent loving messages to her nearest friends—her life was broken, her writing seemed trivial stuff. " Theophrastus Such " was, however, on its way, and in grief and sadness she felt she must do something about the printed sheets lying uncorrected. " What is joy is joy no longer, or what is pain is easier because he has not to bear it." " My everlasting winter has set in." She could not bear to go out of sight of the things he used and looked on. " Each day seems a new beginning—a new acquaintance with grief." Mr. Cross was able to see and comfort her after a time. She thought she was to die, but her physicians said otherwise. Then came the idea of founding a student-ship in memory of Mr. Lewes, and suitable trustees were appointed to carry it out. It was designed to help a young man anxious to carry on Physiological research but without the means of doing so.

" Theophrastus " was thus to appear in a time of sadness, and on reading the proofs the author considered the possibility of suppressing it in its original form, so dissatisfied was she with it. But she was so far committed to the work that she decided to go forward and publish it in the end of May.

It would have been better, perhaps, had its author adhered to her first impulse. But Lewes had sent the manuscript to the publisher and had encouraged her to proceed—a course which makes one somewhat doubt his judgment. He had a sense of humour and possessed real wit, but in this book the humour is so ponderous as to be almost unrecognisable, and the wit is blunt-edged. It was George Eliot's last book—another of apparently a somewhat similar kind was left unfinished—and it seemed as if the splendid brain-power had become somewhat atrophied, or that the middle-aged bachelor who is supposed to write in the form of satirical sketches these quasi-humorous observations on life as he had known it, had taken possession of the real author's mind, and divested her of all the lighter elements, emphasising only the didactic and ponderous. Satire such as this requires the lightest and most skilful hand to make it readable. In "Looking Backward" we have some pleasant recollections of old country days, but less well expressed than elsewhere in the author's writings ; and in "On Debasing the Moral Currency" there is a good lesson but put in tiresome and unattractive language. George Eliot was always critical of those who mocked what others reverenced, saying that those who thought themselves most free from superstition were the most intolerant, and this is one of her points. Then, again, she quotes French writers like La Bruyère without unfortunately following in their steps as regards briefness and lucidity. There is no great writer of fiction so hard to follow in her portentously long didactic sentences as George Eliot at her worst. And in "Theophrastus" we have many of these sentences which neither convey their lesson clearly nor run agreeably to our æsthetic senses. The most direct and natural—because deeply sincere—of her essays is that on the Jewish race and its treatment.

In George Eliot's novels we have revealed the

meaning of the lives of ordinary men and women as they are lived, and there is there the personal touch which is requisite to the true novel writer. She was able to tell us what her contemporaries —men and women—were thinking, feeling and saying. She could do this when the mask was on, and she was projecting herself in her characters, but strangely enough the dæmonic power failed her when she wrote in her own person ; and her essays show this very clearly. The same is evident in her letters where, instead of forgetting herself, the writer hears herself talking : " *Elle s'écoute quand elle parle*," as her French critics say, and she is fatally conscious of how what she has to say will appear. The letters are interesting, because all that is written by an interesting woman is interesting. But we never wish to read them again, as we do any of the immortal letters, like those of Mme. de Sévigné, or even of the naturally low-pitched Cowper. The reason is that letters above all require lightness of touch and forgetfulness of self on the part of the writer in relation to the one who is being addressed. We do not want moral reflections in our letters, else we should feel as if we were having beef-sandwiches at tea : we want directness of expression and not periphrases : we do not want to hear of " juicy blessings " but of strawberries, even though the strawberries may be dealt with in the lightest way possible. Consequently the " Letters " are. for the most part tedious, and the manner of writing the life of George Eliot through her letters is not successful. She had not " a fine voice for writing."

We have only one side of George Eliot's corre-

spondence, for, as we have seen, with her hatred
of " hard curiosity," she destroyed the friends'
letters, which she considered were only meant for
her own eyes. She had an unusual number of
correspondents, some of whom must have been
tiresome even to her affectionate nature. Apart
from those published by Mr. Cross, there is a little-
known book of letters dating from 1872 from an
admiring friend, Mrs. (Elma) Stuart, who continually—and almost too often, one would say—
sent her tokens of the gratitude she bore her.
Occasionally Mr. Lewes wrote in reply, but more
often George Eliot herself, and some of those letters,
especially those to Mrs. Stuart's young son, are
charming and natural. Mr. Lewes always writes
delightfully, and even unbends so far as to call
his wife " Polly," as in strict intimacy he often did,
though the name seemed singularly inappropriate.
On her side she terms herself Elma's " mother "
(the adjective " spiritual " was fortunately soon
given up).* All through there is a pleasant relationship with this artistic woman who made beautiful
articles for George Eliot's use.

In some of those letters there are amusing remarks
of a personal sort. George Eliot was sensitive
about her looks, and always refused to be photo-
graphed—indeed she had a real horror of even
being sketched, as she sometimes was unwittingly.
Hence she trembled at the idea of her friend Elma
seeing her for the first time, since the only portrait
the former had known was that by Lawrence of

* Elma Stuart is buried near George Eliot in Highgate Cemetery,
and on the tombstone she is termed " one who for eight and a half
blessed years George Eliot called by the sweet name of Daughter."

eight years before, which in no way represented her present appearance. " Instead," she says, " imagine a first cousin of the old Dante's—rather smoke-dried—a face with lines in it that seem a map of sorrows." This was her own view, but others speak of the wonderful eyes that lighted up with eager passion and of how " the soul itself seemed to shine through its worn framework with a radiance of almost unearthly beauty."

In April, 1879, George Eliot sent an S.O.S. to Mr. J. W. Cross : " I am in dreadful need of your counsel, pray come to me when you can—morning, afternoon or evening."

She was a woman who was not adapted for facing life alone. She had always been dependent on the love and affection of some other on whom she could lean. And the staff on which she had depended had been taken from her. Mr. Cross had lately lost his mother to whom he was greatly devoted, and was finding fresh interest in the new pursuit of reading Dante. Hence they read the " Inferno " and " Purgatorio " together ; not, as we may well understand, in dilettante fashion, but with minute and careful examination of the construction of every sentence. He writes : " The prodigious stimulus of such a teacher (estanto maestro) made the reading a real labour of love." She, too, was taken into a new world, and so it was a renovation of life to them both. At the end of May, Mr. Cross induced her to play on the piano at Witley again, and she played regularly during his frequent visits from Weybridge. So the life went on. A few friends came, and there was the pleasure of the children of the new gener-ation of Leweses. George Lewes's papers were all the time being arranged, and the " Study of Psychology " published. Madame Bodichon writes in June—" I spent an hour with Marian. She was more delightful than I can say and left me in good spirits for her, though she is wretchedly thin, and looks in her long loose black dress like the black shadow of herself. She said that she had so much to do that she must keep well—' the world was so *intensely interesting.*'" Sir James Paget and Dr. Andrew Clark guarded over her health along with the country practitioner, for illness came from time to time and with it pain, and its depressing influence. John Blackwood's death in October, 1879, was a heavy loss, bound up as he had been with most she cared for in her life for more than twenty years.

The sense of solitude was bitter, but she and Mr. Cross after her return to London in the autumn together visited museums and as he says in his rather prosaic but truthful way, a " bond of mutual dependence had been formed between us." On March 28th, 1880, eighteen months after George Lewes's death, she came down to Weybridge, and on April 9th it was decided that the two should marry as soon and as privately as possible. " You can hardly think how sweet the name sister is to me," she writes to Miss Eleanor Cross, " that I have not been called by for so many, many years. Nothing less than the prospect of being loved and welcomed by you all could have sustained me. . . . Yet I quail a little in facing what has to be gone through—the hurting of many whom I care for. You all do everything you can to help me." Then came a letter to one of her oldest friends, Madame Bodichon, telling her " what will doubtless be a great surprise to her." " I am going to do what not very long ago I should myself have pronounced impossible for me, and therefore I do not wonder at anyone else who finds my action incomprehensible." To Mrs. Stuart, her constant correspondent, she puts the question, " Will your love and trust in me suffice to satisfy you that if I act in a way which is thoroughly unexpected there are reasons which justify my action ? " By the time Madame Bodichon's letter arrived she would be married to Mr. J. W. Cross " who you know is a friend of years, a friend much loved and trusted by Mr. Lewes, and who, now that I am alone, sees his happiness in the dedication of his life to me." As to her care for Mr. Lewes's family it was to make no difference as Mr. Cross was sufficiently provided. On May 6th, 1880, the two were married at St. George's, Hanover Square. " Only Mr. Cross's family were present," she says, " and we went back to the Priory where we signed our wills, then started for Dover."

" Marriage has seemed to restore me to my old self," she writes from Grenoble to Charles Lewes. " I was getting hard, and if I had decided differently, I think I should have become very selfish." That is true, for the danger for George Eliot was always that of getting centred in herself, and as children were not to be hers, she had to have some object of affection constantly beside her. Physically she benefited. " I would still give up my own life willingly if he (the Pater) could have the happiness instead of me," she says to his son ; and to Miss Cross : " I have been uninterruptedly well, and feel quite strong with all sorts of strength except strong-mindedness." One great pleasure was a letter which came to Italy from the brother Isaac estranged since her first union with Mr. Lewes. Indeed, extraordinary as it seems, he would never even mention her name. " Our long silence has never broken the affection for you which began when we were little ones," she says, magnanimously overlooking the long estrangement. The marriage was a blow to some of her admirers, but other friends like Madame Belloc, who had seen her through other crises in her life, wrote sympathetically. " All this, a wonderful blessing, falling to me, after I thought my life was ended," she says to Madame Bodichon. " Deep down below there is a hidden river of sadness, but this must be always with those who have lived long—and I am able to enjoy my newly reopened life." It had to be explained why no inkling had been given of the contemplated step to many who felt somewhat sore in consequence of being left in the dark, and to make matters worse some of the letters announcing the marriage went astray.

Mrs. Thackeray Ritchie tells us that Charles Lewes was certain that his father would have wished his adopted mother to be happy, and spoke with emotion of his debt to her. George Eliot herself dwells on the danger of sinking into self-absorption and laziness. " The whole history is something like a miracle-legend," she says, " but instead of any former affection being displaced in my mind, I seem to have recovered the loving sympathy that I was in danger of losing." After a brief illness suffered by Mr. Cross at Venice, the two made their way home to Witley. George Eliot had apparently been amazingly well, and had

walked a great deal sight-seeing, and never seemed
conscious of fatigue; she looked many years
younger. Whether or not she had overdone herself, this excellent health was unfortunately not
of long duration, for in autumn she had an attack
of a disorder to which she was subject, and Sir
Andrew Clark, " the beloved physician," visited her.
But though there was a recovery of strength, an
English autumn did not suit her. Mr. Cross gives
a delightful account of their last months together.
They read Comte, for whom she maintained her
critical admiration. They began their reading at
Witley with some chapters of the Bible, " a very
precious and sacred book to her," and especially
enjoyed the fine chapters of Isaiah, Jeremiah and
St. Paul's Epistles. "The Bible and our elder
English poets best suited the organ-like tones of
her voice," he says, " which required for their full
effect, a certain solemnity and majesty of rhythm."

Her rich, deep, flexible voice is often spoken of,
and her reading of Milton was specially fine : such
reading Mr. Cross truly says " is an art like singing
—a personal possession that dies with the possessor
and leaves nothing behind except a memory."
They also read Goethe, Shakespeare and Wordsworth, Scott and Lamb, and books requiring intense concentration like Sayce's " Science of Language." Her power of concentration and con-
tinuous thought was astounding and her memory
of books read in the past was extremely good,
though verbal memory was lacking, and quotations
had always to be verified. Cross tells us that "she
spoke French, German, Italian and Spanish
accurately, though with difficulty ; the mimetic

power of catching intonation and accent was wanting." Greek, Latin and Hebrew she could also read, and she even had a hankering after Mathematics; Astronomy and Botany were both delightful studies to her. Her manuscripts were always beautifully written like her letters, free from blur or erasure, and every letter was delicately and distinctly finished.

In December Mr. and Mrs. Cross moved to 4, Cheyne Walk. The house was coming into order and Dr. and Mrs. Congreve and Madame Belloc visited them; the large library was arranged and they went on December 18th as usual to a popular concert at St. James's Hall, where George Eliot got a chill, though she was able to play over some of the music they had heard in the evening, and on Sunday could see Mr. Herbert Spencer. But next day she fell seriously ill, and she died on December 22nd, 1880.

She was buried in Highgate Cemetery, and laid in the grave next to Mr. Lewes. December 29th was a bitter day of sleet and snow, but the cemetery was crowded with men and women of every kind. Her brother Isaac came up from the North. Herbert Spencer, who had been a constant friend since 1851, tells us that there was a movement to have the burial in Westminster Abbey, but that it was concluded that there might be criticisms and the movement was abandoned. Huxley even demurred on the ground that Westminster Abbey is a Christian church and not a Pantheon, though he knew that Dean Stanley would have agreed to an Abbey funeral had it been strongly pressed.

Lord Acton wrote: "It seems to me as if the sun had gone out. You cannot think how much I loved her."

CHAPTER XV

George Eliot and Her Time

ALTHOUGH it is more than a hundred years since Mary Ann Evans was born, she so completely represented the Mid-Victorian era, that we may justly try to consider both how she represented the thought of that period, and how she influenced our own time. It is specially difficult to assign a place in history to a novelist whose writings show such very various qualities as hers. One can, however, say what she has been for a former generation, and what her influence is even in the present day.

Certainly she was born into what was intellectually a great era. She had as fellow novelists the greatest, even setting aside Scott who belongs to an earlier and different time. Dickens and Thackeray were delighting the world with their humour, pathos and satire, the Brontës, very slightly her predecessors, were to outrival their contemporaries in actual force and genius ; and there were a multitude of less outstanding writers of fiction who would have been notable in a less distinguished age. As the delineator of that wonderful age there is perhaps no one in fiction more accurate and informing than George Eliot, whether we regard her as the describer of rural life in the time in which her youth was passed, or as the interpreter of the feelings and sentiments of at least a large section of the people of the Victorian age.

It is indeed impossible to claim that, remarkable as this writer might be, she was a world interpreter. She had no universal message to mankind. In France she had certain keen admirers such as Montégut and Scherer, but it cannot be said that she was read in anything like the same degree as George Sand was read in England. The form in which her tales are put, and the constant pauses for the author to make her own reflections on her characters may not have appealed to the French, who love clarity and directness. But even in Germany there is no evidence that she was a popular writer. Her survey indeed did not extend far beyond the very considerable one of the society and surroundings in which she was placed. But as to that society and time, the period with which she dealt was in the first place extraordinarily interesting because it embraced that great political movement which stirred the educated middle classes to their foundations, and led to the intellectual awakening which Matthew Arnold was to describe so vividly ; and, in the second place, it was moved by moral and religious passions of the deepest order. The very limitations of her outlook enhanced its value, for we could not have a satisfactory description of a time of deep emotion and tense sense of the value of life in itself, without what might seem undue emphasis being laid on the psychological side of things.

Of course there was a happy, jolly life going on in England in the earlier part of last century which paid no account of these problems of existence.

When we read Jane Austen, for instance, we feel that for her the problems had not yet arisen, and we often give a sigh of relief that we may enjoy her meticulously faithful record of the lives of her contemporaries, their sentiments, affections and dislikes, without being called on to make our way too far below the surface, or even to imagine that there were in existence such things as the searchings of conscience and passionate remorse that so pervade the writings of George Eliot. But Jane Austen's world could not survive the great upheaval which followed the French Wars and culminated in the Industrial Revolution. It was this that influenced the typical mid-Victorians and made life an earnest, solemn fact to so many Englishmen, young as well as old. Novelists came to think of the lessons they had to teach, an idea that never entered into the heads of Walter Scott or Jane Austen. Dickens's " lessons " made him free even to those young people who were brought up in strictest piety : the morals were obvious to the most careless reader, and they were morals which were badly needed at a time when reform was just coming into existence and people were waking up to the cruelties and hardships that were going on around them unheeded. Thackeray's teaching was more subtle and was mainly conveyed by satire : it dealt with a somewhat different class and largely with social backslidings, but it was present all the same. Even sixty years ago fiction was only justified to many people by such secondary aims, and to them very many of the writers of the modern day would have been anathema. No wonder George Eliot harked back to Rousseau, one of her favourite authors. The less distinguished writers of the day, such as Harriet Martineau and Miss Yonge, often lost their art in the lessons they tried to teach.

Now, of course, it is not true that instruction in fiction is incompatible with true art, just as it is far from true that it excludes the sense of humour. In the authors mentioned we certainly have art and undoubtedly have humour. George Eliot herself is full of humour when she lets herself go and forgets the weight of responsibility that rests upon her as an interpreter of her times. Dickens's humour is of another sort : it is rollicking and human and appeals to all the world and brightens its drab days. How much poorer an affair would the world be without the immortal Dickens and his fun ! But George Eliot's humour in its own way is quite as real, and has the merit of having not a touch of exaggeration. There are various sorts of humour, from the bright sense of fun which is commonest in youth, or the sense of the ludicrous involving the juxtaposition of oddly incongruous things which is common to all ages, up to the humour which sees the inherent absurdity of much that passes as serious in life. This is the humour that makes life endurable to many people, and to others prevents their pursuing some quite justifiable line of argument or action beyond the point at which humanity allows it to hold good. It is a very subtle thing and difficult to define, but on it turns much of the happiness of men and women. It was merciful that George Eliot had what she had of it, considering the quality of her surroundings, but it seemed to be a development more than a native gift—the development of a great nature. In her letters and essays it seems strangely absent. The humour of Mrs. Poyser, however, cannot be surpassed ; nor can the charm of the children in George Eliot's writings. Swinburne appreciated this characteristic at its full. "No other man or woman, as far as I can recollect, outside the order of poets, has ever written of children with such adorable fidelity of affection as the spiritual mother of Totty, of Eppie and of Lillo." We never wonder how Totty will grow up—"She is Totty for ever and ever, a chubby immortal little child, set in the lap of our love for the kisses and laughter of all time."* One sometimes wonders how anyone who read the early works of the anonymous author was ever at a loss as to the sex of the writer or deceived by her masculine name. No man, however skilled, could have entered into the relationship between Totty and Mrs. Poyser or Lizzie and Mrs. Jerome. Dickens's mothers and children are entertaining and pathetic, but they are drawn from outside and without the true motherly instinct. To George Eliot "motherhood is a most vivid and vital impulse," as Swinburne truly says.

But the quality that strikes us most in reading George Eliot is her intense realisation of the moral side of life, as it presented itself at the period in which she wrote. This side is quite independent of any orthodox religion, and yet sometimes one wonders whether those who did not "experience" religion ever have the same sense of it as those who did. George Eliot knew and understood evangelical teaching as only those brought up in it can do. It was an intensely real thing to her, and perhaps never more real than when she broke with its outward forms. To those who have "got religion" the possession

* A. C. Swinburne, "A Note on Charlotte Brontë," p. 49.

is an everlasting one—all life is looked at from a different point of view, sins committed or described are not the light-hearted and venial errors in judgment that some would have us believe, but desperate wrong-doing—a wrongdoing which proceeds from an inward perversion which, if it is to be in any way made good must be so by deep contrition and sorrow. Its consequences indeed can never be overcome.

The Puritan Fathers could not have been more inexorable than was this woman writer who seemed to see into the very depths of the human heart. We sometimes feel as if it were only through her own deep experiences that she could have known what she did. Charlotte and Emily Brontë painted wicked men, but there was not the terrific internal struggle that we have in George Eliot's wrongdoers. Arthur Donnithorne, weak as he was, sinned against the light, and was made to feel it to the quick. Heath-cliffe's wickedness, on the other hand, was of the objective sort, drawn as it was with a strength of genius that has perhaps never been surpassed. Emily Brontë seems to rise above the limitations of her time, or rather never to have been conscious of their existence. But George Eliot dwells both on the misdeeds of the sinner and the struggle after righteousness made by those whose efforts are in vain so far as outward success is concerned. Seth Bede is a pathetic character who has to find satis-faction in his inward goodness, for success in other matters always failed him. Dorothea's life was outwardly a failure, and yet with all her mistakes we love as well as revere her. The Good to the writer was something far above the attainment of any outside object, however excellent in itself.

In sentiment, again, George Eliot rings true, and in that she is superior to many of her contemporaries. We do not so often feel inclined to shed tears over her sentimental passages as we do when we are reading of Paul Dombey or little Nell. But the sentiment is deeper, or at least more faithful to nature. The pathos of Mrs. Browning is not as profound, and even that of " Les Misérables " is not as genuine. In her saddest passages, like the heart-rending account of Hetty's wanderings, we do not dwell so much on the one pathetic figure as on the pity of it all as it is happening day by day in human life. And in her descriptions of the sorrows of child-life, again, we know that if Maggie suffers it is because she represents the Maggies of the world who have to make their way by the same rough road. It is not so with Dickens. He makes us concentrate our attention on one sorrowful being and uses every art to accentuate the emotion, so that the figure remains with us, for ever burned into our memory. But though this may cause us to try to see that no more David Copperfields or Nicholas Nicklebys shall exist in our land, we know in our hearts that our feelings are being worked upon deliberately, and that we have not the whole unvarnished truth before us. Sometimes, indeed, the subject is made pathetic from some curious abnormality only. The real tragedy is the essential and inevitable tragedy that lies deep in the essence of things, while simple pathos may be related to some one individual fact or person and hence be accidental in its nature.

It is strange that though the latter part of last century was a time in which science and industry were particularly active, and when the scientific outlook was really rather narrow and apt to dominate the general outlook unduly—we see this very clearly in George Eliot's writings—it was yet in another way full of sentiment. Perhaps one of the most unexpected things in George Eliot's novels is the mixture of scientific analysis—not always very convincing—and sentimental reflections. George Eliot herself was constantly in tears, and in these tears even Lewes sometimes joined. They wept over their friends' letters, they wept over the books they read, and George Eliot wept over her own characters. We have been accustomed to think that those things belonged to an age that had already passed ; but in spite of the lofty attitude of philosophic detachment that is taken, the other element is constantly appearing. The sentiment of Tennyson was not very far off, and it is almost a matter of regret that it did not appear more fully in George Eliot's poetry. Had she not from her girlhood trained herself to look dispassionately on life, she would have been even more sentimental than the rest ; as it was, every now and then her sensibility seemed to get the better of her and to cause her despair.

The world in these later decades has changed so enormously on the social side that it is almost impossible for those who did not live through the latter part of last century to realise what were the quality and nature of rural England in its earlier years. The greatest changes in our time have been brought about by a huge conflagration that has affected every man, woman and child in this country. The changes in the century before were brought about only indirectly by war. Our professional army was very small, and its doings seemed remote. But through these wars, and through the changes and revolutions in other countries, there came that process of fermentation that brought forth riotings and unrest, demands for rights and votes, and all the discontent that has never really left us since. Now the interest of George Eliot's earlier novels is that she tells us of the old placidity that we associate with the picturesque life described by Dickens. A hundred years ago coaches were still in their glory, steam engines were half a horrid dread and half a possible coming excitement. The country clergy were undisturbed by tiresome "movements" (though this was not to endure long) and enjoyed their privileges without too much worrying about their responsibilities. The landlord was still rejoicing in the good time brought about by the war, and building those enormous mansions which were to prove the bane and eventual destruction of his descendants. The farmer had not been forced to trouble himself with new methods or to keep annoying accounts. The country-side looked a place of happiness and contentment, until you lighted on the canker at the root. George Eliot, the countrywoman born and bred, knew that things were not really well below the surface. She herself had lived the perfectly happy country life, was well fed and well clad, and yet deep down in her nature there was the same rebellious self that was springing up in all around her, and that shouted aloud for liberty. George Eliot was no fanatic—no iconoclast. She loved her images too well to break them ; but she knew that the surface which she could describe better than almost any of her fellows was not the whole. This gives her writing so much reality for her time and ours. She had the power of expressing herself in wonderful, accurate, telling sentences that were full of pith but never exaggerated, and she used all these powers to show us what life was and is—that with an apparently untroubled surface such as a backwater society presents, life may be a tremendously deep and complicated matter, full of influences of which it is itself scarcely sensible.

This is what people are apt nowadays to call the highbrow view of life, for which the young generation have little use. It is true that George Eliot just missed being a pedant because of her deep sympathy with actual human beings and their doings. She had not for nothing given up her early and impressionable young womanhood to the study of philosophy. That is to say, she had gone about her life work in a way opposite to that of most writers of her kind. She looked first and foremost deep down into the heart of things, and sought out their true significance. Her characters are in this sense like those of her great forerunner Goethe, though she lacked his immensity of grasp and poetic gifts. They are no mere puppets dancing to the transient fancies of the day, but human beings showing forth the truths of eternity. The great awakening which we associate with Carlyle, and which came largely from Germany, did for the educated classes in England what the cruder propaganda of Paine did for the lowest, or that of Owen, Place and Cobbett for education and reform in the early part of the century.

The devotion of Lord Acton to George Eliot is remarkable, and it has always been quoted as a remarkable testimony to the excellence of her work, for, as he states, in politics and religion he was divided from her as widely as it was possible to be, and therefore he cannot be considered to have been blind to her faults. " We must," he says, " never judge the quality of a teaching by the quality of a Teacher, or allow the spots to shut out the sun." And he considered the nature of her character " generally perfect " and her " touch unfailing." " No writer," he declares, " ever lived who had anything like her power of manifold, but disinterested and impartially observant sympathy." Could he say more ? For thus he sets her beside the greatest masters of the age. Gladstone, on the other hand, also a great Victorian, never cared for George Eliot, Acton thinks curiously because of her lack of idealism. But, though Montégut places her amongst the realistic writers— the realism that proceeds from Christianity and especially English Protestantism which glorifies the humble life and modest domestic virtues—her realism had meaning only because she saw the ideal through it.

So that though it is true that George Eliot's writings deal with the realities of common life, no Englishman would consider that they were not permeated throughout with the idealistic spirit. Contemporary Romatics such as D. G. Rossetti did not, however, for other reasons appreciate her work. Coventry Patmore was wholly antipathetic, and others considered that she forgot that art was to please, and insisted on its teaching as well. De Vogüé, on the other hand, asserts that realism in England began with Richardson and culminated in Dickens, Thackeray and George Eliot,* and holds that the last named gave it a serenity and grandeur never equalled.

* " Le Roman Russe," par V. G. M. de Vogüè. Paris. 1912.

Despite his admiration of Tourgenieff and Tolstoy, he maintains that a hundred years hence there will be no hesitation in assigning to George Eliot the foremost place amongst the three.   As he expresses it, page follows page of simple words and simple acts, and suddenly, without any reason or tragic event, the tear drops on the page—why the subtlest of us could not say :   " it simply is that God speaks to us—that is all."   He considers that her writing has the beauty of the Bible because she has religion in her blood.   That is as great a testimony as could be given from a French critic of highest standing. When we come to French writers of our own day, like Proust, we find an almost unexpected appreciation of a writer who like himself deals with situations and human relations rather than events.

*   *   *   *   *

As so much is said about her religious views, it is worth while trying to state George Eliot's position, which was really never very definite.   In those days she was thought unorthodox : in the present she might have been a Modernist.   We have seen what a regard she had for the outward forms of belief, and how she disliked negative propagandism of any sort. She had no sympathy with Free-thinkers, and Lewes and she must have agreed to differ on these matters. Lord Acton was quite wrong in terming her in a letter to Lady Blennerhasset " a perfect atheist " who " had to reconstruct her life without any aid at all from the habits and influences she had rejected." With her intensely conservative feelings, and reverence for what has descended to us from past ages, she looked for its lasting meaning in all religious doctrine.   The days of her admiration for Strauss were long over, and Renan's " Vie de Jésus " did not attract her. The facts of a sacred life were of little value, compared with the ideas that the life set forth. She looked to a development in religion which should have as its dominant quality less care for the personal element and a more deep sense of responsibility to man. In her youth she had dwelt in dreams of a pantheistic sort, but that was of the past. Mechanical and material explanations of life on the other hand had no attraction for her. As to the new ideas of atoms and protoplasm and molecular physics, which during last century became so dominant a feature in scientific belief and systems, she says " One might as well hope to dissect one's own body and be merry in doing it, as take molecular physics (in which you must banish from your field of view what is specifically human) to be your dominant guide, your determiner of motives, in what is solely human. That every study has its bearing on every other is true ; but pain and relief, love and sorrow, have their peculiar history which makes an experience and knowledge over and above the swing of the atoms." There is, it is true, a tale of how Tennyson on a certain spot near Witley when he said good-bye to George Eliot, exclaimed as she went down the hill, "Well, good-bye, you and your molecules," and she replied : " I am quite contented with my molecules." But in spite of that such matters as molecules never really appealed to her, though her close association with Lewes might have made her bound to defend them.

In many respects she was nearest to Positivism and Comtism ; but while she had great admiration for Comte's writings, she was never really a Positivist, though she went so far as to subscribe to the friends of the Body through her warm friends the Congreves. " I will not submit to him my heart and my intellect," she exclaimed regarding Comte. And again she asserted that she was brought up in the Church of England and never belonged to any other body, though she thought it one of the least dignified of all forms of Post Reformation Christianity. She had the deepest aversion to personal statements and commitments, even though she knew that she might be apt to prefer the haze to the clearness. " Deliverances " of all sorts on momentous subjects jarred on her, for she felt she might make them her " own insistent echo of herself." She particularly disliked the " assurance " of a well-known Calvinistic preacher of the day, and expressions such as " Let us approach the throne of God " which seemed to her as though " inviting one to take a chair." Any form of spiritualism again she detested, not feeling " bound to study these spirits more than she was bound to study the special follies of a particular phase of society."

As to worship of a public kind George Eliot recognised its desirability, so far as it expressed the desire of the community for the highest Good, and implied the recognition of a binding spiritual belief of law saving the worshippers from the slavery of unregulated passion. She herself once expressed to a friend her sense of loss in being unable to practise the old ordinance of family prayers. Unless there were strong reason of definite conviction, conformity was better than a nonconformity which has in it nothing but negatives. She recognised that the highest lot was to have that definite belief that one was bound to express. These views were written in early days to Mr. Cross, who presumably more or less conformed. To her there was " one comprehensive Church whose fellowship consists in the desire to purify and ennoble human life, and where the best members of all narrower Churches may call themselves brother and sister in spite of differences." After all, so far as it went, it was a fine creed and not unlike that of the present-day modern churchman.

* * * * *

Few women have had so great a capacity for friendship as George Eliot. She had confidences from every type of man and woman, and was equally ready to lay her hand on the head of a troubled girl and give her comfort, as to put into words all that can be said when the great sorrows came to her contemporaries. Her letters in joy and sorrow are free from any sententiousness and have the human touch which makes them go to the heart. This is the proof of a really great soul ; for it was owing to her depth of human feeling that she was able to write as she did. Her finest characters all have a part of herself in them : the characters that were most difficult were those that were hard like Rosamond Vincy, and with whom she could not sympathise. The gift of true sympathy is a great one ; but it takes enormously from the giver, and she suffered from the freedom with which the wells of such sympathy broke forth.

William Hale White, after seeing the unpublished letters to George Eliot's stepchildren, makes the very true remark that though they are delightfully affectionate and even playful, " the light that lay upon them was uniformly toned and reduced to a kind of sunset tint such as I see now upon the grassy hills opposite to me." " I am glad to find," he writes, " that my feeling towards her has lost none of its intensity, and that as a whole what I thought of her thirty-five years ago is what I think of her now . . . There are submarine caves which she has sounded, into which no plummet but hers has dropped."* " The style of Miss Evans's conversation," he says in another place, " was perfect; it was quite natural but never slipshod, and the force and sharpness of her thought was never lost in worn phrases."†

George Eliot was wideminded in the moral sense. She trained herself to see right wherever it might be, and to be careful of hasty condemnation. And in theory she wished others to have the same widemindedness as herself. She had many friends of the so-called " advanced school " when feminism was starting on its new lines of progress. She was strongly in favour of thoroughness as against amateurishness in work, as her own work showed. The deepest disgrace to her was to do any sort of work badly. She more or less supported, though as we have seen with some hesitation, the new movements in which some of her friends were eagerly engaged. But she was not a " fanatic " in the modern sense, and cannot be regarded as such historically. She was almost angry at the rather tactless suggestion from one friend that she—an æsthetic and not a doctrinal teacher, one who aroused the nobler emotions which make mankind desire the social right and not the prescriber of special measures—should take to the platform. Of course in that she was absolutely

* " Letters to Three Friends." Oxford, 1924.
† The *Bookman* of August, 1902.

correct. But she held fast to the old idea that the main point was that the recognised work of women should be done well, and held sacred. She herself took special pride in being a good housewife and she had some doubts as to whether this woman's work would not be disdained by the daughters of the future. Political measures for reforming society must not take the place of individual effort. In all this she was a Victorian at heart.

* * * * *

We have spoken of George Eliot's sense of humour, which in her early work was of the brightest, but not of her wit, in which she was usually held to be defective. But she certainly had the power of saying apt things on the spur of the moment, as some tales reveal. One of these is related by Herbert Spencer at his own expense. At one time he was fishing in the Highlands and had had, to his satisfaction, considerable success with heterodox flies. He had been explaining in his usual rather sententious form how he had trusted to the carrying out of his aim of making the best *average* representation of an insect buzzing on the surface of the water. " Yes," she replied, " you have such a passion for generalising, you even fish with a generalisation ! " Another instance had reference to a certain friend who was remarkable for his tendency to dissent from whatever opinions another uttered. At last she said : " Dr. A., how is it that you always take your colour from your company ? " " *I* take my colour from my company ? " he exclaimed. " What *do* you mean ? " " Yes," she replied, " the opposite colour ! " But these sallies belong to earlier days and were not frequent in later life.

F. W. Myers in his " Essays " speaks much of the excess of conscientiousness from which George Eliot suffered, while at the same time her spirit had a moral dignity, if not a saintly holiness.   There is a remarkable and striking passage about her visit to Cambridge.   " I walked with her once in the Fellows' Garden of Trinity, on an evening of a rainy May, and she, stirred somewhat beyond her wont, and taking as her text the three words which have been used so often as the inspiring trumpet-calls of men—the words *God, Immortality, Duty!*—pronounced with terrible earnestness how inconceivable was the *first*, how unbelievable the *second*, and yet how peremptory and absolute the *third*.   Never, perhaps, had sterner accents affirmed the sovereignty of impersonal and uncompromising law.   I listened and night fell ; her grave, majestic countenance turned towards me like a Sybil's in the gloom ; it was as though she withdrew from my grasp, one by one, the two scrolls of promise, and left me the third scroll only awful with inevitable fates."

It was perhaps her lack of living the life of her times that had the effect of causing George Eliot to be somewhat out of gear with the world.   Lord Morley truly says that even the Brontës " passed their days in one long succession of wild, stormy, squalid, anxious and miserable scenes—almost as romantic, as poetic and as tragic, to use George Eliot's words, as their own stories."   And this despite the extraordinary remoteness of their outward lives.   George Sand, of course, shared even more in " the passionate tumult and disorder, in the emotions, the aspirations, the ardour, the great conflicts and controversies of her time."   Now the criticism is just that George Eliot did not live this vivid, real life. She had the calm of a philosopher, and no doubt benefited from the fact, because she meditated on the deep things of the spiritual life. One longs, however, for her to have gone out into the open, and seen what was really happening there. She dreaded indiscriminate reading on the part of the young. Even the calm way in which she speaks of her charitable efforts gives one the sense that in her careful weighing she does the wise thing at the expense of her healthy natural impulses, which are stultified. Could she not herself go and see the miseries of the poor and try to suffer with them? But no, she seemed to stand outside, and look on from out of the grille that got ever closer as the years passed on, and as the protecting arms became more closely entwined.

What one wishes, also, is that George Eliot should have had more *joie de vivre*—more real happiness in her great successes. But this was not to be. She had a sort of Puritanical distrust of herself and her works. She felt their imperfections, for her standard was immensely high; and she felt still more strongly, as we have seen, the responsibility she incurred in writing, and the dread that if she had succeeded in the past she would fail in the future. It was only when she returned to her efforts years afterwards that she was really moved and saw that her work was good. She always had the desire to teach, and it was, so to speak, accidental that she could but teach in fiction. Could George Eliot only have written as John Bunyan wrote the " Pilgrim's Progress " from Bedford Jail and as most of the greatest books have been written, without consciousness of writing for any public but just because of the personal joy of writing ; or else with the delight in writing for itself that Scott and many of the great romance writers possessed ! But this was never so with her—she always had an idea to put into form and it was usually a great idea, such as she hoped would remain in the mind of all right-judging men and women, even when the story itself became dim.

* * * * *

George Eliot's outlook tended to be that of the just judge who sees the whole iniquity of the prisoner at the bar, and yet who loves mankind without suffering any illusions regarding it. She believes that there is no escape from the law that we reap that which we sow. Contrition or sacrifice will not save us. This gives the sad tinge to her writings, and yet it is their strength. If her sentiment has no false sentimentality, her satire in fiction has none of the bitterness of Swift. A very beautiful letter to the Hon. Mrs. Ponsonby puts her position clearly. She expresses her longing that men should be able to differ speculatively, and yet be " of one mind " in the desire to give no unnecessary pain and do " an honest part towards the general well-being. Pity and fairness," she goes on—" two little words which, carried out, would embrace the utmost delicacies of the moral life—seem to me not to rest on unverifiable hypotheses, but on facts quite as irreversible as the perception that a pyramid will not stand on its apex." She takes her place thus as a great and noble judge of the foibles of her time, and yet never forgets the temptations that lead to them. And the present generation might well regard these judgments.

The time for romance had passed away as the century grew older, and men and women were facing the strenuous life that met them with the rise of the scientific spirit. Even the excitement of the Oxford Movement had died down, and it was succeeded by a much more general excitement over the new physical interpretation of man and nature, or what was considered such. Science and religion came into violent opposition, and men's beliefs became shattered. It was here that George Eliot's calm judgment was so useful. She seemed to take the ordinary life and convert its ordinariness into something bigger and better. She did not controvert, but she showed that there was truth above the struggles, and also showed that there was a spiritual element running through all the events of life without which they would be incomprehensible. This, for those who were puzzled and troubled over the conclusions that Darwin's and Huxley's reasoning led to, was the greatest possible solace and help. We are not so concerned about science and its relation to the religious and moral life in these days, or at least we approach the question of the reconciliation rather differently. But though our approach may be different, we can still appreciate George Eliot's ethical background ; and the way in which she traces how men's actions are bound up with the happenings of their forefathers and race, is associated with those laws of evolution and heredity that were coming to be so seriously taken into account.

INDEX

A

Acton, Lord, 244, 275, 291, 301, 302, 303.
Ainsworth, Harrison, 199.
Allbutt, Clifford, 238.
Allinghams, Mr. and Mrs., 270.
Arnold, Matthew, 222, 293.
Austen, Jane, 107, 121, 294.

B

Balfour, Lord, 254.
Bashkirtseff, Marie, 159.
Blackwood, John, 114 seq., 130, 135, 137, 139, 154, 173, 179, 217, 256.
Blanc, Louis, 63.
Blennerhasset, Lady, 303.
Blind, Mathilde, 44, 51.
Brabant, Dr., 49, 76.
Brabant, Miss, 49.
Bray, Mr. and Mrs., 44 seq., 56, 67, 88, 90, 94, 103, 122..
Brontës, C. and E., 74, 86, 107, 121, 159, 292, 297, 309.
Browning, Mrs., 298.
Browning, Oscar, 90, 257.
Browning, Robert, 38.
Buckle, Mr., 104.
Bunyan, John, 310.
Burton, Sir Frederick, viii., 191, 215.

C

Carlisle, Richard, 236.
Carlyle, Mrs., 136.
Carlyle, Thomas, 37, 76, 106, 164, 301.
Chapman, Dr., 55, 68 seq.
Clark, Sir Andrew, 287, 290.
Clark, W. S., 191.

Clifford, Mrs, W. K., viii., 272 seq., 282.
Cobbett, W., 235, 301.
Cobden, R., 77.
Collins, Wilkie, 191.
Combe, George, 45, 52, 85 seq.
Comte, A., 305.
Congreves, Mr. and Mrs., 155, 214, 291.
Cooper, Thos., 235.
Courtney, W. L., 255.
Cousin, V., 98.
Cowper, W., 284.
Cross, Eleanor, 287, 288.
Cross, J. W., vii., 191, 239, 270, 282, 285 seq.
Cumming, Dr., 104.

D

D'Albert, Mr. and Mrs., 65 seq., 171, 255.
Darwin, Charles, 6, 37, 174, 312.
Dessoir, F., 98.
De Vogüé, V. G. M., 302, 303.
Dickens, C., 75, 136, 158, 185, 292, 294, 295, 298, 300.
Disraeli, B., 59.
Du Bois Reymond, 98.
Dumas, A., 199.
Du Maurier, 9, 270.

E

Emerson, R. W., 45, 63, 75.
Evans, Christina, 12, 28.
Evans, Elizabeth, 34 seq., 48, 139 seq.
Evans, Isaac, 16 seq., 48, 161, 194, 291.
Evans, Mrs. (C. Pearson), 164.
Evans, Robert, 10 seq., 20, 41 seq., 163, 248.

X